In the wake of the Mexican Revolution, citizens in many parts of Mexico experienced turbulent and uncertain times. This book tells the story of how the people of the Sierra Norte de Puebla emerged from those traumatic years and came to terms with the many challenges facing them in the decade that followed. It also examines the phenomenon of *caciquismo* in the postrevolutionary period as seen in the career of one powerful individual.

Gabriel Barrios Cabrera, leader of the Brigada Serrana, rose from rural obscurity in the tiny village of Cuacuila to a position of unprecedented military strength during the Revolution, and throughout the 1920s he and his brother Demetrio came to enjoy the confidence of the nation's presidents. This work provides an in-depth look at how a local political boss held on to power. Keith Brewster reveals how the story of the Sierra is inextricably linked to that of the Barrios Cabrera family, and he investigates the ways in which this interconnection developed.

Brewster argues that Barrios owed his long prominence to his sensitivity to the region's culture but also shows that the extent of his power was exaggerated by both contemporaries and historians. Barrios was able to develop a working relationship with federal government officials by endorsing their objectives and convincing them of his own indispensability, but his authority depended on the weakness of the federal government and on infighting within the Puebla state government; once both governments stabilized, Barrios quickly lost his grip on power.

continued on back flap

Militarism, Ethnicity, and Politics in the Sierra Norte de Puebla, 1917–1930

Militarism, Ethnicity, and Politics in the Sierra Norte de Puebla, 1917–1930

Keith Brewster

The University of Arizona Press, Tucson

The University of Arizona Press
© 2003 The Arizona Board of Regents
First Printing
All rights reserved

☉ This book is printed on acid-free, archival-quality paper.
Manufactured in the United States of America

08   07   06   05   04   03   6   5   4   3   2   1

Library of Congress Cataloging-in-Publication Data

Brewster, Keith, 1956–
Militarism, ethnicity, and politics in the Sierra Norte de Puebla,
1917–1930 / Keith Brewster.
p. cm.
Includes bibliographical references and index.
ISBN 0-8165-2252-9 (cloth : alk. paper)
1. Puebla (Mexico : State)—Politics and government—20th century.
2. Barrios Cabrera, Gabriel, 1888–1964. 3. Patronage, Political—
Mexico—Puebla (State)—History—20th century. 4. State-local
relations—Mexico—Puebla (State)—History—20th century. 5. Puebla
(Mexico : State)—Militia—History—20th century. 6. Ethnicity—
Mexico—Puebla (State)—History—20th century. I. Title.
F1326 .B74 2003
972'.48082—dc21
2002154102

British Library Cataloguing-in-Publication Data
A catalogue record for this book is available from the British Library.

Contents

Illustrations

Figures

Maps

Tables

Acknowledgments

Militarism, Ethnicity, and Politics in the Sierra Norte de Puebla, 1917–1930, began as a doctoral thesis produced at the Department of History, University of Warwick, England, between 1992 and 1995. As such, I owe a debt of gratitude to two individuals at Warwick who had an important influence upon my academic career: Bill Dusinberre, who during my undergraduate studies aroused my interest in historical research; and Guy Thomson, my postgraduate supervisor, whose patience, time, and knowledge kindled, refined, and sustained that interest. Even after I obtained my doctorate, Guy has continued to be a constant source of encouragement, advice, and friendship. Similarly, the constructive criticism and support of my doctoral thesis examiners, Raymond Buve and Alan Knight, were crucial in sharpening my analysis of several aspects of the study. My postgraduate research and trips to Mexico were made possible by the financial support of the British Academy. During a period when access to such funds is becoming increasingly competitive, I feel honored to have benefited from the Academy's generosity and hope that my endeavors do justice to the Academy's investment in me.

For the last five years, I have had the pleasure and honor to work at the Centre of Latin American Studies, University of Cambridge, England. From my very first days at the Centre I have found it to be the most stimulating and supportive of places in which to convert my thesis into its present form. The friendship and good humor of Clare Hariri, Julie Coimbra, and Ana Gray provide the Centre with the welcoming reputation that it deserves. The steady flow of Latin Americanists passing through the Centre was a constant source of new ideas and inspiration, while the development of this project benefited greatly from the academic stimulation of David Lehmann and David Brading. Most of all, however, I would like to thank my close friend and colleague, Valentina Napolitano, someone with whom I have shared teaching, ideas, anxieties, and many happy moments. My thanks go to all of you.

During my many visits to Mexico, I have been struck by the unfailing kindness and patience of staff in the many archives I have visited. I am especially grateful to the staff of the Archivo General de la Nación, who nursed me through my first days in a Mexican archive, and to General Eulalio Fonseca, who permitted me to consult the invaluable documents contained within the Archivo de la Defensa Nacional at a time when access was extremely difficult to obtain. I also wish to thank Guillermo Zermeño at the Universidad Iberoamericana for writing a letter of introduction that facilitated access to the Defensa archive. Similarly, staff in Puebla city and municipal archives throughout the Sierra de Puebla were enormously helpful. In particular, I must mention two individuals: Sergio, who endures the cold, damp conditions in the Biblioteca Luis Cabrera, Zacatlán, and who had the foresight to accept the valuable RHAM archive when offered it by a member of the Barrios family; and Emma Gutiérrez, who single-handedly fights a constant battle to rescue the Cuetzalan archive from the humidity that makes the village such a beautiful place to visit.

A tremendous number of people within the Sierra de Puebla helped with my research, so any attempt to name them all would inevitably lead to inadvertent omissions. I only hope that I showed my gratitude at the appropriate time. Yet the many members of the Barrios family deserve particular mention, because without their help my research would have foundered. I am particularly grateful to José María Barrios, whose recent death caused my wife and me much sadness, and to Carlotta Barrios, Arnulfo Barrios, Vicente Barrios, and their respective families. In addition, Alejandro Barrios not only has been a good friend, but arranged transport and access for trips into the Sierra that provided me with invaluable verbal and visual images. From the very first moments of my contact with the Barrios family, they all gave me their full cooperation, warm friendship, recollections, and access to family papers. The majority of the photographs in this book come from originals in their collections, and I thank them for allowing me to use them. In seeking to clarify the many ambiguities concerning their forefathers' control of the Sierra, I hope that I have not inadvertently taken advantage of their friendship.

Equally important during my stay in Mexico, particularly during the first lonely months, was the support of my many friends: Rocio, Fernando, Caro, and Lucy Carranza in Xalapa, Veracruz; Daniel Kirk, Mireya Hernández Hernández, the staff of La Panadería "La Vascona" on Calle Tacuba, and my *queridos vecinos* at the "Heartburn Hotel" in Mexico City. In the city of Puebla, a *fuerte abrazo* goes to Marco Antonio Velázquez at the Universidad Autónoma de Puebla. Marco, Gloria, and Cynthia showed me nothing but warmth and encouragement, while Marco's many students at the UAP offered their friendship and interest in my studies. During my many visits to Zacatlán, Liz Macin, Luis Irala, and Liz's family became close friends, while Alberta and Victoria (the *familia real inglesa* in exile) will never quite know how much the *gorditas* they sell at their market stall sustained me after many a long day in the archives.

In converting this study into a book, I have recently made a new set of acquaintances and incurred a new set of debts among the staff at the University of Arizona Press. I thank Patti Hartmann for having enough faith to accept my manuscript for publication; the two anonymous readers for their meticulous reading of the manuscript and their invaluable comments; Nancy Arora for knocking the edges off my British English; and in particular Kirsteen Anderson for editing the manuscript in a methodical and sympathetic way.

Finally, I want to mention those closer to home who have helped to keep my academic endeavors in perspective. These include the memory of my dad, Ken, who would have said little but would nonetheless have been proud, and my mum, Doris, who always keeps a well-stocked fridge and never thought that her name would appear in a book. By far my biggest debt of gratitude is to Claire. As in all other areas of my life, without her this book would have remained incomplete. For her painstaking efforts to improve the drafts of my text, for her companionship during long walks spent resolving issues in the text, and for all the lost weekends and the hours she sacrificed from her own research, it is with love and deep appreciation that I thank her.

Abbreviations

$	Mexican Peso
CGT	Confederación General de Trabajadores
CROM	Confederación Regional de Obreros Mexicanos
INEHRM	Instituto Nacional de Estudios Históricos de la Revolución Mexicana
PCM	Partido Comunista Mexicano
PLM	Partido Liberal Mexicano
PNA	Partido Nacional Agraria
PNR	Partido Nacional Revolucionario
PRI	Partido Revolucionario Institucional
SCOP	Secretaría de Obras Públicas
SEP	Secretaría de Educación Pública

Militarism, Ethnicity,

and Politics in the

Sierra Norte de Puebla,

1917–1930

Introduction

Militarism, Ethnicity, and Politics in the Sierra Norte de Puebla, 1917–1930, tells the story of how the people of the Sierra Norte de Puebla emerged from the traumatic years of the Mexican Revolution and came to terms with the many challenges facing them in the decade that followed. As was true in other areas of Mexico, individuals' experiences depended upon a variety of factors including who they were, what they did, and where they lived. Some communities escaped relatively unscathed from the violent conflict that took place around them, while in others the very fabric of everyday life fell apart. Similarly, many families struggled to overcome devastating personal losses, while some not only survived but prospered from the opportunities that conflict provided them.

Nowhere in the Sierra were the bittersweet fortunes of war felt so keenly as within the Barrios Cabrera household in the tiny mountain village of Cuacuila. Two of four brothers were killed in the Revolution and the violence that followed, while the remaining two, Gabriel and Demetrio, rose from rural obscurity to become the region's most influential figures during the 1920s. Military success afforded them rapid promotion within the federal army, and as commander of the 46th Battalion, Gabriel Barrios led his Indian soldiers to a position of unrivaled military influence within the area. At crucial moments, the battalion made significant contributions to the survival of postrevolutionary administrations, thereby earning the Barrios brothers the confidence of national presidents. The Barrioses soon extended beyond their military brief to become key instigators of rural development in the Sierra. Whether it be the construction of a road, an irrigation channel, a school, or telephone lines, no project of significance took place without the moral or material support of Gabriel and Demetrio Barrios. The rapidity and nature of their rise to prominence attracted admiration and suspicion in equal measure. From the corridors of national power to *palacios municipales* throughout the Sierra, debate took place concerning how to view the emergence of the power base located in Cuacuila. The story of the Sierra, therefore, is inextricably linked to the story of the Barrios Cabrera family; in this book I investigate the ways in which this interconnection developed.

Although their actions were far reaching, the Barrios brothers were just one of many factors influencing the ways in which the people and communities of the Sierra experienced the aftermath of civil war. At the onset of the Mexican Revolution, the Sierra comprised eight thousand square kilometers of almost impenetrable mountains populated by Nahua, Totonac, and Otomí villages.[1] Poor transportation and communications infrastructure meant that mestizo jurisdiction over remote areas was incomplete, and many indigenous communities retained a degree of cultural and political autonomy that was manifest in the survival of pre-Columbian beliefs. Neither Catholic priests nor nineteenth-century Protestant missionaries could fully extirpate deeply embedded beliefs in the spiritual world of native mysticism, where human beings were able to transform into animals, and mountains and rivers were revered as gods. Kinship and patriarchal structures often carried more weight than constitutional authority, and community disapproval was a more effective restraint upon unsociable behavior than was the law. Outsiders who ran roughshod over such sensibilities might gain the obedience of indigenous serranos but were rarely accepted. Those who acknowledged local sensibilities might gain acceptance but rarely enjoyed unconditional support.

In peripheral regions of Mexico the approbation of indigenous communities may not have mattered to those in power, but the Sierra de Puebla's geopolitical importance demanded that mestizo authority sometimes yield to local opinion. At times when broader priorities forced engagement with local consciousness, temporary realignments in social, political, and ethnic balances occurred. The Sierra de Puebla offers an opportunity to study the dynamics of such adjustments, providing a greater understanding of the complex relations between state and community during the 1920s.

Lying within a day's horse ride of the strategic corridor between

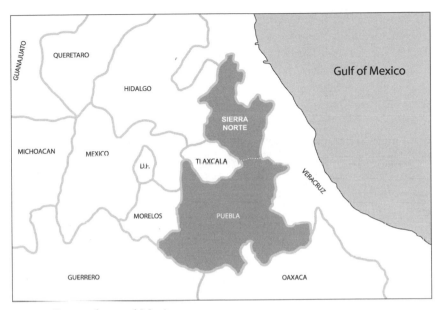

Map 1. States of central Mexico

Mexico City and the port of Veracruz, the Sierra was a highly valued location in times of national turmoil (see map 1). During the nineteenth century, its valleys offered asylum to political activists escaping persecution on the plains below, while its indigenous communities were coveted as a rich source of military recruits and provisions. French and Austrian troops sought to pacify the area during Maximilian's brief reign, and the ensuing guerrilla war of resistance politicized some indigenous communities, which then sought to embrace the benefits of liberal egalitarianism. Many others remained guarded in declaring their political affiliations. Whether from innate conservatism or opportunism, they preferred to work within existing sociopolitical structures to gain their overall objectives. I demonstrate how this discriminating response toward those seeking support continued to evolve throughout the early decades of the twentieth century, a time when the region experienced unprecedented exposure to outside influences. The diversity and dynamics of political postures assumed by Sierra communities, and their motives for engaging in mestizo politics, are central to my analysis of the revolutionary and postrevolutionary periods.

Indigenous mobilization during the Revolution was by no means restricted to the Sierra de Puebla, nor did those who fought do so in pursuit of local rather than national objectives. Yet serrano mobilization in the Sierra produced an almost unique phenomenon in the military history of the Mexican federal army: an indigenous battalion that operated in its own region under the orders of its own commanders. Rather than indicating any measure of mutual trust between the military establishment and indigenous soldiers, however, I believe that this situation resulted from the government's near complete lack of understanding of the situation in the Sierra. The inability of the Guerra y Marina to predict serrano responses led to a hesitancy to act in any way that might jeopardize military support from the serranos. This hesitancy created an environment in which indigenous units of the 46th Battalion were able to mobilize in pursuit of local objectives behind the façade of loyal support for national causes.

One problem facing those serranos who mobilized was how to pursue their personal or community objectives when the need for their military force subsided. Experiences in the late nineteenth century had shown how quickly promises made in the heat of battle were forgotten in more peaceful times. Periodic threats to the postrevolutionary government postponed this dilemma until the mid-1920s, but thereafter their redundancy as soldiers left serranos ill equipped to face a longer-lasting threat than revolutionary violence. Rapid improvements in infrastructure opened up the area to unprecedented levels and facilitated the arrival of new ideas and perspectives that challenged the status quo. An opportunity for one person often represented a threat to another, and vested interests at individual, factional, community, and regional levels all strove to manage such changes to their advantage. With mobilization no longer an option, serranos needed to employ new forms of resistance and negotiation. In this respect, the Barrios family had an important role to play, both as the instigators of change and as the means through which compromises over implementation were negotiated.

The Barrios Family

Official histories of the state of Puebla mention Gabriel Barrios merely as a military general who built a few roads in the Sierra. More detailed accounts invariably portray him as a brutal cacique who prevented his fellow serranos from enjoying the full benefits of the Revolution. This image matches that of the many warlords who thrived during the Revolution and who met their nemesis following the restoration of civilian political authority. Present-day detractors within the Sierra generally concur with this depiction, often embellishing their accounts with adjectives such as "ignorant," "uneducated," and significantly, "Indian." That such a one-dimensional image has remained unchallenged is a disservice both to the memory of Gabriel Barrios and, more importantly, to the memories of the many serranos who were his contemporaries and who refused to be bought or coerced into acting contrary to their individual or collective interests. In reappraising the image of Barrios in this book, I also reappraise the image of the Sierra campesino.

An underlying premise of my study is that Gabriel Barrios's family background equipped him with the necessary personal qualities to engage with a wide range of actors within the Sierra. It makes sense, therefore, to lay out the nature of life within the Barrios household and the early experiences that served him so well in his adult life. Surviving members of the family give different versions of the family's origins. Some believe that Gabriel Barrios's father, José María, moved to the Sierra de Puebla from either Durango or Sonora during the latter half of the nineteenth century;[2] others say he came from Veracruz and fought against the French as a captain under the highly respected Nahua commander from the Sierra, Juan Francisco Lucas.[3] All agree that he settled in Cuacuila shortly after arriving in the Sierra and became Lucas's close friend during a period when the latter enjoyed considerable political influence. Although there is a suggestion that José María was a teacher in Cuacuila (see map 2), this seems doubtful as his sons only mastered the Spanish language in adult life. More likely, he made his living from farming and real estate, perhaps making the most of the wave of *desamortización* that swept through this part of the Sierra during the late nineteenth century.

Few details are known about Gabriel Barrios's mother, María Dominga Cabrera, other than that she was Nahua and native to Cuacuila. She had five children: Amado, Gabriel, Bardomiano, Pilar, and Demetrio (see figure 1). Gabriel's birth was never registered, but the weight of circumstantial evidence suggests that he was born on 18 March 1888.[4] José María's union with other local women, including his wife's sister, produced many more children, and Gabriel Barrios's half brothers would later form a significant element in his *cacicazgo*. María Dominga

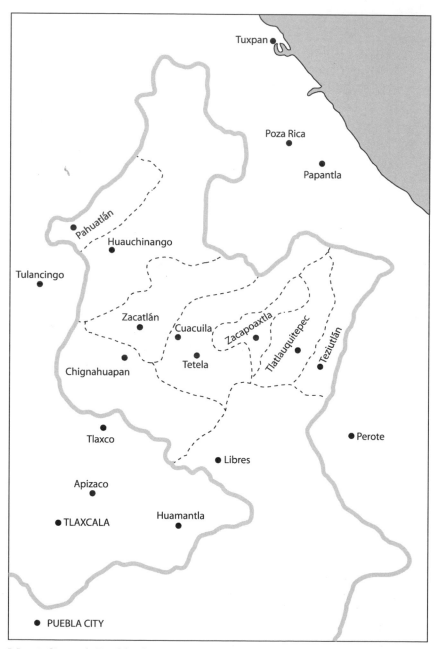

Map 2. Sierra de Puebla electoral constituencies during 1920s

Figure 1. Bardomiano, Gabriel, and Demetrio Barrios (all seated, center)
(Courtesy of Arnulfo Barrios Aco)

died in 1899 and José María, six years later, at which point the four brothers inherited their father's property in Cuacuila.[5]

During the Revolution the Barrios brothers described themselves as farm laborers, although a more accurate description might be *rancheros:* modest landowners who engaged in the raising and sale of horses and who employed neighbors to work on their land.[6] They also speculated in property. When Amado was killed in May 1916, he left property in Cuacuila and in the nearby district of Tetela.[7] In August 1919, the three surviving brothers bought land from Juan Francisco Lucas's son, Abraham.[8] Bardomiano Barrios purchased more land and houses in the nearby market towns of Tetela de Ocampo and Zacatlán, and when he died in December 1923 his widow inherited a considerable estate. Three years later, this estate was sold to Demetrio Barrios, who had already bought numerous plots of land in the districts of Tetela and in Zacatlán, where he spent much of his early military career.[9] Gabriel Barrios also added to the land he inherited from his father. In February 1919, he bought an urban plot in Tetela de Ocampo for two thousand pesos and throughout the 1920s he acquired land in Tetela for modest amounts of money as well as purchasing from several widows the rights to their family's estates.[10] Despite such deals, land acquisition was never a major occupation for Barrios; his main source of income from 1920 onwards was as a professional soldier. Indeed, his most substantial land-holding was the ranch of Zacatempan, a rural settlement close to Chignahuapan, which he inherited on his wife's death in 1940.[11] Gabriel Barrios had married Guadalupe Nava Bonilla, the daughter of a comfortably well-off mestizo farmer, in December 1908. They had four children, although other relationships provided Barrios with many more, both in the Sierra de Puebla and in Chiapas, where he was stationed for several years during the 1930s.[12]

Given the importance I place upon Gabriel Barrios's role as a cultural intermediary between serranos and federal authorities, it is important to analyze how different groups within and beyond the Sierra perceived his ethnicity. Using parentage as the sole criterion, there is no doubt that he was mestizo. Yet although his facial features distinguished him from his Nahua neighbors and soldiers, his bronze skin, slanted eyes, and short stature set him apart from many mestizos. Gabriel and his siblings grew up in the rural environment of Cuacuila. Reflecting the origins of their mother and neighbors, they spoke Nahuatl at home, had Nahua playmates, and later worked their father's land alongside Nahua campesinos. People who met Gabriel often commented upon his faltering Spanish, although many were never quite sure whether he varied his degree of proficiency to suit his audience and interests. These elements of fluidity in the way the brothers, particularly Gabriel, sought to define themselves ethnically perhaps reflected a broader reality of life in rural communities. As Judith Friedlander observed in her study of the Nahua town of Hueyapan in the 1960s, indicators of ethnicity such as language, dress, customs, values, and collective memory were not static and isolated, but instead were frequently influencing and being influenced by the dominant mestizo culture. Importantly, the adoption of particular traits established the parameters of social discourse. Nahuatl, for example, was often used by Indians to exclude external authorities from negotiations, and Spanish was sometimes used to draw distinctions between more "advanced" Indian factions and those they wished to portray as less acculturated.[13] I believe that language and dress became vital tools that Gabriel Barrios used to carve out the political niche he occupied throughout the 1920s.

Whether people saw Gabriel Barrios as Indian or mestizo depended on the time and place. Several influential white families in the Sierra adopted a pragmatic approach. In Zacatlán, for instance, the Barrios brothers established valuable personal ties with the Carrancista politicians Luis and Alfonso Cabrera. For reasons of their own, the Cabrera brothers became Gabriel Barrios's political sponsors and contributed greatly to the success of his early career. Some believe that Luis Cabrera began the false rumor that Barrios was the illegitimate son of Juan Francisco Lucas, to emphasize Barrios's indigenous credentials and make it easier for him to assume the political legitimacy of the old warrior.[14] As he acquired military and political prominence, *gente de razón* within the Zacatlán district overlooked Barrios's rustic, "Indian" ways and became representatives of the Barrios cacicazgo during its heyday. In more distant districts of the Sierra, other factors came into play. Influential families threatened by Barrios's rise to prominence portrayed him as a wild Indian who roamed the Sierra with his equally dangerous Indian soldiers. Some genuinely believed him to be indigenous, whereas others chose to designate him an Indian for political capital. Within the Guerra y Marina, he was valued precisely because he was seen to have deep cultural affinities with the Indian unit under his command. Politicians, on the other hand, preferred to emphasize the professionalism of the 46th Battalion rather than its Indian composition. Only in 1929, when his services were no longer required, did the same politicians and newspaper editors depict his troops as "half savages" who needed to be removed from their bailiwick.

The majority of mestizos throughout the Sierra viewed Gabriel Barrios as a campesino who had made good. Whether they liked him or not depended more upon how he treated them than his ethnicity. In most indigenous communities, Barrios was viewed as a Nahuatl-speaking mestizo because of his influence and relative wealth. Those closer to Cuacuila, however, recognized his respect for their cultural values and his understanding of the challenges of everyday life in the fields. He did not have to feign this respect, as it was integral to his own identity formation. Guillermo Mejía Cabrera, who worked as a servant in the Barrios household during the Revolution, confirms that the Barrios brothers fought barefoot or in huaraches and dressed in the *traje de manta* typically worn by soldiers and campesinos within the region (see figure 2). Not until the 1920s did the brothers wear federal uniforms, and Mejía remembers with great fondness the day when Gabriel Barrios

Figure 2. Demetrio, Gabriel, and Bardomiano Barrios (mounted) in Cuacuila
(Courtesy of Arnulfo Barrios Aco)

took delivery of his riding boots: "What quality boots they were; the
best from Guanajuato."[15] Although his military career often caused him
to spend lengthy periods away from Cuacuila, after every campaign
within the Sierra and after spending years in Mexico City, Chiapas, and
Oaxaca, Barrios returned to live among the Nahua campesinos of his
native village.

Debate concerning Gabriel Barrios's ethnic identity is circuitous and
ultimately inconclusive. Lifestyle, customs, language, and dress all provide cultural indicators, but political, economic, and social realities obscure any objective portrayal. Perhaps the more important observation
is that for a critical period in postrevolutionary Mexican history, the
military potential of the Sierra de Puebla was seen to be overwhelm-
ingly indigenous. All external overtures toward Gabriel Barrios took
place within this context. So although Barrios's detractors within and
beyond the Sierra might denigrate his "Indian" ways, Barrios himself
recognized that he could manipulate his ambiguous identity to good
effect. His apparent ability to engage in dialogue with both federal
agencies and indigenous communities convinced many that he was
indispensable.

Caciquismo and Subaltern Politics

Gabriel Barrios's role as a cultural intermediary fits into a pattern of revolutionary leadership identified by revisionists in the 1970s.[16] Studies of regional and local power brokers confirm that the very survival of the early postrevolutionary state depended upon the support of regional leaders with varying degrees of loyalty toward the federal government. In general, these studies offer a pessimistic interpretation of rural politics during the 1920s [17] Leaders are portrayed as figures who employed a mixture of patronage and coercion to continue the exploitation of campesinos. They often had enjoyed a degree of influence in more peaceful times, and many belonged to the rural bourgeoisie as artisans, small traders, and rancheros.[18] Warfare offered opportunities for social mobility, with the promise of land or the threat of losing it commonly being used to buy support.[19] Scholars developed a hierarchy to locate these hard men of Mexican politics. Distinctions based upon size of following and territorial jurisdiction were made between caciques and caudillos, and between regional and national caudillos. Some writers presented their subjects as charismatic leaders similar to those of the early independence period; others described leaders who gained their positions through "new forms of authority, increasingly civilian and bureaucratic, with sound rational-legal foundations."[20] Broad-brushstroke images appeared in the historiography that depicted Mexico as having fallen under the control of "traditional" or "modern" leaders who used campesinos as cannon fodder in their fight for personal gain.[21] With the eventual consolidation of a stronger state during the 1930s, the writing was on the wall for these provincial leaders. For those with political aspirations, incorporation within the party machinery became the safest option.

That this Machiavellian image of rural leadership has emerged from the genre of caudillo and cacique studies is unfortunate because it paints only a partial impression of what research has revealed. Critics claim that the top-down approach to regional studies denies political agency to campesinos and relegates them to being passive recipients of the changes affecting them. Yet many portrayals of caudillos and caciques contain considerable detail on their efforts to gain support from these very campesinos. They depict the ambiguous position of local and regional leaders, who needed to satisfy the demands of external authorities and local constituencies alike to retain their pivotal role as middlemen between the city and the countryside, between rich and poor, and often between mestizo and Indian. Frans Schryer points out that those figures with political and economic influence recognized the importance and value of appealing to the cultural sensitivities of their constituencies. Similarly, Paul Friedrich reveals how radical leader Primo Tapia adopted a range of cultural postures to help legitimize his position in negotiations with community leaders in the Zacapu Valley of Michoacán.[22] Importantly, a decision to support a regional leader did not amount to a wholesale surrender of local authority; village elders could still retain considerable influence regarding community responses to the demands of warfare.[23]

Ironically, the recent emphasis on understanding power relations from the bottom up might bring about the redemption of caudillos and caciques. Highlighting the political potential of subordinate groups offers reinterpretations not only of state-community relations, but also of how communities imposed checks and balances upon the actions of regional brokers. The ways in which rural leaders sought to maintain their legitimacy provides a point of contact between scholars of caciquismo and those emphasizing the political potential of campesinos. While some studies of caciquismo may overplay the extent to which leaders manipulated local cultural sensitivities in order to gain legitimacy, we should not overlook the manipulative power of campesinos.[24] A strong message coming from bottom-up approaches to rural politics is that campesino leaders had considerable experience in negotiating with external political agents. Even the most influential caciques could not take away such experience. It is equally likely that campesino communities used these very skills to benefit from the contacts that a regional cacique enjoyed. Far from accepting subjugation, communities were able to orchestrate particular circumstances to their advantage. In this respect, by not ruling caciques out of the equation, one might arrive at a yet more subtle appreciation of the negotiating capacity of subaltern groups.

Explaining why rural communities fought during the Revolution has provided gainful employment for several generations of historians; land tenure, local autonomy, and political factionalism often feature among their conclusions. For many revisionists, the destructive spread of rural capitalism provides an answer. Historians and anthropologists have worked under the premise that campesinos fought to avoid the erosion of "traditional" values and structures that provided a measure of social equity and stability. For some, capitalism merely represents a continuation of campesino exploitation by a new means. Luisa Pare, for instance, argues that caciques acted as the lackeys of wealthier patrons who tried to channel campesino mobilization to preserve their dominant position within rural society, by holding back the forces of capitalism or by controlling how it was introduced. Either way the cacique was damned.[25] More recently, Gerardo Otero has suggested that it was more likely to have been the Mexican semi-proletariat—with limited access to land and dependent upon sporadic wage labor—who rebelled in order to reduce their economic vulnerability.[26] The agent may have changed but the link between economic motives and political actions remains. Yet any analysis of Mexican rural politics needs to explain the many conflicts that do not appear to have been influenced by class divisions. Rural communities fought each other over land and natural resources, personal or factional vendettas pitched campesino against campesino, and opposing sides were as likely to seek the material support of a local patron as to embrace class solidarity. Moreover, recent studies question Marxist assumptions regarding precapitalist rural society. Simon Miller, for example, shows that the hacienda system was not as resistant to capitalism as previously thought.[27] Indeed, not all prerevolution rural societies were isolated from the broader economic world. Whereas some remained relatively autonomous, others engaged the mercantilist world beyond their immediate environs in limited ways. For some communities, the harsh realities of rural life necessitated periods of seasonal migration in search of paid labor, which had inevitable social and cultural consequences.[28]

The inadequacy of economic criteria to explain the motives for peasant resistance has encouraged some historians to explore the links between local reception to state initiatives and popular culture.[29] Mary Kay Vaughan summarizes the range of concepts and working categories adopted by cultural historians in recent years to explain the nature of subaltern resistance. She cites space, identity, ritual, and gender as issues through which conflict and compromise can be discerned. Prominent among the conceptual frameworks are postcolonial subalternity and Gramscian notions of discourse and hegemony, carefully modified to suit the Latin American environment. Utilizing such tools, Vaughan invites local historians to revisit archival documents and search beyond obvious vertical power relationships to reveal "the moral codes and power networks among the dominated." Evidence from municipal, regional, and national archives; oral history; testimony; statistics; and a wide range of local cultural paraphernalia can be exposed to new forms of analysis to discover how subjugated groups thought and acted. While many of these sources would already attract the critical attention of most diligent local historians, other more unusual sources, such as proverbs and folk songs, are being subjected to analytical perspectives that challenge previous ways of interpreting history.[30]

Yet even as historians embrace this new, sometimes subjective approach to history, important factors such as time and place should never be overlooked. Recent studies by Tim Henderson and Jesús Márquez Carrillo, for example, portray *poblano* campesinos in the 1920s as being confused about their new position within the postrevolutionary order. Henderson finds strident *agraristas* who, while aware of their newfound rights, still showed deference to the equally determined hacendada Rosalie Evans.[31] Márquez Carrillo suggests that campesino protests revealed "the emotions of a people lacking reliable points of reference with which to replace the societal values that existed immediately prior to the process of change."[32] In her study of rural politics in Puebla, Vaughan notes that although there were signs of peasant consciousness in the 1930s, it was very much in its infancy. Class unity frequently coexisted with, and had to overcome, neighborhood and factional disputes or vertical ties of loyalty to caciques, priests, or landowners.[33] The fact that it is never easy to discard the baggage of the past left the door open for seemingly irreconcilable contradictions to coexist. Similarly, the study of campesino solidarity needs to address the divisive and subjective question of ethnicity. Steve Stern argues that the difficulty of identifying ethnic motives for peasant mobilization has led historians to overlook them in preference for socioeconomic factors.[34] While increased awareness of the heterogeneity of indigenous groups may encourage historians to take up Stern's challenge, in doing so we need to guard against grafting newfound Western sensitivities onto previous generations.[35] In the 1920s, racism played a major role in the way that both rural and urban Mexican mestizos rationalized the "Indian" problem. Furthermore, a "mestizo" to one campesino might be deemed an "indito" to the gente de razón down the road. To complicate matters further, a mestizo campesino in relatively peaceful times might become a "barbarous Indian" during an armed uprising. While such definitional fluidity could drive historians to distraction, if we are to understand the actions of rural, especially indigenous, communities, we have to recognize the differing perceptions of ethnicity at various levels of authority. Furthermore, we need to appreciate that diverse opinions existed at each level and that these were liable to change, often for unconnected reasons.

Applications to the Sierra Norte de Puebla

In chapter 1, I begin my analysis of the Sierra de Puebla during the 1920s with an overview of the immediately preceding decades, specifically the legacy of indigenous mobilization in the nineteenth century. Recent studies on indigenous mobilization elsewhere play down the degree of separation between ethnic groups. In his study of the caste war in Yucatán, Terry Rugeley warns against simplistic dichotomies such as tension between rich and poor, landowners and landless, or creoles and Mayas.[36] Peter Guardino, in his study of peasant resistance in Guerrero, finds that far from being insular, indigenous communities were fully aware of the broader political issues at stake and agreed to fight alongside mestizos to protect their own interests.[37] Similarly, in the case of the Sierra de Puebla, both Guy Thomson and Florencia Mallon emphasize the increased mutual understanding resulting from indigenous soldiers fighting alongside their mestizo allies.[38]

In revisiting their work, I explore alternative interpretations of the nature and significance of nineteenth-century indigenous mobilization in the region. While I agree that participation in widespread conflicts indicated community engagement in crucial political issues, I believe that the underlying motives were more pragmatic than ideological. In this respect, I question whether evidence of "popular liberalism" should more accurately be viewed as the deployment of what James C. Scott refers to as "weapons of the weak."[39] Mobilization in favor of the liberal cause, whether popular or not, may have indicated nothing more than a community's realization that such a posture represented the best hope of achieving their aims. My intention is not to undermine Thomson's and Mallon's arguments, but to question whether all Sierra communities embraced national concepts and discourse to the same extent.

Understanding the true nature of political discourse in the Sierra de Puebla is relevant to my study in that the process of negotiation in the nineteenth century is said to have informed debates concerning implementation of postrevolutionary reforms in the Sierra during the 1930s.[40] Extrapolation of this kind does not sit well with my own analysis that the interim period, particularly the 1920s, was characterized by an almost complete lack of dialogue between indigenous communities and federal agents beyond the Sierra. In chapter 2, I illustrate this weak relationship by focusing upon the major issue on which federal government and Sierra communities held passionate views: revolutionary mobilization and the restoration of law and order. Above all, I explain why the federal government appeared willing to allow serranos of the Sierra de Puebla to fight within their own region under their own leaders. In contrast, local mobilization of indigenous groups in other regions was often seen as a potential threat to mestizo society, and steps were quickly taken to disarm them or transfer them to other parts of the republic. I believe that the Sierra de Puebla's geopolitical importance placed a high premium on its loyalty and forced the federal government to adopt a different approach. An inability to predict how the Sierra would react to the imposition of direct military control persuaded the Guerra y Marina to seek the services of a locally accepted intermediary.

Federal military strategies for the Sierra de Puebla were built upon the mistaken premise that Gabriel Barrios was in complete control of his troops. While he undoubtedly enjoyed the loyalty, even devotion, of some serranos, in many communities Barrios was barely tolerated. His success in retaining serrano support and thereby sustaining his reputation with the Guerra y Marina depended upon him offering serranos something that others could not. In order to discover what this might be, I explore the extent to which elements such as charisma, coercion, and patronage secured the loyalty of his soldiers. Yet the heterogeneity of Sierra communities and the men who fought for him suggests that there were other reasons why Barrios enjoyed widespread, if sometimes begrudging, acceptance. I argue that the overriding consideration that convinced communities of various ethnic and social circumstances to accept Barrios was a shared desire to bring an end to the arbitrary violence of the Revolution. I conclude the chapter by looking at how lawlessness disrupted serrano everyday life and how the absence of stable civilian authority offered Barrios an opportunity to extend beyond his military brief to assume a peacekeeping role. By identifying the community-based structure of Barrios's army, the military nature of local law enforcement units, and the limits that units placed upon their willingness to fight, I illustrate the delicate, ever-changing balance of power between the Sierra soldiers and those who sought to use them.

In chapter 3, I explore the symbiotic relationship between political actors at national, regional, and municipal levels. Mexican politics during the 1920s might be characterized as a process of faltering yet relentless centralization in which provincial caudillos and mass organizations became absorbed within an emerging state. In this respect, developments in the politically important state of Puebla represented a major thorn in the federal government's project of incorporation. For much of the decade, Puebla was beset by caudillo politics and bitter factional disputes that reflected but did not follow national trends. Agraristas and laboristas fought each other and a conservative elite for control of the local congress. This often produced a situation of near anarchy, with violence replacing reasoned debate. The federal government frequently used its constitutional powers to intervene, which invariably led to increased resentment in Puebla and further political chaos.

At one level, the Sierra Norte de Puebla appeared to be detached from events on the plains below. Although agrarian and labor union activity caused conflict in peripheral Sierra districts, for many communities these issues were neither relevant nor contested. I suggest that political instability in the city of Puebla created a vacuum of civilian authority within the Sierra that enabled the Barrios cacicazgo to flourish. In the context of cacique politics, however, I argue that Barrios never enjoyed complete freedom to convert military influence into political capital. Elections in Sierra *cabeceras* were bitterly contested and invariably characterized by violence and accusations of fraud. In such circumstances, it was often left to state and national legislatures to decide the outcome of municipal elections. When Barrios's enemies enjoyed ascendancy in congress, he found it difficult to prevent his opponents from occupying political positions in key Sierra towns. Even though Barrios never showed any ambitions beyond the Sierra, his representatives needed to contest political power in national and local congresses in order to protect his interests within the Sierra. This necessity sometimes produced unlikely alliances, and I conclude the chapter by looking at how Gabriel Barrios established a mutually convenient accord with the intellectual and prominent left-wing politician Vicente Lombardo Toledano. This accord exemplifies the often pragmatic and ideologically bankrupt nature of political life in Puebla during this period.

Having located the Sierra within the national military and political context, the remaining chapters concentrate upon how Sierra communities sought to resolve the problems they faced and to influence the nature of proposed changes. At various points, I refer to the importance of recognizing the ethnic and social heterogeneity of the Sierra. Chapter 4 examines the political consequences of this phenomenon by tracing the differing political economies of Sierra communities. Local politics in district capitals were the domain of gente de razón and wealthy mestizos. As suggested previously, contestation in these communities reflected the broader struggles for power between those supporting or opposing Barrios's continued influence within the region. Of more interest, perhaps, are the myriad smaller towns and pueblos where constitutional politics sustained an uncomfortable coexistence with other forms of local authority. In this chapter I explore how different serrano communities chose their leaders and the extent to which their free will was compromised by Barrios's imposition of nonelected local officials. I test my thesis that his control was never as complete as many would have us believe by analyzing the ways that communities dealt with the need to restore law and order. Community leaders were able to forge compromises that delivered the security both they and Barrios needed while satisfying local sensibilities regarding political legitimacy and authority. They recognized Barrios's strengths and weaknesses and frequently tested the boundaries of cooperation and confrontation. Yet they also recognized his ability to provide them with a measure of protection that enabled them to resume everyday civilian life, and this persuaded communities less than enamored with Barrios reluctantly to accept his latent presence.

Chapter 5 traces how the national trend from militarism to reconstruction developed in the Sierra. Vaughan's study of educational reform in rural Mexico during the 1930s shows that the lack of enthusiasm for many federal schemes in the Puebla state government encouraged conservative elements within Sierra society to delay, or even reject, local implementation. A decade earlier, the lack of any coherent political direction within the city of Puebla had produced a similar vacuum of regional support for federal projects. If we bear in mind Pare's assertion that caciques such as Barrios colluded with local elites to oppose or distort such schemes, then we might expect a similar failure of federal initiatives to take root in Sierra soil. Yet, instead, Barrios seized the opportunity to promote a range of innovations that often reflected, and sometimes preempted, federal government designs. Barrios's role in these projects shows the inadequacy of previous stereotypes of caciquismo. Far from keeping the Sierra isolated, Barrios relied upon his patronage of national projects to ensure his survival as an important player in the Sierra. Paradoxically, these projects would later expose the region to the very influences that would bring about his eventual downfall.

The implementation of these various schemes offers another opportunity to trace the nature of negotiations between political agents at different levels. During the 1960s the Sierra de Puebla attracted considerable anthropological interest due to government initiatives to improve road networks that had fallen into disrepair in previous decades. Anthropologists sought to gauge how indigenous campesinos coped with challenges not unlike those that had faced their forefathers in the 1920s. What the studies revealed was a dynamic process in which campesinos used long-established channels of internal political discourse to decide upon their degree of incorporation within broader mestizo society. It is my contention that similar processes took place in the 1920s as communities decided how to respond to the various changes that Gabriel Barrios sought to introduce. I suggest that, like their descendents did in the 1960s, serranos showed considerable ingenuity in trading acquiescence to major projects they could not halt for the freedom to determine the nature of more modest, local schemes. As in other areas of their lives, serranos charted a route between submission and resistance.

The hills and villages of the Sierra have once more become a battlefield as historians seek to reinterpret the past and give due recognition to political and social actors at all levels of society. Both caciquismo and popular community-based movements have been identified as keys to understanding how this region fitted into the national picture. Revisionists and post-revisionists have delved into the past and found evidence to satisfy their own analyses. In doing so they have, to greater or lesser extents, sought to explain the actions of indigenous rural communities, actions often overlooked by official history. Such a task is not without risk, and it raises serious methodological dilemmas.[41] The recent controversy begun by David Stoll regarding the writing of *I, Rigoberta Menchú* highlights the constraints that the academic world places upon cultures where fluidity in time and space is the essence of all traditions.[42] Referring to this polemic, John Beverley argues that "almost by definition the subaltern . . . cannot be adequately represented by literature or in the university" as they are "among the practices that create and sustain subalternity." The question becomes one of authority to narrate.[43] In her study of nineteenth-century rural politics in Mexico and Peru, Mallon tries to overcome such pitfalls by letting political actors speak for themselves. Yet Beverley criticizes Mallon for never relinquishing her right as a professional academic to have the final word even as she negotiates history with local intellectuals.[44] It would appear that cultural awareness and sensitivity alone cannot satisfy all critics.

In analyzing the political history of the Sierra de Puebla during the 1920s, I seek not to overturn previous interpretations, but to offer what I see as necessary correctives. In doing so, I recognize the limitations of my own perspective but take comfort from two recent observations. Vaughan argues that cultural historians need constantly to provide empirical evidence to substantiate their conclusions and to apply and compare their findings to those produced by economic and political analyses.[45] Improved understanding is best reached through refinement of our approaches, rather than substitution of one approach for another. Commenting upon the vociferous academic polemic in the United States, Daniel Nugent suggests that "rather than surrender to the insuperability of the tensions between 'real social history' and the study of 'discursive effects' or 'bottom-up' and 'top-down' perspectives, we should just get on with our work, uniting the two when the material being analyzed permits, and, for the rest, remaining cognizant of the incomplete character of our historical and political understandings."[46] It is in this spirit that I seek to expose empirical evidence to support innovative analysis. My aim is not to discover the secret formula for penetrating the minds of indigenous communities, but to observe patterns of behavior that offer clues about why they behaved as they did.[47]

What I hope to encourage is a move toward a much less polarized debate regarding the balance of political powers within postrevolutionary Mexico. Portraying caudillos as either dependent upon or autonomous of the emerging state merely sets out the two extremes of a wide spectrum of intermediary roles that such figures assumed. Similarly, studies that depict regional power brokers as conservative barriers to effective state-community dialogue pass up the opportunity to identify the circumstances under which each of these actors gained temporary ascendancy. In many respects, the studies of Howard Campbell and Jeffrey Rubin on rural politics in Juchitán during the early twentieth century illustrate the benefits of taking a fresh look at the role of the local political boss, particularly in indigenous regions.[48] Commenting on Rubin's findings, Vaughan notes that rural politics was characterized by "cacicazgos, or personal dynasties . . . that although paternalistic and authoritarian, sheltered local cultural forms by mediating the impact of federal directives and market forces."[49] Yet many revisionist historians agree that a cacique's ability to retain legitimacy among his followers depended upon his sensitivity toward the cultural mores of those he sought to lead. As such, revisionists and cultural historians are looking at two sides of the same coin, sides that are both complementary and mutually dependent.

My focus upon the political influence of Gabriel Barrios, therefore, is intended not to be a political biography of a petty tyrant, but to use his career to shed light on a range of issues concerning political representation in rural Mexico during the 1920s. What emerges is a picture of uncertainty befitting the times: a weak federal government whose survival depended upon the goodwill of a host of regional leaders who, in turn, faced multiple pressures that forced them to be flexible in their dealings with others. As they strove to pick up the pieces after years of violence, rural communities sought the most effective means of shaping their future. Within the Sierra de Puebla, relationships among local, regional, and national political agents were interlinked and intensified by the ethnic factor. I argue that a hesitancy, even an inability, to establish direct dialogue with such communities convinced the federal government of the need to use cultural intermediaries such as Gabriel Barrios. This reliance, however, did not make Barrios all-powerful. His influence was limited both by the demands of those in Mexico City and by the extent to which his role was useful to communities within the Sierra de Puebla. Not only were indigenous groups aware of the bargaining position that their military potential afforded, but whenever possible they used this potential to modify the actions of Gabriel Barrios as their agent with external authorities. The resulting picture is one that rejects polarities in favor of a more measured, nuanced picture of power relations in rural Mexico during the 1920s.

1

The People and
History of the
Sierra Norte de Puebla

The nature of relationships between social and ethnic groups in Mexico attracted considerable attention during the 1990s. The recent emphasis on the political agency of subaltern groups sheds new light on factors influencing apparent changes in previous patterns of coexistence. Particular focus has been placed upon the turbulent century following independence, when statesmen sought to construct a new Mexican identity that might counter the inherent regionalism of the past. The violent struggles accompanying this process often disturbed the local status quo as different groups traded concessions for temporary alliances. In some regions, conflict served to undermine the position of the social elite and, as James Scott suggests, offered opportunities for subalterns to take up arms in order to redress previous injustices. Times of conflict exposed tensions that remained hidden in more peaceful moments, allowing us to get nearer to the true balance of power between different groups and the dynamics by which this balance might shift.

In this chapter I look at the correlation between ethnic relations and violence during the nineteenth century, with particular focus on the Sierra Norte de Puebla. The region's geopolitical importance meant that many communities within the Sierra were affected by, and were forced to respond to, such violence. Where I depart from earlier studies is in the broader significance I attach to such responses. I believe that the particular concerns of each community were unique and that although communities may have acted in similar ways to the challenges they faced, this need not indicate shared motives. Because my own argument stresses how the heterogeneity of indigenous communities affected the way they responded to outside pressures, it is useful to introduce the area, its inhabitants, and the ways communities developed their own values, traditions, and priorities.

Topography and Society of the Sierra Norte de Puebla

Altitude has a direct bearing on climate, agricultural activities, and resulting socioeconomic characteristics of any given location within the Sierra.[1] The *tierra caliente*, which extends from the gulf coast to the northeastern foothills of the Sierra, is a zone of high humidity and subtropical vegetation (see map 3). It enjoys generous rainfall throughout the year and the climate is conducive to the cultivation of maize, sugarcane, and vanilla. In the early twentieth century, the discovery of oil dramatically increased the economic and employment opportunities of the hitherto agriculturally dependant coastal communities, placing new impetus on long-standing plans to improve roads and communications between the coast and Mexico City.

Moving out of the coastal plain and up the slopes of the Sierra to a maximum of 1,200 meters, we encounter the *tierra cálida*, which is characterized by a blanket of mist that typically forms as the warm gulf breeze meets the colder air of the Sierra Madre Oriental. Humidity remains high, especially in summer and winter, and although cooler than the coast, the area is free of the frosts that threaten agriculture at higher elevations. Several rivers cut deep into the region's slopes, draining the higher reaches and producing spectacular waterfalls and canyons. The climate and fertile soil allow coffee and to a lesser extent sugarcane, beans, chilies, and citrus fruits to grow alongside more established crops such as maize.

At an altitude between 1,200 and 2,200 meters, the *tierra templada* is cooler, with higher rainfall and less fertile soil than the tierra cálida further down the slopes. Although limited to one harvest a year, coffee cultivation is still viable in all but the highest reaches of the zone. Indeed, in communities near Zacapoaxtla coffee has eclipsed maize production to such an extent that serranos now have to purchase maize from other regions in order to satisfy their own needs.[2] As in the tierra caliente, the raising of sugarcane, vegetables, citrus fruit, and chickens supplements the campesinos' diet and income. During the wet season between June and September, the high altitude gives a chilling edge to the heavy rainfall. Social and commercial activity falters as dampness

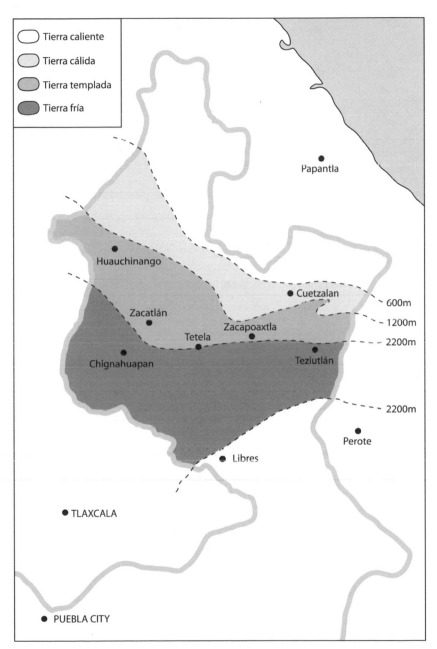

Map 3. Sierra de Puebla climatic zones (based on Beaucage 1973)

pervades food, clothing, and even the body. The rain eventually gives way to the variable weather of autumn and winter. Although there are lengthy spells of warm sunshine, when the *nortes* blow clouds periodically rush to fill the valleys where many serrano towns are situated. These clouds push against the gorge that skirts Zacatlán and frequently spill over to engulf the town. During these periods, dampness returns and temperatures tumble.

The *tierra fría* comprises the highest peaks in the Sierra Norte. Above Chignahuapan (3,400 meters) the land is dry and barren, and the slopes are generally deeply eroded and unsuitable for cultivation. In the more sheltered valleys, however, communities are able to produce subsistence crops, selling pears, apples, and potatoes in local markets. The southern fringes of the tierra fría give way to the *meseta*, the vast high plateau upon which lie the state capital of Puebla and the main route from Mexico City to the port of Veracruz.

Patterns of early settlement were determined by the agricultural activities that a specific area could sustain, and by access to local and regional markets. Although early indigenous migration to the Sierra is still reflected in the concentration of Totonac settlements below the tierra cálida and of Nahua settlements above, there are many exceptions to this neat division. Regional commerce and seasonal migration, particularly from the Sierra to the tierra caliente, have produced kinship ties between communities from widely contrasting local environments, and several communities are now bilingual in Nahuatl and Totonac.[3] In addition, as Peter Gerhart shows, the Otomís have a considerable historical presence south of Chignahuapan and west of the Zacatlán-Huauchinango axis.[4] Bernal García's study of pre-Columbian and colonial demography shows that the region's topography hampered communication, restricted external administrative control, and fostered subtle cultural distinctions between communities with common ethnic origins.[5] These cultural differences are manifest in Alexis Juárez's recent study of present-day popular religion in the Sierra. He suggests that although most indigenous communities share a devotion to the Catholic Church, the unique symbolism that each attaches to daily worship reflects the very different ways in which they have fused indigenous and mestizo cultures.[6] Totonac and Nahua communities have synthesized native and Catholic beliefs to create images of a spiritual world that include a varying mix of holy, supernatural, and magical influences. Even so, anthropologists believe that it is still possible to find similarities within diverse indigenous communities, whether they be in the vestiges of pre-Columbian traits or adaptations to colonial influences. Many communities share a cosmic vision of the world in which humans are a part of nature rather than opposed to it, and where spiritual significance is attached to physical spaces and features. As elsewhere within Mesoamerica, such a vision adds a cultural dimension to any form of community resistance based upon occupancy and use of land.[7] Patriarchal social structures are common elements of Nahua and Totonac communities. Land inheritance follows the male line and acts to bind male offspring to their paternal origins. Political and moral authority often lies in the performance of civil and religious obligations, and the sponsorship of *cargos* affords men a degree of spiritual reverence amongst community members.[8]

Early colonial exposure to mestizo culture in the region was sporadic, varied, and sometimes rapid and destructive. Gerhart shows that non-Indian settlement was light and mainly concentrated in areas close to the trading route that crossed the meseta. San Juan de los Llanos (present-day Libres), for example, became a cabecera as early as 1569, whereas only much later did mining opportunities stimulate mestizo penetration into the more remote areas around Tetela de Ocampo and Teziutlán. Elsewhere in the tierra fría and tierra templada, colonial settlement was slow to arrive and limited in scope. Zacapoaxtla, which in the nineteenth century would become a bastion of non-Indian influence, witnessed its first significant colonial presence only in the previous century. Indeed, nineteenth-century mestizo settlement brought important changes to the Sierra, as established families sought to hold the line against the wave of political and economic migrants from the meseta.[9] Subsequent tensions between these groups quickly assumed the same character as a much broader battle within Mexico over the future direction of the new republic. The majority indigenous population could not help but become a part of the environment of heightened politicization. Previous exploitation of the indigenous campesinos had relied more on the white elite's control of their "voluntary" labor (*topiles*) and of the local market trade. For some communities, however, nineteenth-century migration represented the first major conflict over land tenure and usage. When external pressures threatened to upset previous arrangements, communities faced a choice between submissive acceptance, negotiated compromise, or armed rebellion. Within the Sierra, all three would be employed.

Indigenous Militarism in Nineteenth-Century Mexico

Opinions regarding indigenous participation in nineteenth-century political discourse varied depending upon time and place. In 1848 the Mexico City newspaper *El Monitor Republicano* lamented that the only active role Indians played in national public affairs was "to serve as soldiers in the army, which they are obliged to do by force."[10] This statement probably reflected a common view among *capitalinos* and provincial elites that Indians were apolitical and docile and needed to be forced to honor their duties as citizens in the new republic. Cut adrift from their rural communities and exposed to the vagaries of city life, Indians were often viewed as a "noxious influence and social problem."[11]

Yet this image, and the mestizo confidence it implied, periodically wavered. Indian uprisings in Veracruz in 1787 exposed the weakness of the army in New Spain, and the incumbent viceroy, Manuel Flórez, reflected that if an enemy squadron had appeared off the coast of Veracruz at the same time, Indians could have contributed to the loss of the kingdom. In the early 1800s rumors persisted of a network connecting the nation's Indian communities with a native king in Tlaxcala who was plotting to overthrow white rule.[12] Throughout the nineteenth century opposing mestizo sides sought to recruit Indian soldiers to their cause, an effort that entailed considerable risk. When Juan Alvarez recruited among Guerrero's Indian communities during the 1830s and 1840s, his political enemies accused him of fostering a caste war.[13] In Yucatán during the 1840s, creoles in Campeche and Mérida were sufficiently confident, or desperate, to mobilize and arm Mayas in their struggle against each other and U.S. incursions. When Maya actions showed signs of getting out of hand, however, creoles united under the rallying cry of "caste war."[14] Jan Rus's study of Chiapas during the 1860s shows a similar development. Liberals in Tuxtla and Chiapa were quite prepared to foment friction between their conservative rivals in San Cristóbal de las Casas and the highland Indian communities. Yet as soon as Indians spilled white blood and were perceived to be taking control of their own actions, ladinos closed ranks to protect their race.[15]

Guardino suggests that claims of a caste war in Guerrero were politically motivated, and much the same can be said of Yucatán and Chiapas. Yet this should not obscure the underlying insecurity within non-Indian provincial society that made such a tactic highly effective in uniting rival factions. For the isolated white settlements in outlying regions, a fine line existed between control and catastrophe. Although interethnic contact was more immediate in rural cabeceras than in the cities, this did not necessarily lead to any significant increase in mutual trust. It is true that in many outlying pueblos, mestizos lived alongside their indigenous neighbors and in economic terms may have been barely distinguishable from them. Within rural cabeceras, however, there was often a small but influential sector, sometimes referred to as gente de razón, who sought to sustain the civility of cosmopolitan life enjoyed by their city-based contemporaries While their control of markets, labor, and religion constantly reaffirmed the subordination of the local Indian population, the fact that they were an isolated minority made them very sensitive to perceived threats to their dominant position. It is interesting to note that events in Yucatán were happening at precisely the time when *El Monitor Republicano* bemoaned the reluctance of indigenous groups to embrace national projects and fight for their country. It appears that in soldiery, as in civilian life, the aim was to maximize yet tightly restrict the potential of the Indians. Politicization, especially from the point of view of provincial elites, did not go so far as to encourage Indians to define their rights and fight for them independently.

Was the Sierra de Puebla any different? Until well into the twentieth century, the region shared many of the characteristics of more remote locations: a large indigenous population, a minority white elite concentrated in dispersed cabeceras, and a poor communications infrastructure resulting in nominal external authority. Although living in the same communities, different ethnic groups occupied separate worlds; Nahua and Totonac families lived in flimsy single-roomed houses made of wood or cane and were simply clothed, while gente de razón in Zacapoaxtla, for example, lived in imposing houses filled with furniture from Mexico City and dressed in the latest fashions from Paris and London.[16]

As Friedlander noted in Hueyapan during the 1960s, coexistence has been unable to erode the formidable cultural and social barriers between ethnic groups.[17] Zacapoaxtla's relatively late colonial settlement may have made it an extreme case, but in times of unrest local gente de razón and mestizos in Tetela de Ocampo and Zacatlán displayed considerable hesitancy in unleashing the region's indigenous military potential. As in Yucatán and Chiapas, mestizo politicians eventually put the need for soldiers before their misgivings, but although Nahuas were offered a variety of incentives to fight, social equality was never a factor driving liberal actions: "As far as the Sierra Norte's mestizos were concerned in 1857 armed conflict and competition for recruits required that a popular Liberal agenda be kept alive to attract Indian soldiers."[18] Liberals merely stole a march on conservatives and adapted their approach to ensure continued support.

In giving their military support to the liberal revolution of Ayutla in 1855, and in organizing themselves into locally based national guard units, the indigenous soldiers of the Sierra began a long history of militarism in support of national movements. When in 1862 the defeated conservatives encouraged the French army to intervene in Mexico, the serranos assumed a more conspicuous profile. The 6th Battalion of the Puebla National Guard drew most of its troops from Sierra communities such as Xochiapulco, which had earlier rallied to the liberal cause. A local Nahua leader, Juan Francisco Lucas, rapidly emerged as a natural leader of the soldiers and a reliable supporter of the liberals. Their contribution to the Mexican army's famous defeat of the French on 5 May 1862 near the city of Puebla guaranteed the Nahua soldiers enduring if disproportionate national fame. More immediately, however, the subsequent victory of the European invasion force brought guerrilla warfare to the Sierra, as French and Austrian troops sought to bring the area under control. Skirmishes with foreign troops continued, and when Porfirio Díaz finally led the victorious liberal army towards Mexico City, he could depend upon the military support of the Sierra. Serrano loyalty for Díaz was evident once more in 1876 when he raised a rebellion in Tuxtepec against what he saw as a discredited national government. Díaz's eventual victory began three decades of executive power during which the friendship he had forged with loyal serrano military leaders such as Lucas produced tangible benefits for the region.

If this were the full story, then we might be left with the impression that the Sierra's military contribution was manipulated by mestizo leaders for their own personal or political ambitions. The national conflicts between liberals and conservatives, and between liberal factions, were certainly present in the state of Puebla, and the Sierra was deeply embroiled in these disputes.[19] Recent studies of indigenous mobilization elsewhere, however, show that communities were able to wring important concessions in return for their military services. In the tierra caliente around Papantla, mobilization during the 1810s indicated that rebels in Totonac communities saw the insurgency as an opportunity to address long-standing disputes against local officialdom.[20] Similarly, Thomson and Mallon uncover evidence deeper in the Sierra of indigenous assertiveness in negotiations with various external authorities in later decades. Both argue that Nahuas recognized the liberal political agenda and sought to use it to their advantage.

Thomson provides several reasons for believing that Juan Francisco Lucas played a crucial role in negotiations between Sierra communities and the world beyond. He contends that Lucas used his influence among mestizo politicians to protect indigenous communities from mestizo abuse, shielding them from forcible recruitment into the national guard, service beyond the Sierra Norte region, and excessive taxation. In effect, Lucas filtered many of the harmful aspects of liberal reforms while using legislation to convert liberal ideals of equal citizenship into a reality for some Sierra communities. More directly, as a reward for his military service, Lucas obtained possession of the former hacienda of Xochiapulco on the outskirts of Zacapoaxtla. This land was later developed into a military-style colony that became a liberal model of successful reform and a safe haven for Indians fleeing political abuse and repression elsewhere in the Sierra. Lucas's growing wealth led him to buy more land, some of which he offered to dispossessed Indians and used to establish projects for civic and social improvement. Such actions appealed to the cultural sensibilities of many Sierra communities, which placed considerable importance upon the redistribution of wealth for the greater good. In this way, Lucas's image as a benign patron extended beyond the limited number of communities where he had direct, personal contact.[21]

Lucas was not merely an intermediary in the sense of trading military support for local autonomy. He also allayed local mestizo fears by acting as a mediating force when indigenous anger occasionally flared up, as occurred in the rebellion against mestizo coffee producers in Cuetzalan led by Agustín Dieguillo.[22] The more Lucas could help to moderate Indians' reactions to increasing demands for resources by coffee exploiters, the greater his chances of persuading mestizos to consult with indigenous communities before adopting their plans. The last thing a mestizo entrepreneur wanted was for his investments to be endangered by social unrest. Negotiations over future use of land required a trusted intermediary to articulate the hopes and fears of both sides. By providing such a service, Lucas gained greater respect among mestizos and the various affected communities.

In offering their military services to Lucas, Nahua communities in the Sierra demonstrated a considerable degree of independence. They would fight only under their own leaders, and they would not spend long periods away from their families and fields. The demands of the agricultural calendar had an important limiting effect upon the serranos' political and military commitments. The Brigada Serrana that Lucas eventually commanded, therefore, was little more than an amalgam of national guard units based within Nahua communities and led by local and regional Nahua commanders. The rank and file of the Brigada were campesinos who spent most of their time tending their crops. The question then becomes one of motives and long-term effects of this military cooperation.

Thomson and Mallon share much common ground regarding their opinions of the ability of indigenous communities to use broader political circumstances in pursuit of local objectives, particularly in times of civil war. Where they differ, however, is over the channels through which the detailed processes of negotiation, compromise, and resistance took place. Thomson suggests that in times of great anxiety, a diverse range of Sierra communities were drawn toward the paternalistic protection that Lucas offered. This is the point at which Mallon picks up the voice of those below, viewing conflict as an opportunity for reappraisal not just among various groups within a community, but between communities and external authorities. She argues that family, factional, gender, and generational contestation constantly reshaped community responses to external affairs. Mobilization, for example, afforded a community's young soldiers a level of temporary authority that would have taken years to attain through traditional *cargo* systems.[23]

Reflecting the thoughts of Raymond Williams twenty years earlier, Mallon argues that the relationship between state and community evolved as internal and external factors fed into the equation at different levels of power. In this regard, Mallon points to the unique antecedents of the military colony of Xochiapulco and rightly questions whether rural communities that retained more traditional hierarchical structures could ever have responded in the same way.[24] Drawing from Ranajit Guha's work on peasant rebellion in India, Adolfo Gilly agrees that decisions to take up arms are rarely impulsive but result from protracted internal debate that is informed by the cultural, political, and historical realities of a particular community.[25] Yet given such heterogeneity, how does the local historian overcome the eternal problem of plotting a route toward broader conclusions based on diverse, often contradictory local signposts? For Mallon, the very flexibility of hegemonic discourse becomes the linchpin. While the exact nature of the negotiations between the state and a community might vary for a number of reasons, they take place within recognized parameters that can be applied to all cases. For Thomson, the broad appeal of patriarchal figures offers a better understanding of the state's relationship with Sierra communities. Lucas may not have been seen in the same light by all communities, but he did represent a culturally acceptable figure through whom communities could accomplish their aims.[26]

My problem with both analyses is less with the differing perspectives of how Sierra communities negotiated than with the long-term significance attributed to the act of negotiation. Let us go back for a moment to the earlier insurrections in Papantla. Michael Ducey's study shows that key insurgent figures worked hard to prevent the struggle from being reduced to one based upon "peasant localism." Speeches and circulars reflected the language and rhetoric of the broader political debate in late colonial society, and the potency of this propaganda is exemplified by the way that local rebel leaders, such as Mariano Olarte, issued declarations bearing the hallmarks of Spanish constitutional rhetoric. Yet his messages were modified to address the main concern of Totonac peasants: the demand for increased autonomy that might relieve them from excessive exploitation.[27] If, as Ducey suggests, a central tenet of the insurgency was a vision of the nation that recognized the plurality of pueblos and respected local traditions, this merely reflected a fundamental resistance to relinquishing local autonomy in return for inclusion within a new, homogenous form of national identity. Regardless of the deployment of cosmopolitan political discourse, the village remained the focus of peasant priorities. Crucially, the nature of the relationship between the emerging nation and its multifarious local components had yet to be settled.

Thomson believes that half a century later Lucas helped to facilitate the progress of this relationship in the Sierra. He refers to the collective memory of *vecinos* in the Cuetzalan community of San Miguel Tzinacapan, where Lucas is remembered "not only because he was a good general, but because until the end of his life he was seen as a maseual [Indian] who helped his people." Thomson concludes that Lucas helped stimulate the community's "entry into the modern Mexican nation-state, with Lucas freeing the maseualmej [indigenous population] from the analtekos [non-Indians], leading them into their patriotic sacrifices, and guaranteeing their rights of citizenship."[28] Perhaps we need to step back from such a bold assertion. It is one thing to acknowledge that Tzinacapanecos believed Lucas to have been a good chap, but entirely another to suggest that he was leading them into a brave new liberal world. Indeed, intrinsic to Thomson's assertion that many communities preferred to adopt a "popular," rather than a national, form of liberalism is the fact that most Nahua soldiers were pursuing a fundamentally local agenda. Thomson's comparison of the national guard units of Xochiapulco and Cuetzalan illustrates the point. The first, he suggests, was a "classic creation with liberal ideals incorporating and embracing much offered by the Liberal Constitution," while the Cuetzalan unit used "radical liberal discourse as a means of rescuing local autonomy."[29] However, when political rhetoric and postures were stripped away, both communities sought the same objectives: protection from unrestrained external interference, whether this be forced conscription (*leva*), crippling taxes, or threats to local autonomy. While they were fighting together against a common enemy, mestizo and Nahua soldiers appeared to be in tune; yet this did not mean that all Nahua communities necessarily shared a common commitment to the liberal cause, either popular or national. It may have reflected the fact that during periods of war, when certain avenues for resistance disappeared, the military option offered an alternative. Serranos in Tzinacapan and elsewhere may well have been adding indigenous lyrics to mestizo melodies.

Paradoxically, if we accept that Sierra communities had the political acumen to engage in broader ideological negotiations, then we should also credit them with having the ability to learn from previous mistakes. Throughout the history of their negotiations with mestizo politicians, indigenous communities in the Sierra saw promises made in the heat of battle unfulfilled once the need for soldiers subsided. How often could a community's hopes be dashed before it lost faith in state representatives? Derek Sayer suggests that state hegemony might be the weakest aspect of the state, as it relies on "living what [the participants] much of the time know to be a lie."[30] When living the lie was the only political option available, there may have been a need to keep the pretense going. Yet apparent willingness to negotiate, even voicing eagerness to negotiate through documents or manifestations, may have been the best tactic when other forms of resistance were not feasible. For a community such as Xochiapulco, whose raison d'être depended upon liberal ideals, there was good reason to live the lie longer. But what about Chiconcuautla, a few miles down the mountain tracks? In May 1862 it offered soldiers for the liberal cause at the famous battle in the city of Puebla. The depth of its loyalty was exposed a year later when it entered into negotiations with conservative forces promising to relieve the burden of taxation.[31] While Chiconcuautla and other indigenous communities undoubtedly had the ability to negotiate with the state, it is a matter of debate whether the ensuing dialogue implied any enduring commitment to a particular state project.

Mallon recognizes this pattern of reneged promises and the renewed process of conflict, negotiation, and compromise it produced. Indeed, she argues that this experience better equipped all parties to shape the nature and direction of postrevolutionary reforms in the 1920s and 1930s. But was this the only possible effect upon state-community relations? Any measure of mutual trust forged in the 1860s would have been long buried when the need for indigenous soldiers arose again in 1910. Many of those debating community responses to the demands of the Revolution and postrevolutionary reforms would have been elders who may have fought in the past and certainly would have remembered the checkered history of their dealings with state representatives. Would they embrace the latest ideology coming from the center, transforming it and making it their own, as had happened in certain communities with liberalism? Or would they think twice about negotiating with a state that much of the time was barely able to guarantee its own survival, let alone honor its commitments? As in the past, the heterogeneity of the Sierra provoked diverse reactions. Some communities sought allegiances with national popular movements; others turned inward and kept their heads down. Still others turned to the support and protection of local leaders and, in this respect, Lucas once more became politically significant. Yet if a common motive can be gleaned from those serranos who fought in the Revolution, it was their pursuit of the same objectives that had compelled young national guardsmen and elderly *pasados* to rebel a generation before: defense of their families and community.

2 Indigenous Militarism within the Sierra, 1910–1930

When Demetrio Barrios Cabrera retired in 1961 after a lifetime of military service, he is said to have reflected upon how the Mexican army had changed: "Gone are the days of the Indian soldier. Nowadays they expect you to take exams and speak foreign languages."[1] He may have been thinking of his nephew, José María Barrios Nava, one of a new generation of professional army officers, the first fruit of the seeds of army reform sown in the postrevolutionary period. Yet even so, Barrios Nava's dark skin and short stature singled him out. A senior officer once quipped that the reason why "el indito" Barrios Nava spoke French so well was because in the last century his grandfather had eaten a Frenchman.[2] Behind the banter and latent racism of the officers' mess, however, lay recognition of the Sierra Indians' contribution to the struggles against foreign and Mexican enemies that marred the first century of independence.

Given the treatment of indigenous soldiers elsewhere, the record of militarism in the Sierra de Puebla appears all the more remarkable. When Demetrio Barrios retired, he relinquished control of an Indian battalion that had given loyal service to the federal government for almost a century. Beginning as a cluster of community-based national guard units, the Brigada Serrana saw action during every major military conflict from Ayutla to the Revolution under the leadership of Juan Francisco Lucas. Upon Lucas's death in 1917, Gabriel Barrios performed a similar role until his retirement in 1940, when command passed to his brother Demetrio. Throughout this period, the unit gained a reputation for its swift and loyal response in times of national crisis, and when in 1944 an attempt was made on the life of the poblano president, Manuel Avila Camacho, it was from the Indian ranks of his Sierra homeland that a new presidential guard was formed.[3] While such a history might suggest serranos to have been little more than obedient foot soldiers of the federal government, it disguises a large measure of independent action that, in other places at other times, might have been deemed rebellious.

In this chapter I examine the singular nature of militarism in the Sierra Norte de Puebla between 1910 and 1930, a time which saw indigenous soldiers operating within their own territory under the command of their own leaders. While this attracted vehement opposition from some quarters of the local elite, unlike what happened elsewhere in the republic, such protests fell on deaf ears. For brief periods during the 1920s it appears that local indigenous commanders and soldiers were dictating terms not only to wealthy families from Zacatlán to Zacapoaxtla, but to generals and politicians from Puebla city to Mexico City. How and why this occurred reveals the limitations of federal authority during this period and, in particular, the part that warfare played in delivering political agency to groups more accustomed to a subordinate role.

To explain the nature of the serrano military contribution in the 1920s, I begin with an overview of federal military priorities and the role that indigenous mobilization assumed in other parts of the republic. I then identify how federal generals viewed the Sierra de Puebla's contribution to these objectives and the dilemmas they faced in adopting strategies designed to secure the region's loyalty. I reveal a complicated phase of risk assessment and negotiations from which Gabriel Barrios emerged as an apparently essential intermediary between those who sought and those who possessed the Sierra's military potential. In testing the veracity of this image, I address the broader question of exactly where the Sierra fits into a polarized debate that on one hand sees military leaders like Barrios as unprincipled manipulators of submissive peasants, and on the other portrays indigenous community leaders as experienced campaigners able to deploy a range of weapons in their ongoing struggles with the state.

Federal Militarism: From Pragmatism to Professionalism

Backing the right horse in the Revolution was a tricky, hazardous, but potentially profitable business. With the governments of Francisco

Madero (1911–1913), Victoriano Huerta (1913–1914), Venustiano Carranza (1915–1920), and Alvaro Obregón (1920–1924) each representing
a violent, abrupt departure from the immediately preceding administration, anyone purporting to be a loyal supporter of the national
executive needed to be pragmatic, flexible, and above all, lucky to
emerge unscathed. Any professionalism the Porfirian federal army may
once have possessed was quickly eclipsed as corrupt, often incompetent
officers marshaled conscripted, undernourished, and demoralized soldiers into battle. As Madero's assassination illustrated, placing trust in
the federal army offered little security. With political authority devolv-
ing to individuals with sufficient military clout to get their way, those
with pretensions to national government had to coerce, cajole, or convince a diversity of irregular forces to support them. Why such armies
should do so has been a bone of historical contention for several decades. Land, autonomy, ambition, conviction, and intimidation featured
highly among the factors persuading otherwise peaceful Mexicans to
risk their lives. The problem that postrevolutionary administrations
faced, however, was in satisfying these diverse and often conflicting
aspirations. As in the nineteenth century, promises made in the heat of
battle were more difficult to honor once the fighting had subsided and
the need for civilian soldiers had passed.

From Carranza onwards, each administration sought to demilitarize
the Mexican countryside by exchanging guns for land and ploughs, and
by replacing the discredited federal army with a smaller, professional,
and above all loyal institution (see figure 3).[4] In tacit recognition of
past failings, the Carranza administration threatened immediate dismissal of military personnel found guilty of political interference or corruption. Carranza's generals were frequently relocated to reduce their
chances of establishing potentially damaging relationships with local
elites. Manuals, such as the one written by General Arnulfo Gómez,
extolled the virtues of military professionalism and the need to educate
the rank and file to produce an army "that will always be seen as a
positive contributor to the defense of national integrity and the preser-
vation of internal order."[5] Although the *Universal Ilustrado* cartoon suggests that progress was being made, turning principle into practice was
far from easy. At the most basic level, many revolutionaries experienced
problems in getting their military contribution recognized. Did revolutionary combat for one movement, for instance, merit accreditation by
the federal government, and if so were such soldiers entitled to a mili-

LA EVOLUCION DEL EJERCITO.....

Figure 3. La evolución del ejército (the evolution of the army), by Audiffred (from *Universal Ilustrado*, 24 Sept. 1925, p. 48)

tary pension from a grateful nation? Nonrecognition threatened to foster a reservoir of resentment that could be profitably tapped by potential enemies of the postrevolutionary state.

To compound the problem, until the army became subordinate to civilian rule, the federal executive continued to need the services of irregular armies, to protect itself from both its own generals and external threats. The Revolution had forged many leaders in the heat of battle for whom the prospect of returning to civilian life held little appeal. Many had a good war, accruing some wealth along the way. Having backed the right horse, they quite naturally anticipated a share of the winnings. When it became clear that the cut envisaged was one in the military budget, there was a resurgence of violence. On 6 December 1923 an influential group of senior military officers launched an armed uprising when the Obregón administration attempted to usher Plutarco Elías Calles through as the next president. After considerable persuasion, opposition candidate Adolfo de la Huerta agreed to lend his name to the movement. Within days as much as half the federal army had defected, and for several weeks the government tottered on the brink of defeat. More than ever before, the government's survival depended upon the support of agrarian and workers' brigades.[6]

Although two more army revolts, in 1927 and 1929, and a major popular mobilization against the state's anti-Catholic reforms (the Cristero rebellion of 1926–1929) served as reminders of the violent legacy of revolution, the defeat of the Delahuertistas in 1924 ended the last realistic armed threat to Mexico's civilian government. Incorporation within the Partido Nacional Revolucionario (PNR), formed in 1929, signaled the military establishment's recognition of the fledgling single-party political system in which future disputes would be settled internally rather than on the battlefield. At this definitive point in Mexican national politics, the faltering process of political centralization begun in the 1920s began to bear fruit. The time of military caudillismo had passed. Leaders such as Saturnino Cedillo, who refused to relinquish control of the state of San Luis Potosí, were deemed enemies of the Revolution and met a sorry end. Demobilization or full incorporation within the federal army provided peaceful options for those willing to accept the new political reality.

So where does indigenous militarism fit into this broader picture of political and military centralization? A short answer might be that indigenous soldiers played a significant but largely invisible military role during the 1910s and 1920s. This partly reflected a postrevolutionary agenda diametrically opposed to the continued "otherness" of the Indian. Yet the treatment of Indian soldiers was governed more by pragmatism than the idealism of acculturation. There was no shortage of revolutionary groups seeking the services of indigenous soldiers, but local conditions determined how these services might be tapped. In Chiapas, history repeated itself as ladinos from San Cristóbal used indigenous soldiers from Chamula in their struggle against Tuxtla Gutiérrez. When, in 1911, Chamulans began to use the revolutionary struggle to settle old scores with Indian and ladino neighbors alike, ladinos once more united to prevent a caste war from developing. From that time onward, ladinos tried desperately to keep Indians out of the conflict, seeing them as part of the prize rather than potential allies.[7] In the isthmus of Tehuantepec, Zapotec mobilization in Juchitán rallied around Che Gómez, a mestizo member of the local elite who promised regional autonomy. This revolt was quickly crushed by government forces and although sporadic rebellions continued to threaten local stability, the main military contribution of Zapotec battalions during the 1910s and 1920s was as federal government troubleshooters in other parts of the republic. Ironically, one of these units, the 13th Battalion led by General Heliodoro Charis, played a significant role in the defeat of the Yaqui struggle for independence in Sonora.[8]

Yaqui fighting prowess was valued even more than that of the Zapotecs of Juchitán. Following years of repression, the revolutionary struggle offered the Yaqui soldiers of Sonora one last chance to obtain local concessions by supporting a broader movement. However, Evelyn Hu DeHart argues that those who joined the Revolution did so from a position of considerable weakness. The Yaquis were already a defeated people who saw lending support to revolutionary factions as a means of making the best of a bad situation.[9] Alan Knight, in contrast, maintains that the Yaquis' long history of cultural separateness made them impervious to compromise and that "though their struggle merged with that of mestizo revolutionaries . . . their protest was fundamentally traditional . . . dedicated to the complete recovery and untrammeled enjoyment of their old tribal patrimony."[10] Yaquis and mestizos in Sonora may have fought on the same side, and they may even have shared a desire to satisfy local rather than national objectives, but future events would demonstrate that they did not share the same local objectives. The temporary convergence of local and national ambitions afforded

Yaquis a little space and, for a while, the rare sight of indigenous battalions fighting under their own commanders within a national struggle was observed.[11] Upon the cessation of revolutionary hostilities, however, Yaqui belligerence reverted to being depicted as a threat to national interests. As early as 1917, Calles warned his fellow Sonorans that the only "quick and effective" solution to the Yaqui problem was the "complete extermination of the tribe."[12] Despite the Yaquis' renewed mobilization outside Sonora during the de la Huerta rebellion, Charis's Zapotec army thwarted any chance they had of making political capital out of their loyalty to the federation. As Adrian Bantjes points out, it was not until the presidency of Lázaro Cárdenas (1934–1940) that broader political objectives created an environment that allowed the remnants of Yaqui culture to recover in the Yaqui Valley.[13]

Indigenous mobilization, then, should be seen within the broader context of military and political change. In each of the preceding cases, when the priority was mass mobilization, indigenous communities found a degree of freedom to pursue their own objectives through military means. This freedom sometimes took the form of local rebellions led by Indians or mestizos against external authorities, and these were invariably crushed. In other cases, it took the form of joining the ranks of the federal army, but this most often happened well away from a people's home territory, thereby reducing the chances of Indian federal units pursuing local objectives. It was extremely rare for the Guerra y Marina to sanction, even depend upon, an indigenous battalion operating in its own region under its own commanders. It is in this respect that the Sierra de Puebla is a special case.

Federal Army Recruitment in the Sierra Norte de Puebla

The Guerra y Marina's exceptional treatment of the Sierra de Puebla flowed from its recognition of the region's geopolitical importance and the status of Puebla politics. For much of the 1920s, Puebla politics found itself in a state of turmoil that frequently approached anarchy. Hostile relations between federal and Puebla congresses were often aggravated by the forcible removal of unstable governors and their replacement by federal military officers from outside the region. The state government had neither the continuity nor the resources to sustain its own armed forces, and for significant spells during this period, weak civilian governors or leaders of local agrarian armies offered the only alternative to federally imposed rule. Tension between the state and federal governments often manifested itself locally through antagonism between the governor and the incumbent *jefe de operaciones militares* in the city of Puebla.[14] In times of national crisis, the prospects of moral and military support from the state government were remote. In such situations, the loyalty of the Sierra Norte de Puebla assumed even greater significance to the federal regime.

Given the often acrimonious relationship between national and state politicians, federal officials recognized a need to deal directly with those in the Sierra de Puebla who could deliver the cooperation they coveted. During the early years of the Revolution, this meant reviving old ties with the septuagenarian general Juan Francisco Lucas. But times had changed since Lucas's heyday; the passing of the years had taken its toll on Lucas, and some questioned whether he still possessed the political acumen to shoulder new responsibilities. His persistent hesitation in declaring support for one cause or another provoked criticism from all sides and jeopardized ties with previously loyal Sierra communities that were exposed to the arbitrary violence of revolutionary groups. Other leaders within the Sierra emerged with their own supporters ready to lend allegiance to the various revolutionary movements. In 1913, the more forthright political stance of the mestizo Márquez brothers of Otlatlán, Chignahuapan, attracted considerable popular support among those serranos who viewed Lucas's vacillations as a sign that he was about to support the illegitimate Huerta regime (see figure 4). When Carrancistas opposed to Huerta appointed an outsider, General Antonio Medina, to share military jurisdiction of the Sierra de Puebla with the Márquez brothers, there was a real danger that indigenous military leadership of the Sierra might fall out of Nahua hands for the first time in many decades.[15] At this crucial moment, the Barrios brothers began to make their military presence felt, delaying the eclipse of indigenous militarism in the Sierra for many years.

On 6 June 1913, the Barrios brothers mustered 120 of their neighbors and descended the slopes to enlist in Lucas's Brigada Serrana. Now firmly backing the Carrancista cause, the brigade was incorporated within the 3rd East Division led by Medina, and Gabriel Barrios was placed in command of the new recruits, thereafter called the Cuacuila company (see tables 1 and 2).[16] Throughout the second half of 1913, they comprised part of a greater force under the command of the Márquez brothers that defeated Huertista troops in Zacatlán and Chignahuapan.

Figure 4. The Márquez brothers (seated), Coatepec, Veracruz (Courtesy of Sergio, Biblioteca Luis Cabrera, Zacatlán)

In early 1914, the company united with others in a series of battles from Tlatlauquitepec in the eastern Sierra to Tulancingo in the neighboring state of Hidalgo. In May, they fought under Medina in a number of operations in the nearby tierra caliente of Veracruz, where Barrios's leadership earned him the rank of first captain.

In December 1914 the Márquez brothers' decision to switch their allegiance to the convencionistas prompted the Cuacuila company to return to the Sierra. For the next two years, Lucas marshaled his troops in opposition to the Márquez clan, whose headquarters at Otlatlán lay on the far side of a range of hills separating it from Cuacuila. Previous cooperation gave way to open hostility between the dominant families of two communities that had harbored tensions for several years. Guillermo Mejía offers a poignant indication of the heightened tensions under which both families lived during these times. Each of the Barrios brothers had a house next to the small central square in Cuacuila. As a precaution against surprise enemy attacks, the houses were connected by secret passageways, the entrances being concealed behind curtains or wardrobes.[17] Friction between neighbors was compounded by personal revenge when, in one of the Márquez raids on Cuacuila, Demetrio Barrios was injured and another brother, Amado,

Table 1 Evolution of Federal Military Presence in the
Sierra de Puebla

Name of Battalion	Dates Used
Brigada Serrana	Until 31 Dec. 1919
Serrano de Puebla Infantry Regiment	1 Jan. 1920–2 Feb. 1921
54th Battalion	3 Feb. 1921–4 March 1921
8th Auxiliary Battalion	5 March 1921–4 Aug. 1921
59th Auxiliary Battalion	5 Aug. 1921–31 Dec. 1921
46th Battalion	1 Jan. 1922–7 July 1942

Source: ADN, C, 2-1145, fols. 1346–71.

was killed.[18] Gabriel Barrios, however, flourished in the heat of battle and in September 1915 was promoted to major and given command of one of two battalions that composed the Brigada Serrana. (The other was led by Lieutenant Colonel Tranquilino Quintero, a longtime military and personal adviser to Lucas.)

On 1 February 1917 Juan Francisco Lucas's long and illustrious life came to an end and, amid much grief and ceremony, he was buried in Tetela de Ocampo. Although Quintero outranked Gabriel Barrios, the Guerra y Marina accepted news that Barrios had taken over as temporary commander of the Brigada Serrana.[19] The brigade continued the fight against the Márquez forces, obtaining a decisive victory on 12 August 1917 in an early-morning raid on Otlatlán. Esteban and Emilio Márquez were killed in combat, and later that day Barrios received orders to execute Colonel Gaspar Márquez. After the Otlatlán attack Barrios was promoted to lieutenant colonel and, with the Márquez threat eliminated, the brigade was now free to redirect its endeavors against enemies based on both sides of the Sierra: Adampol Gaviño and Rodolfo Herrero operating in the districts of Zacatlán and Huauchinango; and the forces of Salvador Vega Bernal and others who continued to pose a threat in the district of Zacapoaxtla.[20] In their fight against rebel activities, the Barrios brothers rapidly expanded their original military jurisdiction. By 1919 the Brigada Serrana occupied the districts of Tetela, Zacatlán, Huauchinango, Tlatlauquitepec, and Zacapoaxtla in the state of Puebla, and Papantla in Veracruz. The Brigada Serrana continued its campaign against rebel groups and supported Carranza until the very last days of his administration. In recognition of Barrios's steadfastness, Carranza promoted him to the rank of colonel in April 1920.[21]

Table 2 Military Career of Gabriel Barrios Cabrera

Rank	Date Attained
Second captain and head of the Cuacuila Company of the Brigada Serrana	6 June 1913
Captain (same responsibilities)	8 July 1914
Major and head of the Juan N. Méndez Battalion of the Brigada Serrana	29 Sept. 1915
Lieutenant colonel and head of the Brigada Serrana	15 Aug. 1917
Colonel and head of the Serrano de Puebla Infantry Regiment	27 April 1920
Brigadier general (same responsibilities)	27 Nov. 1920
General of the brigade	16 Nov. 1940

Source: ADN, C, 2-1145, fols. 1346–74.

When Carranza's train was stopped in its tracks at the town of Aljibres, Puebla, on 14 May 1920, the fleeing president was persuaded to take to the hills of the Sierra de Puebla in search of Barrios's protection. In the event, Carranza's bedraggled entourage passed through Barrios's military zone without meeting up with the federal commander, and on the evening following its entry into a region controlled by Rodolfo Herrero, Carranza met his death at Tlaxcalantongo. State congressional *diputado* David Vilchis wrote at the time that Barrios had tried unsuccessfully to dissuade Carranza from continuing his journey through the Sierra into territory controlled by Rodolfo Herrero.[22] The weight of evidence suggests, however, that Barrios was not prepared to accept the responsibility of protecting the president. Indeed, critics accused Barrios of being a traitor and bearing a major part of the responsibility for Carranza's death.[23] Carranza's daughter Julia, however, placed no direct blame upon the cacique, while Barrios's sons point to the dilemma he would have faced had he committed his troops in an uneven battle to protect a president whose executive powers had already been withdrawn.[24] In the event, Barrios neither deserted nor helped his president. In refusing to meet Carranza, he avoided personally betraying the president for whom he had fought during the past seven years. Barrios was no fool. He sidestepped the issue and, instead, used his influence to keep the presidential party informed of their pursuers' whereabouts. In this way he ensured the president's safe passage across his region while avoiding the loss of life that would have been inevitable had he and his troops made a stand. At the same time, although Barrios may not have complied with any orders from Obregón to stop Carranza, his actions did leave the door open for the Aguaprietistas to accept his declaration of allegiance.[25]

Following Carranza's assassination, the military situation in the Sierra Norte de Puebla was subjected to detailed scrutiny. Barrios ordered his troops back to their communities and awaited further instructions from the Guerra y Marina. For several months, Salvador Vega Bernal's troops assumed federal military responsibility for the Sierra, and Vega Bernal warned his superiors that Barrios was poised to rebel. In late 1920, however, Obregón ignored the recommendation of his own military advisers and confirmed Barrios as federal military commander for the region with the rank of brigadier general.

Obregón's faith in Barrios was handsomely repaid during the de la Huerta rebellion. Although rebellions occurred in several states, the strongest threat to the government came from those flanking the seat of national power: Jalisco, Michoacán, and Guerrero to the west and Veracruz, Puebla, and Oaxaca to the east. Barrios's continued loyalty had local, regional, and national implications. When in early December 1923, the Delahuertista forces of General Fortunato Maicotte defeated federal troops in the city of Puebla, their failure to launch an attack on Mexico City owed much to General Juan Andreu Almazán's successful counterattack using reinforcements from Tlaxcala. Had Barrios joined the rebellion, his troops, only hours from Tlaxcala, could have mounted a challenge of such strength as seriously to deplete the reinforcements upon whom Almazán's counterattack depended. This would have afforded the rebels vital time to establish the necessary supply links for an assault on the national capital.[26] Moreover, the de la Huerta army in the east would have presented a formidable front had Barrios's forces united with others in the Sierra to form a valuable link between Marcial Cavazos's rebels in Hidalgo, Sánchez and Maicotte's troops in Veracruz and Puebla, and Higinio Aguilar's forces on the borders of Oaxaca.

In the Sierra, the Delahuertista uprising merely gave a new label to armed violence that had never really gone away (see figure 5). In Villa Juárez, General Lindoro Hernández's belated pledge of loyalty to the government could not hide the fact that for the previous two years he had been in an almost permanent state of rebellion.[27] On the other side of the Sierra in Cuetzalan, Salvador Vega Bernal was a constant cause for concern. Indeed, the Vega Bernal family would offer the only significant military challenge to Barrios throughout his period of influence

Figure 5. Cavalry of the 46th Battalion during the Delahuertista campaign, Veracruz (Courtesy of Jose María Barrios)

in the region. The Vega Bernal brothers were relatively recent arrivals in the town of Cuetzalan, and their attempts to gain local political and economic influence were vehemently opposed by the incumbent elite. Salvador Vega Bernal's son maintains that his father took up arms in 1917 to protest against the brutality of local constitutionalista troops. Baudelio Rivera, a former servant of the family and soldier within their ranks, agrees, adding that they became Villistas to rectify social injustices. In the absence of any statements made by the brothers themselves, it remains difficult to corroborate these claims or to rule out the possibility that, as elsewhere, the Villista label was used to legitimize and mask personal motives.[28] Whatever their motivations, taking up arms placed them in direct opposition to Gabriel Barrios's forces. For several months following the assassination of Carranza, Salvador Vega Bernal was given responsibility for ensuring the military security of the Sierra, and during this time he tried his best to convince the Guerra y Marina of Barrios's unreliability. Upon Barrios's reappointment as the region's military commander, animosity between the two men continued. Throughout 1922 various reports emanating from Barrios's headquarters detailed Vega Bernal's movements in the tierra caliente.[29] Although no clear declaration was ever made, by December 1923 the Vega Bernal brothers were considered to have joined the de la Huerta cause. The campaign against Vega Bernal's men continued until their eventual surrender to Demetrio Barrios's forces in March 1924.[30] Even then, the contest between the Barrios and Vega Bernal families did not subside; it merely entered a new phase in which regional and municipal political factionalism would play a major role.

Barrios's enemies later accused him of having played a double game during the de la Huerta rebellion, feigning loyalty for the federal government while conducting secret talks with the rebels. Despite the rumors, there is no evidence to suggest that Barrios was ever tempted to join his adversaries in converting the Sierra into a de la Huerta stronghold. When the rebellion broke, Barrios swiftly expressed his loyalty to the Obregón administration and, reflecting the trust he enjoyed at the Guerra y Marina, was allowed to increase his troops to one thousand. Even if Barrios had been tempted to take a more neutral stance, the personal tragedy of his brother Bardomiano's death in battle against the rebel General Cavazos made it inconceivable that any accord would be found in the future.[31] By remaining loyal, Barrios greatly aided the federal army's recovery of Puebla city and thereby considerably reduced the chances of a successful rebel assault on Mexico City. The defeat of the Delahuertistas in Veracruz was a crucial factor in the outcome of the entire campaign, as it released scarce federal resources to the western front. Subsequent federal victories in the west brought an effective end to the rebellion.

The image of steadfast serrano loyalty continued throughout the 1920s. On 2 October 1927 President Calles informed the jefatura de operaciones militares in Puebla that General Arnulfo R. Gómez, (the author of the military manual promoting loyalty and discipline) had left Mexico City and was planning to launch a rebellion in either Puebla or Veracruz. On receiving the news, Barrios expressed his loyalty to Calles and was allowed to recruit volunteer auxiliary forces to fortify the various garrisons of the 46th Battalion. Throughout the emergency, Barrios cooperated with neighboring federal forces in Veracruz and Hidalgo to counter rebel movements.[32] Similarly, Sierra troops remained steadfast in their support of the federal government during the Cristero rebellion.

Nineteenth-century liberalism had already tempered Catholic fervor in many areas of the Sierra. Indeed, by 1917 the Catholic Church no longer had a presence in Tetela de Ocampo.[33] Even in Zacapoaxtla, where Catholics among the gente de razón were to orchestrate a popular backlash against socialist education in the 1930s, there is no evidence of significant Cristero activity during the 1920s. Although Demetrio Barrios occasionally led forces to quell disturbances by "religious fanatics," such incidents were isolated and never challenged the military strength of the 46th Battalion.[34] Conversely, Barrios's enemies employed the familiar tactic of trying to discredit him by associating him with the federal government's enemies. An anonymous letter sent to the Guerra y Marina accused him of being a "romanista" and of using religious fanatics to cause disturbances in the Sierra.[35] Like all the other accusations against Barrios during this time, it failed to cut much ice with his military superiors.

Although these episodes in Mexico's political history underline the value of the Sierra Norte de Puebla's loyalty, they do not explain why the federal army continued to use local Nahua leaders to guarantee such support. After all, while Lucas had provided reliable service in the past, during the Revolution his leadership was seriously questioned by successive administrations. Part of the reason may have been because indigenous military leadership represented the lesser of two evils. Although the federal government could have chosen to trust local mestizos instead, government suspicion of their loyalties was well founded. Political ambition had led the Márquez brothers into betraying the Carrancista cause, while Salvador Vega Bernal was almost constantly rebelling. Nor did the imposition of outsiders seem promising. Following his transfer to the area, Carrancista General Antonio Medina displayed a weakness that affected many of his peers by letting his political ambitions override military professionalism. Medina was soon suspected of colluding with Lucas to convert the Sierra into an independent political enclave. The transfer of his 3rd Division to the south of Puebla in 1917 is a prime example of Carranza's tactic of relocating his military generals to avoid such circumstances. Similarly, when General Marcelino Arrieta attempted to impose a measure of federal military authority over the region in 1918, Puebla governor Alfonso Cabrera warned Carranza that due to his "lack of tact," Arrieta had produced a "degree of discontent in the Sierra that was threatening to turn serranos towards the enemy camp."[36] Cabrera may well have been motivated by his ongoing battle of wills with Arrieta's commander, jefe de operaciones militares General Cesareo Castro, but the nature of his warning was well chosen.[37] The possibility of an ill-conceived move turning the Sierra against the federal government had always troubled the Guerra y Marina and affected their treatment of the region.

With a mestizo alliance promising little more than fleeting, unreliable support, the track record of indigenous military leadership appeared more appealing to the federal government. While Lucas's early prevarication had weakened his position, his reputation as a loyal supporter of the federal government survived. Although he may have harbored a dream of making the Sierra a separate political entity, he never came near to achieving this. More limited and feasible ambitions were to secure political positions for his two sons. The refusal of Carranza's generals to allow either of them to assume military control of the Brigada Serrana when he died may have been a move to prevent the establishment of a Lucas dynasty. It could also have resulted from their concern that his city-educated sons lacked the personal and military skills to command the respect of the brigade's indigenous soldiers.[38] When Gabriel Barrios informed the Guerra y Marina that Lucas had died and that he had assumed command of the troops, he relieved the federal government of a major headache. Even when Barrios's ambitions became evident, his political enemies had to acknowledge the strength and source of his support. As Porfirio del Castillo related to the members of the national congress in July 1921,

> the cacicazgo that Gabriel Barrios now enjoys was inherited from the patriarch Juan Francisco Lucas, who was an idol to those Indians and who, in his final moments, called his Indians together and made them understand that Gabriel Barrios was his successor, and that they should obey him because he would look after their interests. We are agreed that we need to free the spirit and will of these people, and that it is necessary to move on from this patriarchy, this cacicazgo of the Sierra de Puebla; we agree in the need to eradicate all such cacicazgos, but now you will see that this one has deep roots; Gabriel Barrios continues to live with the Indians in the mountains, conversing with them in Totonac [sic.], and this has given him a decisive influence over them that he still preserves today.[39]

Whatever misgivings the federal government may have had about Barrios were insignificant compared to the possible consequences of relying upon untrustworthy mestizo representatives. The national executive and Barrios thus entered into a marriage of convenience that was to last more than a decade; and like all such relationships, minor transgressions were overlooked as long as it remained useful to stay together.

The Honeymoon Period

By focusing upon Gabriel Barrios's rise to power it is easy to distort the true degree of influence that he enjoyed. At no time did the Barrios cacicazgo attain full independence from federal government patronage. Barrios never controlled the state government and had no major sources of independent financing. His operations required funding and good-will from several government departments, and the government could have forcibly dislodged the brothers from the region if it were deemed necessary. To do so, however, might have involved long-term military occupation in a mountainous region with a potentially hostile local population. At the very least, dislodging Barrios would have required the deployment of federal troops that were badly needed elsewhere. Provided Barrios offered loyalty and stability, therefore, the federal government chose to ignore some of his more questionable actions. The ways in which this arrangement operated reveal the delicate balancing act between the military establishment and its regional and local commanders during the 1920s.

Charges of disloyalty, corruption, and abuse of power litter the Barrios brothers' military files, and there is a clear pattern of official responses. Military investigations were made either directly by Guerra y Marina officers or by the jefatura in Puebla city. A lack of witnesses or corroborating evidence frustrated such charges, and various jefes de operaciones militares in Puebla invariably concluded that the charges either had no substance or were politically motivated.[40] Following the death of Carranza, for example, national and regional newspapers, and reports from Salvador Vega Bernal and others within the Sierra, warned that Gabriel Barrios was a Carrancista diehard plotting against the new administration. While a military investigation dismissed the charges, the investigators did suggest that "it might be wise to separate [Barrios] from the many supporters he possesses in different factions, in order to avoid possible occurrences that would be harmful to our government."[41] Similar claims were made in 1922 by interim state Governor Froylán Manjarrez, and again in 1926, when Governor Claudio Tirado warned President Calles that Barrios was "in open opposition to the state government, creating a state of anarchy so serious and delicate as to warrant the radical and decisive action that only you can order."[42] Yet it was Barrios's accusers who suffered government sanctions. In 1920 Vega Bernal's troops were disbanded, while in 1922 and 1926, shortly after making their charges, both Manjarrez and Tirado were removed from office. The closest the federal government ever came to admonishing Barrios was to send reminders via the jefatura in Puebla city that he should refrain from any activities tantamount to political interference, while being fully aware that he was doing exactly that in one municipality after another.

Charges of corruption were equally vociferous yet ultimately unproven. The most eloquent, or certainly the most flamboyant, accusation came in April 1920 from someone calling himself Alejandro Berriozábal. In a lengthy letter, Berriozábal launched a tirade against Barrios, claiming that "the actions of the most hardened criminal are insignificant compared to those committed by this troglodyte." After listing the murders committed by Barrios's troops, Berriozábal accused Barrios of using intimidation to accumulate "magnificent urban properties in Tetela and Zacatlán and enviable country estates. This new Ali Baba boasts a fortune that includes $100,000 in coins and $200,000 in gold. . . . Like a sultan he has a harem which he lavishes with gifts and scandalizes society. Like a petty tyrant, he treats every person in this region as a subject. Like a dictator his will becomes the law."[43] While Berriozábal's colorful vocabulary gave clues to the sectors of society from which he might come, despite exhaustive efforts the true identity or whereabouts of Berriozábal were never found.[44] In the absence of the accuser to ratify his accusations, the tribunal was left with no alternative but to find Barrios innocent of all charges.[45]

Yet it is quite clear that the charges of corruption made by the mysterious Berriozábal and other anonymous figures had substance. The federal government must have been aware of financial irregularities in Barrios's military operations at various times in his military career. Inflation of troop numbers, nonpayment or partial payment of wages, and the continued receipt of wages for soldiers killed in battle were all employed by the Barrios brothers to accumulate funds. Indeed, the assumption of a deceased officer's identity by one of his half brothers was the quickest way for Barrios to place a family member in a position of influence.[46] It is equally clear, however, that the Barrios brothers were careful not to push their sponsors too far. At vital moments—such as when Lucas died, when Carranza was assassinated, and during the cull of military officers following the de la Huerta rebellion—Barrios almost fawned to federal authorities. In December 1917, for example, Barrios returned sixty thousand pesos in federal funds judged surplus to requirements. This earned him an honorable mention in dispatches in recognition of his efficient reorganization of the Brigada Serrana.[47] Similarly, in September 1920, Barrios offered to reduce his troops by three hundred men to "benefit the finances of the Republic."[48] In June 1924, Barrios again offered to cut troop numbers from 1,000 to 609 men for the same reason. Obregón expressed deep gratitude to Barrios for the "spirit of cooperation shown by reducing the numbers of [his] troops."[49] Given that Barrios was not above the unauthorized use of military funds, one can be excused for adopting a certain cynicism regarding these voluntary financial sacrifices. When issues of loyalty, corruption, and military expenditures were high on the agenda, Barrios made appropriate gestures that were gratefully received by a federal government desperate to retain support while reducing its overhead.

The underlying premise behind this marriage of convenience, of course, was that following the death of Lucas, Gabriel Barrios was seen to hold exclusive access to Nahua militarism in the Sierra. In this respect, it made sense for the Guerra y Marina to allow Barrios a large measure of latitude. This does not mean, however, that Barrios actually enjoyed this degree of influence. I believe that the Guerra y Marina's dependence upon Barrios, and the federal government's inability to establish direct links with recruiting communities, led them to overestimate the degree of control Barrios enjoyed. Barrios's value to the Guerra y Marina was based upon a false impression of the composition, structure, and size of his army, and of the relationship between officers and troops. Given that previous studies point to the development of considerable mutual understanding between the state and serrano soldiers in the nineteenth century, I realize that my contention challenges the extent to which such dialogue continued in the early twentieth century. It is to this issue that we now turn, in order to examine the nature of power relations between the Guerra y Marina in Mexico City, the Barrios brothers as regional commanders, and the Sierra communities that provided the troops.

Community Mobilization

Not everyone within the Sierra de Puebla greeted Barrios's rise to military power with enthusiasm, but official responses to isolated protests reveal much about how the Sierra's military contribution was viewed more generally. As elsewhere in the republic, the mobilization of local Indians within the Sierra de Puebla provoked cases of apparent hysteria among the non-Indian minority. Weeks after the assassination of Carranza, the jefatura in Puebla city received alarming reports from the Sierra district of Huauchinango. In a letter offering a vivid portrayal of ethnic tensions, the authors described themselves as gente de razón who had brought "civilization" and "progress" to the area. Accusing their Indian neighbors of never missing an opportunity to show hatred toward them, the correspondents expressed alarm that the Indians now had a leader. They maintained that Gabriel Barrios was invading the area with two thousand Indians from Tetela de Ocampo, drawing upon the "traditional animosity" between races in order to expand his sphere of influence:

> With this intent of exterminating the gente de razón, he has invaded this military sector, which is not within his jurisdiction, and has been giving arms to all the indigenous. . . . They are now embarking upon a true crusade against us, they come to houses inhabited by people who speak Spanish, enter them, search them, and take what they want. They immediately take all males prisoner, insult them, curse them, tie them up, and then line them up as if to execute them. The terrorized families cry and fall on their knees before these savages, begging them not to carry out their intentions. And then these vile individuals laugh, mock them, and say, "Why are you crying, are you a coyote?" This is how they describe the gente de razón.[50]

Bear in mind that the fear of indigenous mobilization acting as a catalyst for widespread ethnic violence had defined the so-called caste wars of Chiapas and Yucatán, and had informed the ways in which Indian soldiers were used elsewhere in the republic. The Huauchinango claim of a caste war was not unique; another was made in Cuetzalan and, as in Huauchinango, it was stimulated by the recent arrival of Barrios's troops into the community. Yet despite these claims, fellow mestizos in other parts of the Sierra did not rush to these communities' aid, and neither the state nor the national government ever seemed to believe that a caste war was likely. Such responses suggest that few perceived Barrios's mobilization to be based upon ethnic tensions. While there may have been some who feared that indigenous men would take advantage of their new status as soldiers to settle old scores, most serranos were more relaxed. Indian mobilization in the Sierra had a long history and race wars had never featured in the past. In both cases the accusations appear to have been made by political cliques who saw Barrios as a threat to their authority and used the race card as a last means of defense.

If not ethnic antagonism, what was it that persuaded indigenous men to risk their lives in battle? What was the nature of indigenous mobilization in the Sierra, and what degree of control did the Barrios brothers have over their troops? In order to answer these questions, we need to consider the structure of the army. When Barrios assumed control of the Brigada Serrana, he inherited several clusters of irregular Nahua troops centered around Lucas's stronghold of Xochiapulco and Tetela de Ocampo, along with his own troops from Cuacuila and those of Tranquilino Quintero across the valley in Cuautempan.[51] While leadership of the brigade was officially divided between Barrios and Quintero, it soon became clear that the Guerra y Marina favored Barrios. Quintero was given command of a division on the far side of the Sierra, and within fifteen months he had been replaced by Demetrio Barrios. At this stage, the soldiers were Nahua part-timers who had fought directly under Barrios in the past or alongside his troops in the Brigada Serrana. By 1922, when the unit was incorporated into the federal army as the 46th Infantry Battalion, the Barrios brothers had strengthened their grip by promoting half brothers and associates to senior positions in garrisons in the southern Sierra: Zacatlán, Tetela de Ocampo, Zacapoaxtla, and Tlatlauquitepec.

The geographic expansion of Barrios's jurisdiction to encompass the whole of the Sierra, and the extension of the roles performed by his men, demanded a new layer of military support. The regular army garrisons each supervised a network of armed security forces located within nearby communities. These groups were led by *jefes de armas*, who were responsible for maintaining stability within their locality and for controlling the actions of the *cuerpos voluntarios* under their supervision. It is clear that many members of the cuerpos voluntarios were unaware of their military status. Correspondence suggests that they regarded themselves as quasi-military units; jefes de armas referred to their own armed men as soldiers and addressed Gabriel Barrios as "*mi general.*" Despite this, the cuerpos voluntarios were never formally incorporated into the federal army and remained irregular forces who were occasionally mobilized for coordinated military campaigns. Only then did they receive a wage from the battalion paymaster.

As Barrios's cacicazgo grew, so changed the character of his armed support and the means by which he tried to keep these individuals on board. Oral history within the Sierra concurs with the Guerra y Marina's impression that Gabriel Barrios offered strong leadership and maintained strict discipline among his troops. Yet this image applies mostly to the regular soldiers that fought in the old Brigada Serrana, many of whom were neighbors of the Lucas and Barrios families. The irregulars were more numerous, however, and the strength of their loyalty and obedience toward Barrios varied. The true nature of this relationship was concealed from the Guerra y Marina and contributed to the ministry's inflated impression concerning the influence that Barrios held within the Sierra communities. As Porfirio del Castillo's comments to the federal congress in 1921 illustrate, the federal government believed that Barrios's military and political strength in the Sierra owed much to him being accepted locally as the legitimate heir to Lucas's authority, and to his living among the Indians and speaking their native language. (That Castillo's mistake in believing Barrios to speak Totonac, rather than Nahuatl, was not mentioned during the congressional debate further illustrates the degree of ignorance about the Sierra in Mexico City.) That the federal congress and the Guerra y Marina believed Barrios to enjoy more legitimacy than he actually did is largely due to the illusion that Barrios created. This image also depended upon his ability to convince serranos that, despite their diverse ethnic backgrounds, his presence was a positive influence upon their everyday lives. He did this by overlaying the use of patronage or coercion with a more subtle blend of social and cultural gestures that helped to strengthen allegiances while confusing and reducing opposition.

The creation of images was a common feature of political discourse in postrevolutionary Mexico. Many studies of military and political leadership highlight how a sensitivity to popular cultural mores could produce political results. At the national level, a central theme within postrevolutionary state initiatives to regain political control was a cultural project designed to create national, universal heroes out of partisan figures such as Emiliano Zapata.[52] At regional and local levels, characters such as Carrillo Puerto, Juvencio Nochebuena, and Primo Tapia recognized the value of respecting local cultural values, languages, and traditions to gain the trust of potential supporters. So successful were these projects in creating cult heroes that many followers bestowed mystical powers upon their leaders. Within the Sierra de Puebla, Elías Masferrer Kan argues that by satisfying secular demands, Juan Francisco Lucas obtained a degree of legitimacy that put him into the category of leaders who were both secularly and spiritually revered.[53] Marentes Bravo's oral history of the Revolution in the Sierra goes further, relating the widely held belief that Gabriel Barrios was Lucas's illegitimate son and thereby inherited some of his powers.[54] Barrios's servant denies the claim but insists that his former employer was truly respected and loved by his serrano neighbors, who bestowed near-godlike status upon him.[55]

Such an image is, of course, partial and partisan, but one that Barrios did little to dispel. Within Zacatlán and Tetela de Ocampo, Barrios's ability to assume Lucas's mantle was greatest. Like Lucas, he spoke Nahuatl and was rarely seen in the Sierra dressed in anything other than the simple garments of a serrano peasant. A cultural affinity with and an understanding of the dilemmas facing rural communities afforded him much grace, and this was unfaltering. In this area, the enduring impression of Barrios is of an extremely shrewd character, a great tactician who left nothing to chance. Stories persist of him as a shadowy figure: a man who never appeared to need sleep, who was seen in two places at the same time, who would rest at night in one village and appear early the next morning in another many miles away, and who conducted secret meetings with his local commanders under cover of darkness. While such images conform to the actions of a wise military strategist who left nothing to chance, in a local Nahua culture in which the boundaries between the worldly and spiritual were already thin, military prowess could easily be mistaken for mystical mastery.

While Barrios's family background suggests that much of his self-identification as a Nahua campesino was genuine, he also recognized the need to cement his position as military commander of the Brigada Serrana by capitalizing on his indigenous background. Military, political, and economic aspects all played important parts in this process, but Barrios also sought allegiances that went beyond material reward. A seemingly frivolous example nonetheless exposes an aspect of his attempts to manage his own and, by extension, his troops' image. Every community in the districts of Tetela and Zacatlán knew when the tiny village of Cuacuila was staging its fiestas. Whereas most fiestas in the

Figure 6. Chargers used for explosives during Cuacuila fiestas (Photo by Keith Brewster)

area were punctuated by the distant sound of fireworks, Cuacuila went one better. Gunpowder was packed into iron chargers and, according to *cuacuileños*, the explosions were so powerful that they made the mountainside shake and caused considerable structural damage to the village's buildings (see figure 6). The symbolism was clear. No community did things bigger or better than Cuacuila, heart of the Barrios *cacicazgo*.

Similarly, music played a strong part both in Cuacuila's ritual and social calendar and in Barrios's broader strategy. While no self-respecting community went without a band, Barrios made sure that Cuacuila had the most proficient, best-equipped musicians in the region. Professional teachers from Puebla city and mules bearing brass instruments, drums, a marimba, and even a grand piano all struggled up the mountain tracks to Cuacuila. Barrios used music to invade public and private space. Serranos from neighboring settlements would often hear an eerie blend of classical and popular music flowing down the slopes from Cuacuila and filling the night air. The 46th Battalion's band comprised Nahuas who, although they could not read Spanish, could play a repertoire of music with such mastery that communities competed for them to grace their own fiestas (see figure 7). In a region where *mayordomos*

Figure 7. Military band of the 46th Battalion in Zacatlán (Courtesy of Arnulfo Barrios Aco)

gained considerable local respect by sponsoring memorable fiestas, Barrios lent out his band to establish significant ties of goodwill, gratitude, and obligation.[56] While patronage of this type might be seen as reinforcing cultural values in many indigenous communities, Barrios's contribution to civic celebrations in mestizo cabeceras sent an equally symbolic, if differently coded, message of power. Here, the presence of a professional band playing classical music did much to allay fears that Barrios's troops were nothing more than a group of illiterate Indians with guns.

Other aspects of Barrios's cultural image helped soothe anxieties within mestizo society. As in other areas, the ranchero background of the Barrios family afforded a certain local prestige. In Tetela and Zacatlán, Gabriel Barrios was respected for his knowledge of horses. His skill in military tactics was recognized by all, and his standing as a courageous fighter grew in line with his rapid promotion through the ranks of the Brigada Serrana. In time, his reputation as an admirer of thoroughbred horses was surpassed only by his reputedly even greater passion for women.[57] Guns, horses, and women, the accoutrements of the Mexican hero, helped him gain admiration among members of the non-Indian serrano society for whom mysticism had no place.

By raising the issue of cultural affinity, I am not suggesting that Sierra communities, whether white, mestizo, or indigenous, could be easily won over. I do believe, however, that within Barrios's home territory, such an approach added a valuable string to his bow, and it was from these communities that most of his regular soldiers came. As the cacicazgo expanded and sought new adherents, the brothers had to offer more than a few tunes, fireworks, and fine words in Nahuatl. Expansion often involved stepping on the toes of white and mestizo local elites. When Barrios's forces moved into Zacapoaxtla to combat rebels, for example, the municipal president complained to Governor Alfonso Cabrera that "rebel actions are made worse still by the conduct of government troops led by ignorant Indians who use their military might solely to terrorize gente de razón."[58] The emotive language reveals the subjectivity and symbolic power of racial stereotypes. In Zacatlán, people knew the Barrios brothers as both traders and soldiers, and for the most part viewed them as respected mestizos. In the district of Zacapoaxtla, however, they were an unknown quantity, and in an environment of hostility and suspicion, prominent families judged Demetrio Barrios by local criteria; one day's horse ride across the Sierra had transformed him from a respected mestizo into an ignorant Indian.

Negotiations were equally tough as the Barrios brothers pushed down the gulf-facing slopes to incorporate Totonac communities. Compromises had to be reached to satisfy community needs while allowing the brothers a measure of overall authority. It is in communities at the margins of a cacique's natural constituency that one finds evidence of the limitations of cacicazgos such as that of Barrios during the 1920s. Let us look again at the Sierra's response to the de la Huerta rebellion, at a time when Gabriel Barrios was firmly established as the region's federal military commander and the framework of his cacicazgo was nearly complete. Bear in mind, too, that the Sierra's response came at a crucial political crossroads for the Sierra, the state of Puebla and, conceivably, the federal government as well. The headline of an article published in *Excélsior* at the height of the de la Huerta rebellion confidently stated, "10,000 armed serranos offer their services to impede rebel incursions into that region—they have munitions—they have remained armed since the days of the patriarch Juan Francisco Lucas." News of the serranos' affiliation to the federal government was attributed to Major Luis F. Cabañas, who had recently visited the Sierra. The article went on to note that "as with the Zacapoaxtla Indians of the past, they are grateful to the present government that has offered them every consideration and given them land. As a result, they are determined to defend the constitutional authorities that offer them complete protection." Only later in the article is it apparent that such support came with an important qualification. What the Indians were offering was to seal off all points of entry into the Sierra in order to prevent the region from becoming a rebel retreat. They argued that by remaining in the Sierra and protecting their homes from rebel incursions, they were "best contributing towards the federal government's campaign."[59]

Several aspects of this newspaper article are interesting. The first concerns the degree of propaganda in the newspaper coverage of the rebellion. Even if Cabañas had established direct links with Sierra communities, he would have been hard-pressed to have secured the loyalty of ten thousand serranos. The support for the federal government claimed to exist in the Sierra seems to have been more wishful thinking than reality. In addition, the supposed gratitude of the Sierra campesino for the government's agrarian reforms appears misplaced given that much of the Sierra did not experience such reforms. Apart from the *Excélsior* report, there is no evidence that agrarian communities in the Sierra had sought a direct dialogue with the federal government. Neither Obregón nor any of his military chiefs ever received a pledge of military support from Sierra communities, and in no assessment of the region is there any evidence of mobilization other than that conducted by the Barrios brothers.

The report also sheds light on the perception of the armed forces in the Sierra. Nowhere in the article is Barrios's name mentioned, even though he was the recognized federal military commander of the region. This may well be because Cabañas was referring to serranos who appeared to be not soldiers, but civilians vowing loyalty to the federal government. What Cabañas failed to recognize, however, was that it was precisely these Nahua and Totonac campesinos who comprised Barrios's battalion, an informal army of soldiers-cum-peasants who lived and worked in their communities and rallied to Barrios's call when necessary. So when Barrios asked Obregón's permission to increase his troops to one thousand to combat Delahuertismo, it was these very serranos that Barrios mobilized.[60]

A third aspect of Cabañas's report is a strong sense of regional identity that, when combined with the community-based structure of Barrios's troops, provides a valuable key to understanding the true nature of the serranos' reactions to successive national crises. Like their nineteenth-century predecessors, the troops of the 46th Battalion rarely ventured beyond the Sierra de Puebla. Their names are not to be found among the list of heroes who retook the city of Puebla in late December 1923. Their military action was closer to home: in the eastern Sierra against Cavazos's troops and on the gulf-facing slopes of the Sierra against Salvador Vega Bernal's rebels. Throughout the emergency, the Indian army of the Sierra felt that its "best contribution to the national cause" was to mount a local response.[61]

The Sierra's military response to the de la Huerta rebellion is consistent with the way it fought the Revolution. The army that Lucas mustered was never a federal army unit, but rather a special force that answered directly to him. This fact reflected a common fear among serranos that incorporation within the federal army would lead to lengthy spells away from their fields, families, and communities. Indeed, Lucas risked incurring the wrath of the Madero administration by refusing to send serrano troops to fight outside Puebla. Similarly, when Huerta asked Lucas to deploy his troops to neighboring states, Lucas replied that this was impossible, as his troops would refuse to fight outside the Sierra.[62] While Thomson portrays this as a political tactic by Lucas to retain influence and a measure of unity within the Sierra, it is equally likely that Lucas's soldiers would have refused him had he tried to comply with Guerra y Marina orders. When Barrios took control of the Brigada Serrana, he never sought to test his strength by asking his troops to fight more than a couple of days' march from their villages. This, too, might be seen as the Barrios brothers securing their bailiwick and, indeed, it seems likely that the Guerra y Marina held this impression. I believe, however, that Gabriel Barrios could never have persuaded serranos to leave their communities against their will. Even when the Brigada Serrana was incorporated into the federal army, the previous arrangements remained essentially intact. Serrano soldiers answered directly to the Barrios brothers and accepted no orders from officers beyond the region.

If Sierra communities could attach such conditions to their military service, how were they ever convinced to fight for Lucas and later Gabriel Barrios? In many studies of the 1920s, the issue of land tenure is seen as crucial in attracting popular support for provincial leaders. Dudley Ankerson and Romana Falcón both identify Saturnino Cedillo's charismatic leadership in San Luis Potosí as based upon the blatant linkage between land grants on military colonies and a willingness to mobilize.[63] Heather Fowler-Salamini shows that the agrarian governor of Veracruz, Adalberto Tejeda, derived influence through the creation of local agrarian leagues. By controlling the centralized bureaucratic system of patronage that linked these leagues, Tejeda established an impersonal but nonetheless effective control over the *veracruzano* campesino. Knight suggests that a varying mix of the desire for autonomy or agrarian reform convinced campesinos to take up arms.[64] Yet none of these scenarios quite fits in the case of the Sierra de Puebla. While regional autonomy was close to Lucas's heart, incursions by revolutionary groups had shown that the Sierra could never return to some form of splendid isolation. Nor does unquestioning support of a charismatic leader offer an adequate explanation. Many who fought for Barrios had little personal contact with him. Similarly, while the promise of land often spurred campesinos into action elsewhere, such tactics were not easily transferable to the Sierra. With the notable exception of violence resulting from coffee exploitation in the district of Zacapoaxtla, the region was largely free from agrarian conflict.[65] The Sierra's topography and climate generally inhibited large-scale agriculture. The voluntary division and sale of land on larger estates before and during the Revolution meant that many campesinos had acquired their own plots and generally accepted the sacrosanct nature of private ownership. (I discuss the agrarian issue at greater length in chapter 5.)

Thomson believes that a legacy of previous political discourse offers an alternative motive for indigenous mobilization in the Sierra. He finds that in the case of the soldiers of Xochiapulco, "their struggle between 1910 and 1917 was much more a continuation of the revolution of Tuxtepec—a revolution to restore respect for the constitution of 1857—than a twentieth-century social revolution concerned with achieving structural changes."[66] It is curious, then, that the archives give no indication of such dialogue taking place during the 1920s; nor is revolutionary rhetoric demanding respect for the new Constitution of 1917 a common theme. What does appear time and again is a desire for stability. Municipal archives abound with reports from local authorities relating incidents of bandits attacking settlements and stealing money, horses, and provisions. In such an environment, any village that tried to remain neutral became an undefended target for all combatants.[67] It follows, then, that the most common reason for serranos to follow Lucas and Barrios was that it was one of the few options available to reduce the arbitrary violence visited upon their families and communities. As Thomson notes, by the spring of 1914, an all-out war was taking place in the Sierra. Forces from outside the region were accused of all manner of abuses and theft. The breakdown in civilian law and order and the lack of any firm military discipline left communities at the mercy of both revolutionary forces and opportunistic criminals.[68] Similar levels of disorder continued after Lucas's death and, although the so-called violent revolution may have ended elsewhere in the republic, indiscriminate violence continued to hamper social and economic activity in the Sierra. Throughout the early 1920s, there was little change from the immediate past; bandits, rebels, and bandits-in-rebels'-clothing continued to cause havoc to everyday Sierra life. While many serranos still harbor hostile and frequently contradictory memories of Barrios, even his former enemies concede that he transformed a previously violent, lawless Sierra into a region where locals felt safe to use the mountain tracks. During a period when Barrios went to considerable effort to demilitarize and regularize civil peacekeeping within the Sierra, permission to carry weapons and to organize local law enforcement groups depended upon being recognized as one of Barrios's jefes de armas. In much the same way that their forefathers had been motivated to fight for Lucas, a new generation of serranos saw enlistment into Barrios's informal ranks as a means of gaining much-needed protection.

Just as serving as a federal soldier did not mean that Sierra Indians accepted a designated role within postrevolutionary Mexican society, so fighting for Barrios did not imply complete submission to his will. When Cabañas found serranos adding caveats to their pledges of support against Delahuertismo, he was confronting the same uncompromising reality that had so often accompanied Indian mobilization in the Sierra. Had the 46th Battalion been asked to fight beyond their territory, the veneer of support for the federal government would have been swiftly tarnished. The Guerra y Marina took the refusal to fight outside the Sierra as a sign of Barrios's determination not to be separated from his stronghold, and for as long as the armed services needed the region's military support, his position was never challenged. Yet during the de la Huerta rebellion, Barrios's hesitancy to operate beyond his patch reflected as much his own inability to persuade his part-time soldiers to do so as it did his preoccupation with leaving his power base unprotected.

Conclusion

The nature of indigenous militarism in the Sierra de Puebla raises central issues regarding the character of military leadership in postrevolutionary Mexico and challenges previous assumptions concerning the relationship between external authorities, regional military leaders, and those they purported to lead. Several studies suggest that throughout Mexican history mobilization within rural communities was just one of a range of tactics designed to limit the damage of external threats.[69] Peter Guardino reinforces this view by arguing that peasants in colonial Guerrero felt justified in rioting against bad government.[70] In this regard, the Sierra Norte de Puebla was not unique; disputes between factions, neighboring settlements, *sujetos* and cabeceras, and ethnic groups were a part of everyday life. However, on the rare occasions when national and local conflicts coincided, Nahuas and Totonacs in the Sierra de Puebla found alternative methods of contesting local power. With many of the major military crises confronting Mexico taking place within or close to the Sierra, local disputes often became enmeshed within broader imperatives and long-standing local quarrels were settled under national guises.[71]

So how should indigenous mobilization under the leadership of Gabriel Barrios be interpreted? The fact that serranos, many of them indigenous, were able to negotiate terms with regional and national military leaders adds strength to Mallon's argument that Sierra communities actively engaged with the state. What I question, however, is the degree to which community leaders, be they elders or young soldiers, possessed direct links to state representatives. Thomson and Mallon both stress that a large measure of mutual trust developed between Nahua and mestizo soldiers as a result of years of military service. But what was the exact nature of this trust, and what significance did it have for future mobilization? Some poorer mestizos had always lived among their Nahua vecinos and quite likely fought alongside them. At higher levels of authority, mutual trust may have developed between mestizo commanders and their ethnic intermediary, Juan Francisco Lucas. Yet such trust never developed to the extent that these commanders could be confident that Nahua soldiers would accept their direct command and follow them into battle. Throughout the Revolution and the 1920s, the federal government drew back from trying to impose direct military jurisdiction over the Sierra for fear of driving serranos toward the enemy camp. The very reason that the federal government afforded Barrios more respect than his control over the Sierra merited was that the state enjoyed even less influence than he among the diverse Sierra communities.

Like their counterparts elsewhere, indigenous communities of the Sierra de Puebla took up arms in pursuit of local objectives. The difference was that whereas in other areas such mobilization was quickly channeled or suppressed by ladinos and mestizos, the Sierra de Puebla's strategic importance enabled indigenous mobilization to be played out in a different way. During and immediately after the Revolution, many communities judged their best interests to be served by lending their military support to Barrios. As in the case of Namiquipa during the nineteenth and early twentieth centuries, military support for the federal government was, to a certain extent, coincidental and mainly instigated by local imperatives.[72] Widespread, arbitrary violence was having a direct and immediate affect upon serranos' ability to protect their livelihoods. Such violence undermined local autonomy more deeply than anything they relinquished by accepting Barrios's overall military authority. Moreover, in doing so they attracted a measure of federal government endorsement that made local opposition ineffective, even counter-revolutionary. As the case of Huauchinango reveals, for as long as the military demand existed, gente de razón were forced to bite the bullet and merely watch as their Indian neighbors converted military potential into political capital.

Events in the Sierra Norte de Puebla indicate that we need to re-examine indigenous militarism as a form of rural resistance. Examples of sustained indigenous opposition are rare in Mexican history. When such a phenomenon occurred it was often violently repressed by mestizo authority. Yet, in certain circumstances, some native military leaders were able to collaborate with outside powers in a way that did not compromise their own position. Such cooperation need not signify a willingness to accept all or part of a designated role within broader

society. Far from exposing their followers to manipulation or open acceptance of state projects, native leaders took advantage of contemporary circumstances, usually political or strategic, to avoid or at least
postpone efforts to subjugate them. This is not to say that the Indians
were politically aware in the sense that they embraced a national political discourse, but they did follow leaders who were able to conduct
such discourse in a way that would deliver what they most wanted: a
measure of protection for their families and communities. They did not
suddenly act differently in the late 1920s; they merely fell victim to a
changing political environment in which their main bargaining card,
their fighting potential, had lost its value. When this option became
obsolete, negotiation did not end; rather, other, nonmilitary "weapons
of the weak" became more prominent.

3 Politics from the Center and Implications for the Sierra

Just as revolutionary violence presented threats and opportunities to the Sierra de Puebla, so the political volatility of the 1920s closed down some channels while creating others that communities and local leaders could exploit. The state's project of political centralization made little impression in a region devoid of effective communications between different levels of representation. National, regional, local, and individual priorities competed for ascendancy; such contestation sometimes produced unlikely alliances. In this chapter, I approach the issue from a macro level by analyzing the extent to which the fluctuating fortunes of national and regional political groups affected the Sierra. Simultaneously, I show how prominent figures within the region reacted and contributed to the broader political debate. In the remaining chapters of the book, I investigate the degree to which Sierra communities and leaders were connected to this process, in order to discover any correlation between external political instability and the fate of local initiatives.

Following the fall of Carrancista Governor Alfonso Cabrera in May 1920, the governorship of the state of Puebla changed hands no less than fifteen times in eight years. Such instability reflected the diverse interests that sought to influence the local congress. During the Porfiriato, the strong government of General Mucío Martínez stifled social unrest, but the Revolution gave rise to the mobilization of popular labor and agrarian movements, which vied for political dominance, both among themselves and against a small but powerful bourgeois elite that sought to maintain the status quo. The consequent volatility provoked a series of interventions in which federally imposed governors assumed temporary control of Puebla. Ernest Gruening summarizes the malaise that beset political leadership during the 1920s:

> Since 1920 but for a brief interlude—the administration of the young intellectual Lombardo Toledano—the governorship has been going from worse to still worse: General José María Sánchez, "author" of the attempted assassination of [Luis] Morones in the chamber of deputies in November 1924, in which affray an innocent bystander of a diputado was killed; Froylán Manjarrez, who after looting the state joined the de la Huerta rebellion in search of still more loot; Alberto Guerrero, a drunkard; Claudio N. Tirado, who stole at least a million pesos by the simple device of paying no-one and keeping the state revenues, seeking immortality by cutting his name on every new stone erected in the state during his term; and General Manuel P. Montes, the agrarian agitator.[1]

It must be said that Gruening rarely had a good word to say about any Mexican, so his rather jaundiced view of Puebla governors should be taken with more than a pinch of salt. As will be seen, Lombardo Toledano's administration proved to be less than effectual, while to focus upon the deficiencies of other governors detracts from the underlying struggles taking place in Puebla city between major players in national politics. At the subregional level, political theory and practice rarely coincided. District elections were more a contest between factions than manifestos, with the intimidatory presence of caciques often taking precedence over the free will of the people. It fell upon the relevant legislature to resolve the many disputed election results, but often the ensuing debates had an air of unreality to them. Politicians with little knowledge of a municipality sought to uphold democratic principles that bore no relation to realities in the area. Often broader political interests decided the outcome, and contesting diputados were installed, removed, or sometimes governed simultaneously, depending upon the balance of power in state and national capitals.

Given the importance of Puebla to national politics and the fragile tenure of many of its representatives, Gabriel Barrios's enduring presence in the Sierra must have offered the federal government some solace. To maintain the image of stability, he had to strike a balance between remaining aloof from factional politics in Puebla city while becoming sufficiently involved to ensure that he never became a casualty of the struggles that were taking place. Part of his strategy was to establish close working relationships with his commanding officers in Puebla city, and these became crucial in protecting Barrios from his political enemies at local, regional, and national levels. Furthermore, although his military position excluded him from political activities, the extent of Barrios's ambitions for the Sierra made it imperative to have influential voices in both local and federal congresses to defend his position and promote his initiatives. The structure of this network of allegiances reveals the dynamics between military and political actors at all levels of authority in postrevolutionary Puebla. In order to appreciate the complex nature of this relationship, however, it makes sense to begin by reviewing the main movements in national and regional politics.

Political Representation in Postrevolutionary Mexico

The more radical articles of the Federal Constitution of 1917 raised expectations among Mexico's popular groups, and representative organizations soon appeared to pressure a less-than-enthusiastic Carranza administration to honor its commitments. The formation of the Confederación Regional de Obrera Mexicana (CROM) in May 1918 marked the beginning of a process in which affiliated factory unions and agrarian committees sought to establish links with sympathetic elements within the national government. CROM leader Luis Morones pledged political support to Obregón's presidential aspirations in return for firm commitments to labor reform. The political wing of the CROM, the Partido Laborista, was formed in December 1919 and along with the Partido Nacional Cooperatista and other smaller, independent labor organizations, it openly supported Obregón's campaign.[2] Carranza's death and Obregón's eventual assumption of the presidency in 1920 heralded another phase of political lobbying. Radical elements within the labor movement were unhappy with Morones's moderating influence, and the consequent split gave rise to two new organizations, the Partido Comunista Mexicano (PCM) and the Confederación General de Trabajadores (CGT) both formed in February 1921. Class unity gave way to bitter, often violent clashes between members of the different organizations, and during the de la Huerta rebellion, CGT members flocked to the rebel side as it became clear that the CROM enjoyed close links with the presidential candidate, Calles.

As Heather Fowler-Salamini suggests, both the CROM and the CGT saw peasant organizations as secondary to their urban objectives, and while these groups were in the ascendancy in national politics, peasant leaders were forced to seek whatever opportunities came their way. The Partido Nacional Agraria (PNA), formed by Díaz Soto y Gama in 1920, sought to push a radical agrarian agenda but made little headway with President Obregón, who used the party more as a counterbalance to Morones than as a vehicle for social change in the countryside. While the federal government remained militarily weak, the campesinos' strongest bargaining card was in wringing piecemeal concessions in return for military support. In this way agrarian caudillos, such as Saturnino Cedillo in San Luis Potosí, Adalberto Tejeda in Veracruz, and José María Sánchez in Puebla, converted military potential into political influence. But postrevolutionary politics was more about managing popular movements than backing them.

During the Calles administration, the CROM reached the pinnacle of its political fortunes; Morones became minister for labor and industry and seven other CROM members occupied cabinet posts. Brutal suppression of strikes not sanctioned by the CROM served the dual purposes of stifling rival union organizations while deterring excessive worker demands. As long as Morones held his post, agrarian reform remained sidelined. When more radical agrarian elements formed the Liga Nacional Campesina in 1926, its leaders similarly failed to gain much support from Calles.[3] The future aspirations of the Liga and the PNA lay in whatever deal they could reach with Obregón as he stood for a second term of office.

During the 1928 presidential campaign, the Partido Laborista's outspoken attacks on Obregón made it clear that they saw no future in backing the federal government. Conversely, agrarian leaders looked forward with anticipation to a better deal under the new president. Obregón's electoral success and his subsequent assassination merely deepened the sense of political crisis. Agrarista leaders angrily accused the CROM of complicity, prompting the resignation of Morones, Celestino Gasca, and other CROM officials from Calles's administration.[4] The formation of the PNR a year later eclipsed the national prestige of the CROM and forced it to retreat to those provinces where it still held influence. It was precisely at this moment of generalized laborista decline that the state of Puebla offered its activists a last chance for political prominence. Such were the political fortunes of Puebla that it was often directly influenced by, but not necessarily in alignment with, trends at the national level.

Puebla Politics in the 1920s

Politics in Puebla during the 1920s was characterized by a conservative group of influential textile mill owners and landowners trying to hold the line against two distinct popular groups. Puebla's textile industry represented a large industrial base in which radicalism thrived. Alfonso Cabrera had brutally suppressed a strike by textile workers in May 1918, and throughout the 1920s they suffered periodic repression, the most infamous case being the massacre of strikers in the textile town of Atlixco in 1925. Similarly, as graphically portrayed in the correspondence of the U.S.-born hacendada Rosalie Evans, agraristas were beginning to enjoy considerable influence, sufficient indeed to convey their leaders to the governorship of the state.[5] Studies by Henderson and Márquez Carrillo clearly show, however, that popular political consciousness was still in its infancy; campesinos shifted uneasily between feudal deference and collective action. Class struggles became confused as rival groups fought for ascendancy, while federal intervention often turned tense situations into bloody chaos.[6]

When Alfonso Cabrera joined his brother Luis and the president in fleeing into the Sierra de Puebla in May 1920, poblanos were suddenly left without a governor. Federal military officers acted as stopgap governors until July 1920, when former Carrancista Luis Sánchez Pontón was given the task of steering the state toward fresh elections later that year.[7] The choice of Sánchez Pontón may indicate federal government uncertainty regarding local reaction to the death of Carranza. Persistent rumors that the Cabrera brothers were plotting a rebellion did little to allay such fears. The subsequent elections became a straight contest between two extremes. The many surviving Carrancistas, backed by the Partido Liberal Constitucionalista, rallied around Sánchez Pontón's candidate, Rafael Lara Grajales; Obregón, on the other hand, barely disguised his preference for his longtime political ally and *compadre*, the former Zapatista caudillo José María Sánchez. The election results were bitterly contested, with the federal government appointing Claudio N. Tirado as interim governor until June 1921, when the congress declared José María Sánchez the constitutionally elected governor with a four-year mandate. Indicative of the uncertain times in national politics, the CROM supported Obregón's efforts to get Sánchez installed only for the new governor then to repress cromista activities in Puebla.[8] Indeed, when an attempt was made on the life of Morones on the steps of the federal congress, many believed Sánchez to be the author of the crime.

When it became evident that Sánchez was intent on unleashing a program of radical agrarian reform upon his fellow poblanos, a majority of local deputies withdrew recognition of Sánchez's executive powers and transferred congressional proceedings to the town of San Marcos. Social and political divisions within Puebla once again threatened to draw the region into violent conflict. In March 1922 the federal congress moved to impose Froylán C. Manjarrez as governor to defuse the growing tension. The choice of Manjarrez, a Sonora diputado closely aligned to de la Huerta, indicated the ascendancy of the pro–de la Huerta Partido Nacional Cooperatista within national politics.[9] In the event, the appointment merely exported federal political disunity into a state that was already bitterly divided. Manjarrez's fortunes were inextricably linked to those of de la Huerta, and when de la Huerta was passed over for the presidency, Manjarrez pledged swift support for the subsequent rebellion. While the preemptive strike by the federal military commander General Juan Andreu Almazán prevented Manjarrez from converting Puebla city into a Delahuertista stronghold, the federal government's control of military affairs proved to be as fragile as its grip on Puebla politics. Despite Almazán's move, within the first turbulent days of December 1923 the governorship passed from federal to rebel and back into federal hands, reflecting the changing fortunes of Almazán and rebel general Fortunato Maicotte.[10]

With Puebla city secured, the federal government responded favorably to the many telegrams from unions in Puebla requesting that Lombardo Toledano continue as interim governor.[11] His tenure proved to be brief. Although a rising star within the CROM, Lombardo Toledano failed to understand the social and political realities of a state in conflict. While Rome or, to be more exact, parts of Puebla burned, Lombardo Toledano and his intellectual friends set about redirecting government energies toward educational initiatives that would introduce the sons and daughters of campesinos to the classics. This may have saved him from the sharp edge of Gruening's pen but, as Lombardo Toledano ruefully reflected, the poblanos viewed him and his government "as rare animals, not a government but a Greek tragedy, nothing more than intellectuals."[12] The federal government replaced him with Alberto Guerrero in June 1924 and scheduled fresh elections for the beginning of 1925. Three main candidates stood: Luis Sánchez de Cima, Lauro

Camarillo, and Claudio N. Tirado. The first two represented increasingly polarized sectors of Puebla mass politics. Camarillo's support was based upon a rising laborista movement, while Sánchez de Cima's strength stemmed from agrarista mobilization. Tirado's support came from a mixed bag of smaller political parties, the local PNA, and several caudillos and caciques.[13] In the event, both Camarillo and Tirado claimed victory, and it was left to the federal government eventually to accept the credentials of the latter.

Tirado's actions as governor reflected underlying trends in national politics. As Calles reined in the more radical elements of agrarismo, so Tirado sought to moderate the pace of agrarian reform. One of his more unpopular measures was to require campesinos to vacate land acquired by force and petition for the same land in accordance with agrarian legislation.[14] In April 1925, teachers in Puebla city went on strike demanding the right to belong to a union. They were backed by the Confederación Sindicalista de Obreros y Campesinos, a local organization with many campesino members that, in theory, was affiliated with the CROM. Its unilateral decision to support the teachers, however, was interpreted as a challenge to the CROM's monopoly on recognizing strike action. As a consequence, the CROM instructed its members in Puebla to withdraw support for the teachers. Simultaneously, the federal government sent eight thousand soldiers to the city to deter further demonstrations.[15] Calling Morones a traitor to the working classes, the newspaper *El Machete* added that "the 'agraroid' leader Tirado did not have shame, and seeking the protection of the bourgeois constitution, shot, imprisoned, and persecuted workers."[16] With more than a little irony, the article questioned the agrarian credentials of a governor whose lack of leadership led to such repression. With few local allies and widespread unrest, Tirado became an easy target for his many opponents. When former governor Lombardo Toledano accused Tirado of unconstitutional actions, the federal judiciary upheld his claims, and in November 1926 Tirado was removed from office.

Tirado's fall from grace and the subsequent naming of Manuel Montes as provisional governor appeared to revive the flagging fortunes of agrarismo in Puebla.[17] Rogelio Sánchez López examines possible motives for the appointment of an agrarian leader to govern a state where agrarismo was being trounced by a laborista political bloc. He suggests that Calles may have recognized that Montes enjoyed a level of local prestige that Calles's supporters found hard to resist. This being the case, Calles may have been prepared to expose the agraristas' limited agenda by allowing them to fail in state government. In addition, although Montes was linked to the Liga Nacional Campesina, Calles may have perceived him as less of a threat than other possible gubernatorial contenders, such as Crisóforo Ibañez, a vociferous member of the PNA. In the event, the increasingly laborista local congress allowed Montes little freedom to pursue his policies. By July 1927, with the state government once more in turmoil, the federal government again intervened and replaced Montes with General Bravo Izquierdo. According to Sánchez López, Calles imposed Bravo Izquierdo as governor to rein in the wayward state and bring it under central control. Certainly, agrarian reform all but ended as campesino organizations felt the "iron fist" of the military leader.[18] Within a month, Montes was dead, killed by a group of cromista workers. Reflecting upon his death, the Liga Nacional Campesina claimed that "the reason why Montes was killed is the same one that caused the death of Primo Tapia in Michoacán. . . . Montes was the indisputable leader of the Puebla agrarian movement . . . he was a man of action and was respected by thousands of organized campesinos. This explains everything."[19]

If the CROM leadership was implicated in Montes's assassination, the murder of President-Elect Obregón in July 1928 brought even stronger charges from its agrarian opponents. But the two events had different effects. At the national level, Obregón's death indirectly led to the decline of the CROM, as Calles sought to defuse the national crisis by laying the foundations for the PNR. In Puebla, Montes's death left the local agrarian movement devoid of an influential leader, and cromistas seized the opportunity to convert Puebla into one of their few remaining strongholds within the republic. The task of restraining this development fell to Bravo Izquierdo's successor, the brother of the region's former federal military commander, Leonides Andreu Almazán, who was elected governor in November 1928. Almazán shared the prevailing view that the future of representational politics lay in incorporating disparate masses within a common cause. Forming the Partido Socialista de Oriente, he sought to establish institutional links with diverse political factions in the hope that disputes might be resolved through negotiation rather than bloodshed. He allowed the local CROM organization to name the secretary of labor in his administration, actively encouraged the formation of the Confederación Campesina "Emiliano Zapata," and renewed the impetus for agrarian reform. For a crucial period, national and regional politics moved in the same direction. Both agreed on the need to harness the potential of popular groups and, equally importantly, to rid the Mexican countryside of what Calles viewed as a national malaise: the specter of military caciquismo. It was not long before attention focused on the Sierra Norte de Puebla.

Friends in High Places: Barrios's Protective Network

Throughout the 1920s Barrios's political shrewdness was evident in his use of military and political connections to help him convince successive federal governments that he posed no risk to their broader ambitions. The nature of Mexican politics often meant, however, that past loyalty soon became a liability. Luis Cabrera's position within Carranza's cabinet had been vital in enabling Barrios to strengthen his hold over the Brigada Serrana in 1917, but in the unsettled days that accompanied Carranza's fall from grace, Barrios's close ties to the Cabrera family became something of a poisoned chalice. During the months following Carranza's death, the federal congress braced itself for a possible Carrancista backlash. Many believed the Cabrera family and the Sierra Norte de Puebla to be the most likely source of such a response. As early as 3 May 1920, *El Monitor* reported the withdrawal of Alfonso Cabrera's state government to Zacatlán, where it was said to enjoy the protection of Barrios's men.[20] A week later, *El Universal de Puebla* speculated that Carranza himself was receiving Barrios's protection in the Sierra and that the Carrancista generals in the Guerra y Marina had supplied the Brigada Serrana with "large quantities of arms and ammunition."[21] In order to counter suspicions, in June 1920 Barrios wrote directly to the permanent commission of the federal congress, denying that he was about to rebel and pointing out that he had never failed to carry out his duties as a loyal federal officer.[22] Later that year the federal congress discussed allegations that Barrios was using heavy-handed tactics to ensure the election of Cabrera candidates as diputados in Zacatlán. Díaz Soto y Gama referred to a delegation from the Sierra Norte de Puebla who asked Calles, as head of the Guerra y Marina, to remove Barrios. They claimed that Barrios had stashed a cache of 500,000 bullets and weapons in a cave and was waiting for Cabrera's order to rebel. He reflected, "The pernicious existence of cacicazgos is still so strong in this region that the federal government feels impotent in attacking Gabriel Barrios, the legitimate heir to Francisco Lucas's cacicazgo. Faced with such impotence, Barrios has taken control of the Sierra and, as a consequence, the dominance of Cabrerismo also continues."[23]

Yet the idea that Barrios sought to convert the region into a Cabrerista stronghold was misguided. Had he been tempted to do so, it would have made more sense to make such a stand when Carranza entered the Sierra in search of his protection. That Barrios was aware of his own political vulnerability is shown in the gestures of reassurance he made to his military commanders following the fall of Carranza. He quickly needed to replace former political patrons with others who would do his bidding in federal and state congresses, and above all, in the jefatura in Puebla city.

During his time as military commander of the Sierra, Barrios recognized the vital importance of attracting the support of the various military chiefs in Puebla city. Declarations of loyalty, backed by unhesitating military support for the federal government, did much to allay the suspicions aroused by his refusal to operate beyond the Sierra. He steadfastly opposed all rebel activity during Obregón's presidency and during the de la Huerta campaign forged ties of mutual respect with his military superior, General Juan Almazán. Barrios had already received strong support from his new commander when, in May 1923, Almazán sent a detailed report to Calles exonerating Barrios from any blame relating to charges of abuse and political interference.[24] Accusations sent to the president, Guerra y Marina, or governor were eventually relayed back to the jefatura in Puebla for further investigation. The friendship between the two men protected Barrios from the attacks of others and reduced the chances of a critical report being sent back to Mexico City. Similarly, when General Roberto Cruz replaced Almazán in 1924, Barrios wasted little time in establishing good relations with his new boss. By November 1924, Cruz confirmed to Obregón that he considered Barrios a good friend and an officer who always carried out his duties in a loyal and obedient manner.[25]

After Cruz's departure things began to change, and the jefatura became increasingly unwilling or unable to protect Barrios from accusations of political interference and abuse of military power. In June 1926, the incumbent jefe, General Guadalberto Amaya, warned Barrios not to push his luck by giving his political enemies ammunition that could be used against him.[26] Later that year, Amaya voiced public concern that federal troops were interfering in the political process in Teziutlán, and in April 1927 Amaya's replacement, General Pedro J. Almada, curtly reminded Barrios to "abstain absolutely" from political conflicts in the Sierra.[27] Even so, Barrios still had many friends within the military. Correspondence between Barrios and General Bravo Izquierdo, then chief of infantry at the Guerra y Marina, displays a measure of friendship that goes beyond military fraternity.[28] While none of his immediate military superiors could have protected Barrios from a presidential order to remove him from the Sierra, by deflecting criticism they were able to delay the time when this might happen.

Although Gabriel Barrios had strong opinions on the best means of achieving postrevolutionary development, these did not lead him to give recognizable support to any political party. He was above all a pragmatist who sought the best way of retaining a position from which he could develop his ideas for the Sierra. While this demanded frequent engagement with political debates in Mexico City and Puebla city, he never considered giving up his military career to conduct such negotiations personally. Like his troops, he preferred to operate within his own land, using others to do his bidding beyond the Sierra. In the formative years of his cacicazgo, he was greatly aided by the politicians who had advised Juan Francisco Lucas. Demetrio Santa Fe and Ricardo Márquez Galindo had been faithful supporters of Lucas, and both purveyed a brand of liberal ideology for which the western Sierra had become famous. Upon his father's death, Lucas's son Abraham chose to resume a political rather than a military career, and together with Santa Fe and Márquez Galindo, worked closely with Barrios as a representative of the Partido Liberal del Estado de Puebla.[29] Santa Fe, who saw himself very much as an intellectual, wrote various essays relating to the need to develop the Sierra, many of which bore a striking resemblance to policies later adopted by Barrios. In the elections following Carranza's death, Lucas and Santa Fe became state diputado and *suplente* for Tetela respectively, as members of the Partido Liberal Independiente, which backed the candidacy of José María Sánchez for governor. The party's manifesto stressed loyalty to the federal government, and a desire to promote regional peace and stability through economic and educational developments.[30] Above all, however, with Lucas and Santa Fe in the local congress, Barrios found respected, articulate spokesmen to counter his many detractors.

The political alignment of Barrios's representatives with agrarian candidate José María Sánchez did not convince all observers that Barrios had relinquished the Carrancista cause. A report in *El Monitor* in

January 1921 suggested that Barrios had tried to implicate Sánchez in a rebellion in the Sierra town of Ahuacatlán, while during a period when the election results were unresolved, *El Universal de Puebla* and *El Monitor* continued to speculate that Barrios was about to launch his own rebellion in the Sierra.[31] Furthermore, *El Monitor* noted Barrios's hesitation to take action against the Carrancista former governor, Luis Sánchez Pontón, for his use of violence in attempting to take possession of an hacienda near Chignahuapan.[32] The inference was that Barrios had little sympathy for José María Sánchez's agrarian agenda and, to a large extent, this was true. In common with many serranos in the western Sierra, the Barrios brothers respected private ownership of land; they believed campesino development lay in individual endeavor rather than collective action. This being the case, endorsement of Sánchez's candidacy by Barrios's representatives should not be seen as support for agrarismo. Rather it indicated Barrios's acceptance of Obregón as legitimate leader of the Revolution.

When Sánchez eventually assumed the governorship in June 1921, Barrios's public image in Puebla city underwent a transformation. In July, Barrios asked Calles for financial help to initiate projects of "vital importance to the Sierra." The idea that Barrios was using his influence for progress, rather than repression and exploitation, slowly gathered pace and secured Barrios several years of favorable press in regional and national newspapers.[33] As it became clear that his loyalty to the federal government was firm, Barrios gradually became seen as a pillar of stability amid an increasingly chaotic political scene in Puebla. When the state congress withdrew recognition for Sánchez in late 1921, *El Monitor* reported that the governor had tried to buy Barrios's loyalty by offering him the future governorship. The paper reassured its readers that Barrios was too shrewd to fall for such a trick and portrayed him as a force for law and order in a state that regrettably saw violent opposition as the only means of combating the inadequacies of its governor.[34]

Barrios's progressive policies also made it easier for respected politicians to risk association with a cacique. Abraham Lucas, Márquez Galindo, and Santa Fe provided faithful political support for Barrios throughout the 1920s and remained on his side until the final moments of the cacicazgo.[35] During these years, Lucas constantly occupied positions in state or federal congresses, often under the banner of Márquez Galindo's Liga Revolucionaria de Puebla.[36] In 1926 Barrios provided financial support for Lucas's campaign to become suplente to the senatorial candidacy of Rafael Lara Grajales, the former Carrancista politician who had failed to become governor of Puebla in 1921.[37]

Márquez Galindo was an important link between the Barrios brothers and the federal executive. During the de la Huerta crisis in particular, he maintained frequent contact with both Obregón and Calles. As Barrios's loyalty became increasingly apparent at a time when others were defecting, the subsequent flow of trust and goodwill ensured that Márquez Galindo and others representing Barrios's interests received a sympathetic response within the corridors of power. Similarly, other Barrios supporters gained a foothold in federal and state politics. Rodolfo Hernández served as state diputado between 1925 and 1928;[38] Salustio Cabrera, cousin of Luis and Alfonso, continued to support Barrios throughout the 1920s, and as the Liga Revolucionaria de Puebla's candidate, he won the federal diputado elections for Zacatlán in 1928. Another strong advocate of Barrios's cause was Constantino Molina, federal diputado for Zacapoaxtla during the mid-1920s. His role became apparent during Barrios's most significant political challenge, his bitter confrontation with Claudio Tirado, a politician from Zacapoaxtla who held the governorship on two occasions during the 1920s. In the rest of the chapter I concentrate on this conflict because it clarifies several issues: the extent of Barrios's political aspirations and influence; the interrelationship between local, regional, and national political agendas; and the intricate web of military and civilian ambitions that occasionally produced extraordinary allegiances.

The Struggle for Hegemony in the Sierra: Barrios Versus Tirado

As long as Barrios made the right noises, the Sierra's strategic importance meant that the federal government allowed, and even encouraged, the expansion of his military supremacy over the whole region. It is important to point out, however, that such influence did not automatically provide Barrios with corresponding political control. Given events in the western Sierra, this might seem surprising. The victory over the Márquez brothers eliminated one source of political opposition, but there remained the challenge of Tranquilino Quintero. Following the death of Juan Francisco Lucas in 1917, rivalry between Barrios and Quintero polarized into a struggle for overall command of the Brigada Serrana. Quintero never recovered from the Guerra y Marina's preference for Barrios as commander and, following a short spell in charge of Carrancista troops in Teziutlán, he resigned his commission and announced his intention to follow a political career. In June 1922 Quintero ran as the Club Independiente "Ignacio Zaragoza" candidate for diputado in Tetela. Days later, the Club Independiente accused Barrios of interfering in political affairs to the detriment of opposition candidates.[39] Quintero had an influential ally in Miguel Lucas, son of Juan Francisco. Unlike his brother Abraham, Miguel never accepted Barrios's right to assume the mantle of his father and, by lending support to Quintero's military and political ambitions, he sought to weaken Barrios's position. Such hopes ended, however, with Quintero's death at the hands of Delahuertistas in March 1924.[40] Miguel Lucas never again overtly displayed his personal objections to Barrios's rise to power.

The demise of the Márquez and Quintero threats would have appeared to leave the road clear for Barrios to assume political control of the western Sierra. Yet, in both cases, he was considerably aided by federal government support. The limitations of his political autonomy were displayed in 1920, when the federal congress rejected the credentials of Barrios's preferred candidate for Zacatlán, Rodolfo Hernández, and recognized Gonzalo González as municipal president.[41] The presence of González in the heartland of Barrios's territory was the thin end of a much larger wedge of political opposition that determined how the Sierra connected to regional and national politics during the 1920s.

Expansion of the Barrios cacicazgo into territories where he was not well known inevitably produced new challenges, and nowhere were these stronger than in the district of Zacapoaxtla. Political rivalry within the district was already keen, as factions within the long-established gente de razón fought among themselves and against more recent mestizo arrivals for the lion's share of the economic spoils. In the main, this competition did not turn into violent combat during the Revolution. Fighting was for the Indians; the gente de razón generally kept their heads down and adopted positions most likely to achieve their underlying personal and political ambitions. By 1920, the prolonged process of tactical maneuvering in Zacapoaxtla had produced two distinct groups: one led by Carlos Macip y Alcántara and Moisés M. Macip, the other by two brothers, Wenceslao and Ignacio Macip, and Rufino A. Landero. With political and military instability in Puebla city resonating in the Sierra's various districts during the 1920s, the strength of each faction's claim upon Zacapoaxtla became dependent upon it securing a powerful patron. Initially, Carlos and Moisés Macip sought to retain a neutral political stance, but reluctantly they recognized the benefits of cooperating with Barrios. For the opposing group, Claudio Tirado represented their best hope. Although not from the established landed elite, Tirado had by 1920 gained sufficient prestige within Zacapoaxtla society to become the district's federal diputado.[42] The ensuing struggle between Tirado and Barrios was to have local, regional, and national repercussions.

During the July 1922 electoral campaign, Tirado wrote to the jefe de operaciones militares in Puebla city, alleging that Barrios's men had intimidated his political supporters on several occasions. He underlined the detrimental effect of Barrios's presence in the Sierra:

> Here, I feel as though I am entering enemy territory where neither the authority of the president of the republic nor the state governor are recognized. In their place, one finds "Gabriel No. 1," the "señor de Cuacuila" as he is commonly known within the region. . . . Barrios's irregular army constitutes nothing less than an armed political party that, by its very nature, enjoys an unfair advantage over all those political parties in opposition to its policies.[43]

In a dismissive reply, Barrios assured his superiors that Tirado's charges were completely false and were motivated by his desire to acquire total political domination of the region. Declaring himself free from political ambitions, he invited the Guerra y Marina to send a commission to the Sierra to ascertain the true nature of the situation.[44]

That Barrios was far from immune to political attacks was underlined in March 1922 when the local congress accepted Wenceslao Macip's proposal that Froylán Manjarrez be appointed provisional governor.[45] Having a sympathetic state governor made it easier for the anti-Barrios faction to counter the expansion of his political influence. Soon thereafter, supporters of José María Flores—Barrios's important local ally in Cuetzalan—accused Governor Manjarrez of ousting Flores as municipal president and "brutally imposing" Victor Vega Bernal (brother of Barrios's old adversary, Salvador) in his place.[46]

In the face of a sustained campaign of accusations against Barrios, the military authorities in Puebla city were forced to react. In April 1923, General Juan Almazán made a tour of the Sierra to investigate the various allegations. After extensive inquiries, the military commission found no substantial evidence to support the complaints. Almazán concluded that the main accusers, Gonzalo González and Zacapoaxtla federal diputado Wenceslao Macip, "had endeavored to collect every account and rumor they could find in order to criticize Barrios (even those of *comadres*). Moreover, hearsay was presented as firm evidence without any investigation of the origins or the validity of the claims." Almazán further claimed that specific charges made by Macip and the municipal president of Zacapoaxtla, Rufino Landero, betrayed something more sinister: "The Macip family is closely linked to the Vega Bernal family of Cuetzalan, and both are subordinate to the will and interests of Senator Claudio N. Tirado, also from Zacapoaxtla. Together they operate a true political hegemony . . . as a result of their monopoly of all the important public offices throughout this area."[47] Almazán was referring to a complex set of alliances. Wenceslao Macip was federal diputado; his brother, Ignacio, the tax collector; Victor Vega Bernal was municipal president of Cuetzalan; Arnulfo Ortega, brother-in-law of the Macips, was the local judge in Cuetzalan; and Salvador Vega Bernal enjoyed a continued military presence in the region thanks to an armed escort funded by the Guerra y Marina. These individuals, by family or political ties, represented a continuous chain of patronage that flowed from the state governor to the municipal judge.

During and immediately after the de la Huerta rebellion, Barrios and his political allies temporarily gained the ascendancy. Yet much of this advantage was neutralized in August 1925 when Tirado used his executive powers to remove the local council of Cuetzalan, claiming that it had fraudulently taken possession with the help of Barrios and José María Flores.[48] Certainly, Flores was actively impeding Tirado's efforts to strengthen his authority within the region and was relaying details to Demetrio Barrios of the attacks against Tirado that his friends in the federal congress were launching. Flores added that a short list of candidates to replace Tirado had already been drawn up, only to have the decision delayed by a disagreement between President Calles and Gilberto Valenzuela.[49] In the following months Flores and Márquez Galindo constantly lobbied the president and federal congress to remove Tirado from office.[50]

In August 1926, with Governor Tirado fighting for his political life and Barrios proving to be a dangerous enemy, Tirado unleashed one final assault by sending Calles a list of seventeen incidents in which Barrios and his forces were accused of various abuses and of issuing death threats to noncompliant local officials. Tirado warned that since the Sierra de Puebla, from Teziutlán to Huauchinango, was under Barrios's military control, the entire region was in danger of being "in open rebellion against the state government."[51] These accusations were so extreme that Calles ordered an immediate investigation. Within a week, Francisco Heredía's team had begun collecting evidence that would amount to a damning report corroborating many of Tirado's more serious charges. With reference to violent intimidation of local officials in Zacatlán and Cuetzalan, Heredía confirmed that Barrios's men had encouraged a political battle between "groups of armed Indians" (obviously referring to cuerpos voluntarios) and groups loyal to the state government. He surmised that similar political contestation existed in communities throughout the Sierra and that Barrios's supporters probably were guilty of committing abuses when their wishes were not satisfied by the civil authorities. He drew particular attention to the recent federal elections, suggesting that the tension between the distinct groups had been escalated by Barrios's apparent condoning of abuses against authorities loyal to the governor. Significantly, however, Heredía concluded by observing that apart from isolated incidents "the whole of the Sierra enjoys a situation of total peace, with complete security for all those using the roads within the region."[52]

Heredía's account could have been enough to seal Barrios's fate. This independent report offered unequivocal proof of Barrios's interference in the political process. Yet Heredía's overall conclusion that the majority of the Sierra enjoyed a state of peace and security may have been enough to persuade both Obregón and Calles to ignore successive warnings of the consequences of leaving Barrios in control of the Sierra. Such security was rare in a state where revolutionary violence and lawlessness were proving hard to eradicate. Furthermore, Barrios continued to receive the strong support of his military superiors in Puebla city. In forwarding Barrios's response to Tirado's charges, General Amaya enclosed a covering letter to Calles in which he pledged full confidence in Barrios and suggested that the recent difficulties in the Sierra had been aggravated by Tirado's decision to remove democratically elected local authorities. He judged this move to be a tactic by Tirado to strengthen his position before the forthcoming state elections. In conclusion, Amaya expressed his conviction that "if all your supporters worked with the loyalty and sincerity that Señor Tirado displays, then your supreme government would be lost and the Revolution would fall into the most sorrowful collapse."[53] Given that only two months earlier

General Amaya had warned Barrios to stay out of politics, Amaya's comments may have reflected tension between himself and Tirado rather than a willingness to protect Barrios. Nonetheless, the effect was the same. As long as Barrios's contribution toward political stability outweighed any negative consequences of his actions, he continued to receive federal tolerance.

An aspect that further weakened Tirado's accusations against Barrios was a concerted campaign taking place in Mexico City to undermine the governor's credibility. The details of this campaign reveal the extent of Barrios's political network. In September 1926, federal diputado Constantino Molina wrote to Barrios expressing his desire "to defend Barrios's peacemaking, progressive, and patriotic labors from their mutual enemies in the Sierra."[54] Molina, a member of the Zacapoaxtla faction opposed to Tirado's local clique, assured Barrios that up to fifteen other Puebla diputados were pressing for a formal commission to reveal Tirado's charges as groundless and to expose Tirado's intrigues. He added that efforts were being made to attract favorable press coverage and that a propaganda campaign had already been launched to raise awareness of the great benefits that Barrios's initiatives were bringing to the Sierra. The fight against Tirado, then, fostered alliances of convenience in which Barrios's natural supporters joined others who, for one reason or another, wanted to see Tirado defeated. It is within this context that we see the "señor de Cuacuila" joining forces with one of the *siete sabidos* of the Revolution: the intellectual from the Sierra town of Teziutlán, Vicente Lombardo Toledano.

The Cacique and the Intellectual

The paths of Gabriel Barrios and Vicente Lombardo Toledano did not cross as a result of any deep-seated affinity. Apart from their serrano origins, the two men had little in common: Barrios, the "Indian" soldier who preferred to live in rural obscurity, and Lombardo Toledano, the laborista who forsook his native Teziutlán for the stimulating environment of Mexico City. A coincidence of time and space forged an unlikely alliance that lasted several years before their natural differences brought the inevitable rupture.

Lombardo Toledano's enduring image rightly traces the development of his political career from his early work within the CROM. Less attention is given to his inconspicuous period as interim governor of Puebla and the murky battle that ensued as he sought to become federal diputado of his hometown in June 1924. On replacing Lombardo Toledano as interim governor, Alberto Guerrero immediately removed all the *ayuntamientos* that the former had sanctioned during his governorship.[55] Lombardo Toledano's endeavors to become Teziutlán's federal diputado suffered a setback when Guerrero made it clear that he was supporting the rival candidate, Manuel Villavicencio Toscana. Describing his opponent as "an impostor, unknown within the state and a political turncoat," Lombardo Toledano sought Obregón's help in a battle in which his supporters had "no weapons for the fight except honor, clarity of ideas, and hopes for a brighter future for the republic."[56] Two weeks later, Villavicencio Toscana countered by sending an urgent telegram to Obregón: "Intervention of Barrios forces permitted abuses by laborista elements / collecting officer pleads protection if forces in excess of those needed for peacekeeping are not withdrawn / forces constitute threat to civil liberties / Guerra y Marina has been contacted, request you do likewise."[57]

While Lombardo Toledano's appeal to the president and Barrios's subsequent actions might have been unconnected, Lombardo Toledano had the intellect to recognize the substantive help that brawn could give to brain. Reports in *Excélsior* accused Barrios's forces of producing illegal documentation in favor of Lombardo Toledano, even though Teziutlán's municipal president had already recorded a clear majority in favor of Villavicencio Toscana.[58]

The outcome of the battle between Lombardo Toledano and Villavicencio Toscana cannot be isolated from the struggle between Camarillo and Tirado for the state governorship. Tirado's victory over the laborista candidate appeared to deal a decisive blow to Lombardo Toledano's claim of victory in Teziutlán. Lombardo Toledano accepted a post as a councilor in the Mexico City municipal government, where he contested the election results before the federal congress. He maintained a warm correspondence with Barrios and was in regular contact with Barrios's representatives in congress.[59] In October 1925, diputado Márquez Galindo advised Demetrio Barrios that the parliamentary bloc had resolved "the case of Lombardo Toledano" and that Lombardo Toledano would shortly enter the chamber.[60] This suggests that Barrios's supporters in the federal congress were working actively to gain

Lombardo Toledano's admission. A week later, the federal congress overturned Villavicencio Toscana's victory and Lombardo Toledano became diputado for Teziutlán.[61]

In Lombardo Toledano, Barrios's political group had an influential, eloquent ally against the increasingly beleaguered governor of Puebla. This alliance represented a certain political logic. Márquez Galindo, Abraham Lucas, and Demetrio Santa Fe were all members of the Liga Revolucionaria de Puebla, a group professing laborista sympathies. The recruitment of Lombardo Toledano into the fight against Tirado had two motives, the most public being Tirado's removal and replacement with an interim governor more sympathetic to laborista ambitions. More important, however, was the fact that under the guise of a broader political assault, Barrios was able to eliminate his major rival for political hegemony in the Sierra Norte de Puebla.

Once installed in the federal congress, Lombardo Toledano quickly used his rhetorical skills against his political adversary. Being careful not to implicate Calles or Morones too closely in the repression of Puebla teachers, he accused Tirado of tricking the president into believing that the university teachers' claims were unjust. An extract from congressional debates reveals how he played upon Tirado's widely recognized vanity: "There are three figures who symbolize our history: Hidalgo, who gave us our nation; Juárez, who created a public conscience; and Calles, who reconstructed the motherland. . . . Hidalgo, Juárez, and Calles, and Tirado, the second Calles.—(Laughter. Applause) The fourth figure in Mexican history, humbly, without pretensions, the fourth figure in national history, this is Señor Tirado!" Lombardo Toledano was joined in the attack against Tirado by another diputado from Puebla, Gonzalo Bautista. In the name of all Puebla diputados affiliated to the Bloc Socialista, he accused Tirado of being unworthy of the office he held, describing him as a man "who far from attending to the affairs of state, passes the hours playing the guitar (laughter) and drinking cognac."[62] Specific reference to Barrios's role within the rising chaos of Puebla politics was made when a petition from state diputado Adalberto Martínez was read before the federal congress in November 1926. After listing numerous charges against Tirado, including protecting Catholic priests from the rigors of the new federal laws, Martínez accused Tirado of widespread violence during the July elections. Only in the Sierra Norte, Martínez noted, did Barrios's presence prevent such abuses.[63] The image of Barrios as a force for stability within an environment of chaos was once more emphasized in the corridors and chambers of power.

Teziutlán again became the battleground for familiar rivals as members of the Partido Laborista accused pro-Tirado local authorities of intimidating and torturing their members. The local leader of the Unión de Obreros y Campesinos, for example, accused the municipal president of abusing his position and of sending union members to Puebla city in chains on the spurious charge of rebellion. Barrios wrote to Amaya supporting CROM national leadership claims that the municipal president had committed crimes against unarmed workers. Tirado replied that the charges had no substance and were nothing more than part of a systematic attack on state authorities by Lombardo Toledano and his allies.[64] Irrespective of the truth of individual accusations, the sustained campaign had a cumulative effect, and when the federal congress acceded to Lombardo Toledano's request for an inquiry, it was only a matter of time before Tirado fell.

Better the Devil You Know

During the final days of Tirado's governorship, Gabriel Barrios wrote a lengthy letter to Márquez Galindo in which he expressed his hopes and fears for the future of Puebla politics. Barrios's language in this private correspondence with his trusted political ally reveals his deep concern for political stability and unity in Puebla city. He recognized the corrosive nature of factional politics and its detrimental effect upon state and federal initiatives. He believed it was essential "to find a responsible figure who has the capacity of governing in unison with the efforts of the sincere elements within the state."[65] It is significant that Barrios did not see a direct role for himself within the political future of state government; as in the past, he was content to let others do his bidding. He provided a list of possible candidates that included many of those who had supported him in the past, including Generals Bravo Izquierdo, Juan A. Almazán, and Roberto Cruz, and civilian politicians such as Abraham Lucas. Barrios's emphasis on stability and unity, rather than constitutional democracy, reflected both the political reality of Puebla politics during the 1920s and his own philosophy on governing the Sierra. In his view stability depended on good management and, judging by his inclusion of three military candidates, a firm hand at the helm.

Perhaps more revealing than Barrios's preferences are the names missing from his list. In defining "well-intentioned revolutionary elements," for example, he excluded Tirado's eventual replacement, Manuel Montes. In doing so, he displayed not only his opposition to agrarian reform, but also his doubts that such a figure could play the necessary unifying role for Puebla's future. Even more surprising was the fact that Barrios did not believe Lombardo Toledano merited the position of governor. The reasons for his exclusion are a little more complex. A shared loathing for Tirado did much to bring the two men together, and during this period Lombardo Toledano was at pains to compliment the Barrios brothers for their positive influence in the Sierra. As we have seen, Gabriel Barrios sought to place Lombardo Toledano in a position from which he could make an effective contribution to the anti-Tirado campaign. Barrios's hesitation, then, may have been due to Lombardo Toledano's close association with the CROM. His partisan allegiance, together with his unpromising period as governor in 1924, offered little comfort to those seeking someone with the skill to unite opposing factions. These factors alone may have been enough for Barrios to consider Lombardo Toledano inappropriate. In the following years, the differences between the two men became more apparent. With Montes's removal and subsequent assassination, it is clear that Barrios's concern over the direction of regional politics did not abate. While Barrios may have been happy that poblano agrarismo had been dealt a serious blow by Bravo Izquierdo's appointment as interim governor, the 1928 presidential and state gubenatorial elections threatened to drag Puebla into yet another period of conflictual politics.

As the nation debated the legitimacy of Obregón running for a second term of office, dominant themes within this discussion were the varying fortunes and political realignments of agrarista and laborista blocs, and the continuing, sometimes violent rural discontent concerning anti-Catholic legislation. Back in the Sierra de Puebla, Barrios and Márquez Galindo's Liga Revolucionaria came out in full support of Obregón's candidacy. During the early months of 1928, the national press speculated that Barrios was considering running for governor of Puebla. Obregonista political parties from various parts of Puebla contacted Barrios encouraging him to stand. Presumably unaware of Leonides Almazán's future candidacy, his brother Miguel also sent a letter of encouragement and pledged his support in the forthcoming campaign.[66] The widespread nature of the rumor and the absence of any swift denial implies that Barrios was testing the waters. In the event, his chances of success were few. While he might be able to secure the Sierra districts, he would find it hard to obtain significant support beyond the region. Rather than risk public humiliation, Barrios hedged his political bets by putting Ricardo Márquez Galindo forward as his gubernatorial candidate.

The Liga's electoral propaganda suggests it was a middle-of-the-road political party. Its doctrine was graphically portrayed in an anecdote that appeared in its campaign magazine, *La Voz de la Sierra*:

On board a transatlantic liner three gentlemen conversed:

"Without capital, one cannot produce anything," stated the capitalist.

"Without an army, there is neither respect nor order," added the military officer.

"Without religion, there is no morality," said the priest.

A passenger in the third class listened to the conversation, smiled, and regretted that he was not allowed to join in.

During the night the ship capsized in a terrible storm. The four men survived and reached the shores of a deserted island. They cut wood, made a fire, built a shelter, gathered fruit, and hunted animals. And while eating by the fireside, exhausted from the exertions of the day, they felt content and looked forward to resting on the pile of dried leaves that they had gathered to form a bed.

Then the third-class passenger summarized in five words, what he had wanted to say to his companions during their conversation aboard the ship:

"Without work, there is nothing."[67]

Yet, although the Liga expressed sympathy with the working classes, it fell short of advocating collective bargaining and mobilization. It promoted constitutional values, including agrarian and labor reform, but also emphasized a need to respect public and private property rights. Such values were very much in line with those stressed in 1920 when Lucas and Márquez Galindo represented the Partido Liberal Independiente. What had changed was that in the 1928 elections, the Liga comprised an identifiable political entity. Furthermore, in supporting Obregón's candidacy, the Liga placed itself in opposition to Lombardo Toledano, the CROM, and laborista opponents of Obregón. Whereas in previous campaigns Liga candidates could always rely upon the

support of important figures in federal or Puebla politics, in 1928—
particularly after the assassination of Obregón—they were much more
isolated.

Barrios and his political representatives became legitimate targets for
attack from all sides. From within the Sierra, local parties ranging from
laboristas to agraristas began to accuse Barrios of political intimidation
and interference.[68] Just as Lombardo Toledano had been a valuable ally,
so he proved to be a formidable opponent. As early as March 1928, he
indirectly challenged Barrios when he published an article warning of
the inherent dangers of continued rural isolation:

> Not land disputes, commercial competition, interchange of products, mass
> exodus, nor frequent individual travel occur in this region. Life revolves
> around the family hut and, as a consequence, the horizon of all anxieties
> lies at the ridge of the nearest hill. Such a land will only defeat caciquismo
> and the perpetuation of barbarism if it embraces intellectual and physical
> stimuli.[69]

Times had changed. In 1925 Lombardo Toledano had gone out of
his way to praise the Barrios brothers for their efforts to open up the
Sierra by road-building schemes, and in 1926 he had defended Barrios from accusations of political interference in Teziutlán.[70] By August
1928, however, Lombardo Toledano had asked the central committee
of the Partido Laborista to lodge complaints before the president and
the Guerra y Marina over the victimization of laborista supporters in
Teziutlán by Barrios's forces.[71] A couple of months later, similar accusations were made at the laborista gubernatorial nomination convention.
A Cuetzalan delegate spoke of the persecution of CROM members and
of large-scale fraud through which Bravo Izquierdo's state government
had allowed funds destined for road projects to reach the pockets of
Barrios and his cronies. Lombardo Toledano openly attacked his former
ally, alleging that Barrios had for all intents and purposes become the
legal, executive, and military chief of all Sierra communities.[72] While
Lombardo Toledano's own political ambitions suffered a setback when
convention delegates elected Leonides Andreu Almazán as the laborista gubernatorial candidate, it did little to stop the attack on Barrios.
Lombardo Toledano was from the Sierra, his word was respected, and
the insight that he gave to politics in Sierra communities added grist to
the mill of a new governor trying to establish executive authority over
all, rather than parts, of the state.

Conclusion

The political instability of Puebla politics during the 1920s was not the result simply of a class struggle between bourgeois and popular interests, but included deep divisions with labor and campesino organizations that were often settled by violence rather than negotiation. A vital contributory factor was the interference of the federal government. This interference came in various guises: national congressional refusal to approve Puebla governors or diputados, attempts by consecutive presidents to impose interim governors sympathetic to their causes, and the deployment of federal troops to combat rebellions and suppress demonstrations. The backdrop to this was a generalized drift towards political centralization that included the faltering move to depoliticize the military, to harness or neutralize the potential of mass organizations, and to reduce the influence of the Catholic Church. In a state such as Puebla, where a close-knit economic elite clashed with political and military leaders who purported to represent the interests of militant rural and urban groups, the consequences were perhaps inevitable. Years of violent revolution were followed by more than a decade in which regional government singularly failed to take the lead, by either democratic or authoritarian means. Whereas in Puebla city there may have been too many political initiatives, there were too few in outlying regions such as the Sierra de Puebla. An absence of gubernatorial authority within the region meant that it was left to its own devices. In such an environment, Barrios and Tirado emerged as the two main figures who tried to gain control. Neither was able to achieve this to their satisfaction.

This political vacuum presented both opportunities and dangers for the Barrios family. The lack of regional authority meant that it was easier for the brothers to gain influence within the Sierra. Whether through federal restrictions or its own instability, the Puebla government could never deploy a state militia or police force into the Sierra that might make Barrios's military presence obsolete. On the contrary, the very absence of such a force made it imperative that he stay. It is clear, however, that when Barrios's political enemies gained the ascendancy within the Puebla congress, his actions became much more restricted. The most prominent case was Tirado at various times between 1922 and 1927, but similar pressures resulted from those opposed to the Cabrera family in 1920–1921, and from Leonides Andreu Almazán in

1929. So, although Barrios controlled the Sierra for much of this period as its military commander, he faced political challenges in Puebla city that were played out in both local and federal congresses.

Yet even as we talk about a specific case of postrevolutionary caudillismo, it is clear that we are not looking at a straightforward example. Firstly, unlike Saturnino Cedillo, Adalberto Tejeda, or Emilio Portes Gil, Gabriel Barrios never controlled the state government nor had the financial resources that governorship would yield. At times his political representatives had influential voices, but they were often a minority and on the defensive. Nor were they able to rely upon the patronage of a strong leader who did have control of the state. Mújica's relationship with Primo Tapia in Michoacán or, more appropriately perhaps, Cedillo's patronage of Gonzalo Santos in San Luis Potosí are clear examples of political hierarchies in which subordinate leaders knew their role and acted within defined limits. In Puebla, both José María Sánchez and Manuel Montes represented Cedillo-like figures, but neither had sufficient strength to retain power. More importantly, Barrios had little or no affinity to agrarian caudillos from the meseta, so he had to look to Mexico City for political patronage.

As I have argued, Barrios's most effective means of gaining this support was to portray himself in word and deed as a faithful, reliable, and useful federal officer. The stalwart support of successive commanding officers in Puebla city bears witness to his able portrayal and, taking a more cynical view, perhaps the reluctance of commanders to admit that Barrios was beyond their control. Barrios's actions within the Sierra, however, quickly extended beyond a purely military brief. Through necessity and with federal government blessing, he deployed his soldiers to organize a range of tasks more usually left to federal or state civilian authorities, such as policing duties, road construction, and agricultural diversification projects. As I discuss in chapter 5, the way in which these tasks were carried out upset many people and provoked a wave of criticisms that stretched beyond the Guerra y Marina's portfolio. From the earliest days, Barrios's actions were debated in federal and state congresses, and it was imperative that he had representatives who could defend him against his detractors. The problem was that his personal representatives alone were never sufficiently strong to repel vociferous attacks. Barrios's men needed to establish an accord with a broader alliance of diputados from Puebla, some of whom represented districts beyond the Sierra with distinct political problems and who did not know Barrios but nonetheless temporarily shared with him a common enemy. With national and state politics being swayed by the polarization of specific groups, the best means for Barrios to attract the support he needed was to adopt a politically neutral line, one strong on constitutional values but weak on policies. Such a stance was hardly earth shattering, but provided he combined it with overt support for the federal executive, he stood a good chance of attracting continued support from diverse interest groups.

Barrios's problems really began when the federal executive no longer needed him. The crisis caused by Obregón's assassination began an irreversible process of incorporation in national politics. This included a campaign against the remaining military caudillos in the provinces who had survived the 1920s. In particular, the subordination and political neutrality of the federal army was seen as paramount, and federal officers such as Barrios were faced with a stark choice of subjugation or rebellion. Within the state of Puebla, laborista politics was enjoying an Indian summer. Agraristas had been routed, and the embracing arm of single-party national politics had not yet stifled independent political action. For once, if only briefly, federal and state political objectives coincided. Both sought political subordination, and the federal government's assault on military caudillismo complemented Governor Leonides Almazán's own attempts to establish regional stability based on civilian authority.

4 Coercion and Compromise in Local Sierra Politics

Rivers run deep in the Sierra Norte de Puebla. The opinions of one's neighbors matter. Whether in mestizo cabeceras or indigenous pueblos, peer pressure has always acted as a restraint upon unbridled, persistent wrongdoing. The sensitivity that members of the Barrios family still show when confronted by Gabriel's categorization as a cacique serves as a reminder of the significance of language, the elasticity of time, and above all, the intricate, often personal nature of history, politics, and society within small communities. Memories and reputations outlive the life spans of their subjects, and the juxtaposition of past and present, public and private, fact and fiction combine to construct the intricate fabric of society. The power of gossip, that quintessential feature of rural life, should never be underestimated. It has the potential to allow unsubstantiated past deeds to shape present and future actions. It can create a degree of suspicion so great as to thwart the best designs of policymakers and enthuse a level of local resistance that no number of manifestos and declarations can wear down. So as we move from the city to the hills to discover the nature of politics and society during the 1920s, we need to acknowledge the diverse, sometimes ethereal influences behind individual and community actions.

Trying to understand the political economy of Sierra communities raises many questions. Which individuals sought to represent a community, how did they acquire such a position, with whom did they connect, and what restraints were placed upon their actions from within and beyond the community? Of equal interest is the nature of such dialogue. What issues compelled communities to enter into discussion? Were these issues purely related to their own communities? How did the nature of these topics vary according to the communities' size, location, and ethnic composition? How and to what extent did hearsay, rumor, and reputation play a part in local politics? Answers to these questions provide clues about how Sierra communities and their leaders made the transition from warfare to reconstruction. The sporadic violence in the Sierra throughout the 1920s confirms that there was no neat delineation between these two phases. Rebellion and civil disorder coexisted with regenerative projects to improve communications and agriculture. Yet the prerequisite of economic development was law and order, so in this chapter I focus on the implications of this priority on the composition and functioning of local government and how an improved communications infrastructure contributed toward these underlying objectives. Having done so, in the following chapter I explain how economic development eclipsed security as the new imperative and analyze to what extent such initiatives affected the influence of different political actors within the Sierra.

Political Representation in Sierra Communities

The theory and practice of municipal politics in postrevolutionary Puebla rarely coincided. The new Puebla Constitution of 1917 clearly defined the relationship among the electorate, municipal authorities, and state and federal governments. At the most basic level, voters in a pueblo annually elected a mayor, councilors, and trustees who, together with the civil registrar, reported to the municipal president of their respective cabecera. Municipal councilors were also elected annually, and they would choose one of their number to become municipal president. The secretary, tax collector, and municipal judge were externally nominated and not subject to periodic reelection by the community. Through the municipal president, local government was subordinate to the authority of the state governor. Local authorities were responsible for managing finances and providing education and, while each community was expected to muster its own law enforcement agents, these individuals were ultimately controlled by state and federal government directives and, on occasion, augmented by state and federal forces.[1]

That such a situation rarely existed in Sierra communities was ably demonstrated by two respected observers. At the height of his battle with Tirado over local elections in Teziutlán, Lombardo Toledano sought to inform federal diputados about the political realities in the

Sierra and "a thousand other rural districts": "While people often view
the election of the governor or president of the republic with a certain
disdain, everyone is interested in the election of the local council; people are more interested in who becomes the municipal president of their
town than [who becomes] the president of the nation. The federal president is a distant figure, so too is the governor, but the municipal president is very close."[2] In his tour of the Sierra less than a year later, Moisés
Sáenz offered his own views concerning the façade of local politics:

> There is no significant action, no important decision that is taken without
> the presence of the municipal president, his representative, or the council.
> As far as the Indians are concerned, these are the symbols of authority,
> power, respect, and order. If the municipal president says something, his
> word is accepted. But the Indians are fully aware that it is the secretary
> who directs community affairs, and they are forced to realize that it is
> Gabriel Barrios who gives orders to the secretary. Nonetheless, with philo-
> sophical docility, they maintain a form of government in which they speak
> their own language and convince themselves that they are in charge. One
> might view them as children within a make-believe republic created by
> their teacher. In effect, this is how it appears. But these "children" are
> aware of the façade and accept it with a philosophy that leaves them
> content to the extent that, like the dramas of Pirandello, one does not know
> who is fooling who: if it is the mestizo who erected the façade in order to
> govern or the Indian who accepts it with open eyes, knowing that only in
> this way can he preserve unviolated the remaining dignity of his race.[3]

Neither of these comments should be taken at face value. Although a
serrano by birth, Lombardo Toledano spent little time in his native
Teziutlán and even less in other Sierra communities. His comments
were made within the context of a political assault upon the Teziutlán
ayuntamiento by Governor Tirado, and it was in his interests to underline the deep significance that locally elected representatives had for
rural towns such as Teziutlán. Indeed, the town's inhabitants were not
as closed to externally derived politics as Lombardo Toledano's portrayal of rural insularity suggests. Much of the tension within the town
during this period revolved around the efforts by local miners, bakers,
and other workers to improve working conditions and become affiliated with the CROM. Sáenz had even less experience of the Sierra.
Gabriel Barrios organized his tour and accompanied him for part of his
journey. Displays of deference or goodwill toward Barrios were, no

doubt, influenced by his presence, while given the short amount of time he spent in any one community, we might question the accuracy of Sáenz's impressions. In addition, as undersecretary of education, Sáenz had his own political and social agenda that was linked to the department's broader ambitions to rescue these "children" from obscurity, exploitation, and ignorance.

Nonetheless, Lombardo Toledano and Sáenz both possessed considerable political experience, and in some ways their observations coincide. Placing faith in the municipal president could be seen as the ultimate accolade of local democracy, with the elected official enjoying the full backing of the community. Yet they shared a more jaundiced interpretation, lamenting the insularity of rural communities that impeded them from engaging in broader political debate. Lombardo Toledano did not go so far as to suggest that local democracy was a sham, but this may have been because he based his observations on the comparatively developed town of Teziutlán. For Sáenz, the situation was much clearer in the many smaller rural communities where few spoke Spanish and the secretary was often the only gente de razón; the only, as he put it, "civilizing influence" for miles around. It was this nonelected official, the secretary, that Sáenz believed could breach such insularity and that, as a result of his dialogue with external political actors, enjoyed real political authority within a community.[4]

Robert Redfield's study of Tepoztlán, Morelos, provides a useful comparison for understanding the situation in the Sierra de Puebla.[5] While the town's annual election of the municipal council resembled that of Puebla, Redfield suggests that the council members were in practice appointed by the state government in Cuernavaca based on their obedience to the state government. He adds that the municipal council held little real power or prestige, functioning merely as a local administrative body of the state government. Councilors invariably came from "los locos," the less educated sector of society. Due to the relative impotence of local politics in Tepoztlán, Redfield concludes that politics fell into the same category as the organization of religious fiestas: a form of play enjoyed by the less influential sector of the community. Despite the solemnity and internal respect associated with the performance of such duties, local politics in Tepoztlán was a trivial pastime for the masses, while important decisions were made elsewhere. The more educated sector of Tepoztlán society, Redfield argues, viewed local politics with disdain and found that their personal and commercial connections with the state capital provided a more effective method of introducing progressive reform into the community.

Something fundamentally different was occurring in the Sierra de Puebla. A distinction should be made between the power struggle in cabeceras, which were similar to Tepoztlán in size and constitutional importance, and the situation in the pueblos. In the Sierra cabeceras, it was not the "locos," but the gente de razón who contested control of the municipal councils. While the state governor often sought to impose his own people in the cabecera ayuntamientos, those who took office were members of the local social and economic elite, the same group that in Tepoztlán viewed such positions with contempt. These Sierra cabeceras became the political battlegrounds between factions aligned to the state governor and those loyal to Barrios. Throughout the 1920s, towns such as Zacatlán, Tetela de Ocampo, Zacapoaxtla, and Teziutlán witnessed fiercely contended elections. The degree to which Barrios could retain control of cabecera politics served as an indicator of his changing fortunes in the Sierra as a whole.

If Sáenz's observations were accurate, it is in the smaller municipalities and pueblos that we see a political economy more akin to that described by Redfield. Within many Nahua and Totonac communities, legitimacy was afforded through participation within a more or less elaborate *cargo* system, where the respect of one's neighbors was earned through performance of civil or religious duties. What Sáenz noted, therefore, was the grafting of this system onto a bureaucratic framework, which ensured that those who gained internally bestowed legitimacy occupied constitutionally recognized offices. As in Tepoztlán, the solemnity with which Sierra indigenous communities participated in local government reflected their desire to uphold a chosen method of selecting community leaders or, as Sáenz saw it, "to preserve unviolated the remaining dignity of his race." The vital difference in the Sierra was that the nonelected officials who formed part of the "façade to govern" were imposed not by the state government, but by the Barrios family of Cuacuila. In this way, Sáenz concluded, Gabriel Barrios operated "a style of benevolent feudalism, a strong and loving paternalism that, perhaps, offers a key to governing, administering, and civilizing many other regions of Mexico, the many other 'Sierra Norte de Pueblas' that wish they had such a form of government."[6]

Before I invoke a state of apoplexy among those readers who advocate political agency among subaltern groups, I should stress that the evidence does not support Sáenz's image of a region in mild political submission to the Barrios family. The considerable independence shown by serranos in choosing how and when to mobilize undermines such a conclusion. Just as indigenous groups elsewhere took advantage of the administrative hiatus caused by the Revolution to resurrect community social and political structures, so too the political vacuum created spaces in the Sierra that took time to fill.[7] Yet neither were Sáenz's conclusions groundless. During the 1920s the Barrios brothers constructed a remarkable network, and in some communities their influence did render local politics devoid of anything but symbolic value. In Cuacuila, the Barrios family owned much of the community's land, employed many of its inhabitants, and directly or indirectly monopolized political and economic activities. In other communities, wealthy mestizo families enjoyed similar influence. More numerous and diverse, however, were the myriad of other Sierra pueblos where internal influence was contested or where authority was vested in criteria other than economic or political strength. Coercion might force the obedience of some communities, but long-lasting stability could come only through negotiation and cooperation. In this respect, serranos had the opportunity to convert the "façade" into a working relationship.

Political Office: Imposition and Independence

It is clear that Sáenz was correct in suggesting that political patronage had a significant influence upon the appointment of local officials. Bardomiano Barrios's letter to Fernando Sosa in San Mateo offers compelling evidence:

> My apologies for the inconvenience, but as it has been necessary to transfer the present secretary, Manuel Hernández, to another pueblo, this leaves a vacancy in San Mateo. I should appreciate it if you could talk to the municipal president and the councilors and persuade them to allow Señor Francisco Arroyo, a competent and diligent individual, to fill the vacancy. I trust that the local authority will agree to my proposal and that Señor Arroyo will soon receive news of his appointment.[8]

The façade of democracy that Sáenz noted three years later was already evident. Bardomiano Barrios wrote in a matter-of-fact way regarding the need to switch secretaries from one community to another, even though he had no authority to do so. That this letter was written at precisely the time when General Juan Almazán was in the Sierra investigating claims that the Barrios brothers were interfering in politics gives some measure of the confidence they felt concerning their relationship with their military superior.

On other occasions, the brothers barely paid lip service to local democracy. There is no doubt that they directly interfered in the local democratic process, imposing councilors, municipal presidents, or whole ayuntamientos in order to guarantee compliance.[9] In other cases the vetting of candidates negated the need for more direct intervention. Simón Torres, jefe de armas in Tlapacoya, asked Demetrio Barrios to endorse a list of candidates for the community's next ayuntamiento.[10] Artemio González of Villa Juárez did likewise, adding that all had been assessed and shared "your own ideals and each would work for the benefit of the people."[11]

Recognition of Barrios's power to wield unconstitutional political authority is also evident in correspondence directed to him. In one example, a political ally asked Demetrio Barrios to consider his father for a forthcoming vacancy.[12] On another occasion, Señor Meza y Mora, a former secretary, asked Barrios to help him resolve a personal predicament:

> My main purpose in writing is to ask if you could find me employment in Zacatlán or elsewhere in the Sierra, as I am considering returning to the region shortly. Although I presently hold the position of tax collector here in Papantla, my income is not sufficient for my expenses. As you know, I have a large family and with the prices of even essential commodities being very expensive here, I find my expenditures rising daily. Here in Papantla, the climate is very hot and unhealthy, there is a great deal of sickness, and I find it impossible to continue living in such conditions. Since we arrived here, my family and I have suffered constant sickness. Not wishing to take up any more of your time, I hope that you will be able to respond favorably to my request.[13]

In a clear demonstration of how patronage functioned, Meza y Mora strengthened his request by recalling past connections with the Barrios family, notably his cooperation in electoral matters. Yet this example also suggests that being one of Barrios's men was not tantamount to unbridled freedom to enrich oneself. The propensity of communities to complain to Barrios tended to constrain the actions of such officials. In

January 1925 the vecinos of the pueblo of Chicontla sought Demetrio Barrios's help in dealing with a corrupt secretary who had stolen money through extortion.[14] Three years later, the vecinos of Jopala asked Barrios to remove their corrupt secretary.[15] Similarly, in April 1929 the president of the *junta auxiliar* of Concepción, Atlequizayan, asked Demetrio Barrios to replace a secretary who had demanded "increasingly excessive wages while doing very little during his seven years as secretary."[16] In June 1925, the jefe de armas of Caxhuacán sought Barrios's guidance regarding an attempt by local people to replace the municipal president with someone the jefe deemed unsuitable.[17] In each of these cases, complaints should have been directed to the state government in Puebla, yet serranos found it more effective to petition the Barrios family.

To show that political patronage was an integral part of the Barrios cacicazgo is one thing, but it would be too great a leap to suggest that Barrios had a similar level of control throughout the entire Sierra. At various times, Barrios's political enemies held influence within state and municipal governments, representing possible alliances for any community seeking to maintain a more independent, even democratic stance. It is strange, then, that little evidence exists of resistance to Barrios's political authority at the local level. Incidents of confrontation were sporadic and only indirectly challenged Barrios's right to manipulate local politics. As earlier examples show, if a community had a problem with a public official, it sought a resolution from the Barrios family rather than the local constitution.

Part of the problem for local authorities who wished to oppose Barrios was the lack of any reliable state governmental authority. The case of Miguel Manzano, municipal president of Tetela de Ocampo, illustrates this point. In October 1926, Manzano wrote to Gabriel Barrios referring to the lukewarm response he had received to his efforts to establish friendly cooperation with him. He presumed that this was because Barrios thought him to be a Tirado supporter. Manzano assured Barrios that while he had a constitutional responsibility toward the governor, he was not an unconditional follower of Tirado. Indeed, he added, he had always spoken in support of Barrios when the occasion arose.[18] This illustrates the difficulty for diligent public officials. While Manzano's responsibilities were to the governor in the distant city of Puebla, his safest option was to defer to the cacique who lived on top of the hill overlooking his town. Given the average life span of each governorship, local officials in the Sierra may have judged Barrios a more reliable patron. Tirado's dismissal only weeks after Manzano wrote his letter serves to underline the point.

If Manzano's dilemma was compounded by the proximity of Tetela de Ocampo to the center of Barrios's cacicazgo, did communities further afield fare any better? What can be said of Xochiapulco, for example, where local history maintains that teachers like Manuel Rivera unhesitatingly followed Juan Francisco Lucas's call to arms in order to turn the revolutionary slogan *"el sufragio efectivo no reelección"* into a reality.[19] Mallon states that Xochiapulco and other liberal villages participated "enthusiastically on the side of the Constitutionalists during the Revolution" after which "the 1920s and 1930s were a period of political consolidation that attempted to articulate earlier popular struggles to the emerging legacy of 1910."[20] Furthermore, Vaughan illustrates that the community strongly embraced initiatives by the Secretaría de Educación Pública (SEP) to foster education; the village's federally sponsored school became an exemplary model of rural education during the 1920s. Far from seeking isolation, the community strongly desired the construction of a road between it and the railway station at Zaragoza: a practical and symbolic demonstration, perhaps, of Xochiapulco's desire for inclusion within broader Mexican society.[21] If ever there were a Sierra community likely to oppose Barrios's cacicazgo, Xochiapulco was surely a prime candidate. Yet evidence of such resistance is scarce. It is true that Sergio Gutiérrez, director of the federal school in Xochiapulco, claimed to be representing "the proletariat of the Sierra Norte de Puebla" when he accused Barrios of being an unworthy successor to Juan Francisco Lucas. He also argued that Barrios was "sacrificing the individual liberties of the poor" by forcing them to work on a nearby road construction project.[22] Undoubtedly, Gutiérrez believed Barrios lacked legitimacy and sought to persuade President Obregón of his argument.

Given Xochiapulco's proud liberal heritage and the readiness of its inhabitants to petition for education and land rights, it seems strange that Gutiérrez appeared to be a lone voice in his opposition to Barrios.[23] There was never any prolonged campaign against the Barrios cacicazgo, even though at its worst, the cacicazgo might have destroyed the political culture upon which the community was founded. Why should this be the case? There are several explanations, the most obvious perhaps being the fear of reprisal. Yet Donna Rivera's retrospective look at this period does not reveal any deep resentment of Barrios nor any incidents of local intimidation by Barrios's troops. Secondly, Gutiérrez's letter was not countersigned by other villagers and cannot be separated from the ongoing battle between Barrios and Salvador Vega Bernal, for whom Gutiérrez had served as a military officer in 1920. Resentment against Barrios within Xochiapulco may not have been as deep as Gutiérrez portrayed. Was this because other villagers accepted Barrios as Lucas's successor, or was it that the nature of the Barrios cacicazgo never affected the everyday lives of the majority of Xochiapulco's inhabitants? A further explanation might be that Xochiapulco, like many other Sierra communities, took a positive decision to tolerate Barrios in return for greater benefits. Again, the social context of the 1920s needs to be taken into consideration. Sierra society was severely hampered by high levels of crime and banditry. For "individual liberties" to flourish, as Gutiérrez demanded, then peace and security had to return. The period of "political consolidation" that Mallon describes might best be understood in light of the imperative to restore law and order. It is to this topic that we now turn.

Restoration and Preservation of Law and Order

It would be misleading to suggest that revolutionary violence in the Sierra rendered everyday civilian life untenable. Military action was sporadic and did not affect all communities to the same degree.[24] Nonetheless, serrano society often displayed signs of strain. Low public morale was manifest in the increased levels of petty crime, defaults on tax and education contributions, and refusal to maintain thoroughfares upon which social and economic life depended. There are many examples of the pressures to which serranos were subjected. In May 1913, a group of people from Zapotitlán raided the nearby community of Zongozotla, seized local officials, and took more than four hundred pesos of public funds for the "revolutionary cause." In June 1914, Ricardo Márquez Galindo reported the alarming frequency with which bandits not recognized by any revolutionary group were stealing goods and money. Even large towns such as Huauchinango were severely affected by revolutionary and criminal activity. Those communities that sought to keep their heads down to avoid trouble merely became more vulnerable.[25] The people of Tonalapa, Tetela, wrote to the state governor complaining of the havoc wreaked upon them by all sides in the conflict.

After having complied with rebel demands for provisions, they now feared that federal forces might attack them as sympathizers to the rebel cause. The underlying purpose of their letter, however, was to argue that economic disruption had made it impossible for them to satisfy their tax obligations, and they appealed to the governor to waive their debt.[26] Did revolutionary violence really disrupt economic life in Tonalapa to the extent claimed, or was such disruption exaggerated in order to avoid taxation? Or did it perhaps reflect an unwillingness to pay taxes to an illegitimate Huertista administration? In the chaotic times of the Revolution, loyalties, motives, and social norms became stretched and ill defined.

According to the Puebla Constitution of 1917, the ultimate responsibility for restoring and guaranteeing law and order lay with the state and federal governments. However, political instability in Puebla city meant that the Barrios brothers represented the only authority within the region capable of doing the job. This does not mean that various alternative solutions were not proposed. During the height of early revolutionary violence, Demetrio Santa Fe proposed a network of community-based civil defense groups.[27] In 1917, following the death of Lucas, he made similar proposals. Noting that as much as half a campesino's time was disrupted by banditry, he suggested that communities should organize civil guard units of up to twenty-five men under the control of a local commander.[28] By September 1917 Santa Fe was calling for a coordinated network of civil guards and other law enforcement groups.[29] Less than a month later Governor Cabrera himself petitioned President Carranza for permission to recruit armed regional security forces, although Cabrera's main concern was to counter rising levels of crime on the streets of Puebla city caused by the "plague of rats arriving from Mexico City."[30] As with Santa Fe's proposal, these were to be locally recruited forces under the command of a local leader who would answer directly to the state governor. Under no circumstances would they be subject to the authority of the Guerra y Marina.[31] Few of these security forces were ever established in the Sierra and when, in 1920, the Cabrera government fell, the whole question of law enforcement lapsed into disarray once more. Similarly, in May 1922 the jefe de operaciones militares in Puebla city allowed each cabecera to organize a civilian force of up to ten men under the orders of the local authorities. Within six months, the de la Huerta rebellion had erupted, and these nascent steps toward a civilian police force were swept aside by a new national emergency.[32] In December 1926 the provisional governor authorized the town of Libres to establish its own civilian force, but this was overruled by the jefatura, who feared that such a move might cause friction between local civilian and federal forces.[33]

Only much later does evidence appear of a changing philosophy on the question of law and order. In May 1929, the state government issued a letter to one of Barrios's men stating that, in accordance with a presidential decree disbanding ad hoc law enforcement organizations, he was no longer the "commander of forces" for the community.[34] This letter coincided with a more general move by the state government to stamp its authority on the Sierra de Puebla.

The inadequacy of civilian law enforcement in the immediate aftermath of violent revolution meant that Sierra communities increasingly turned to Barrios to resolve nonmilitary problems. In February 1918 the authorities in Tetela de Ocampo asked Gabriel Barrios to help capture a suspect accused of rape.[35] Later the same year, members of Huitzilan's ayuntamicnto petitioned Barrios to investigate charges of abuse of power against the municipal president and to maintain public order while the process continued.[36] In September 1919, Barrios sent ten soldiers to help guard Tetela de Ocampo's jail at the municipal president's request.[37] Similarly, in July 1920, Barrios responded positively to a request from the municipal president of Zacatlán for the deployment of troops to nearby Ahuacatlán, as the community's sole police officer was unable to cope with the high incidence of crime.[38] In October 1921, the provisional council of Zacatlán asked Bardomiano Barrios for troops to assist in the pursuit of a dangerous criminal.[39]

Most of these examples come from communities close to Barrios's military headquarters in Cuacuila, from people who knew him and recognized his legitimacy. Yet during turbulent times, it was difficult to draw a line between matters of public and military security, and communities from an increasing number of Sierra districts approached Barrios's nearby garrisons for protection. In January 1921, *El Monitor* reported that Barrios's troops in Teziutlán had captured a bandit leader, Odilon Almonte, together with thirty to forty of his men, "thus bringing an end to a reign of terror against local campesinos and landowners."[40] In August 1922 Barrios informed his regional superiors that sixty of his troops had captured, killed, or injured rebels responsible for a wave of atrocities in Entabladero, Veracruz.[41] In May 1925 several municipal presidents from throughout the Sierra sought Barrios's help in combating banditry and, in some cases, abuses committed by members of their own ayuntamientos.[42]

A situation in which soldiers were constantly having to define and maintain a distinction between rebels and common criminals was fraught with difficulties. Yet while Barrios had many critics, there were relatively few complaints against the actions of his regular soldiers. Several incidents arose in which troops escorting suspects appear to have applied the so-called *ley de fuga*, where individuals were shot "while trying to escape." Such arbitrary justice attracted the attention of Ernest Gruening, who commented on the execution of four suspects by Barrios's men in Tuxpan, Veracruz, despite their having successfully secured an *amparo* from a federal judge.[43] Others relate to the use of force, including murder, against alleged opponents of the Barrios brothers' designs for a particular community. Yet the number of written complaints is comparatively small and is counterbalanced by a similar number praising Barrios for restoring law and order. Given an atmosphere of intimidation and a political battle between Barrios and Tirado in which "even comadres" were persuaded to make unsubstantiated claims against federal troops, how are we to judge the true impact of Barrios's presence? It is at this point that anecdotes and lasting impressions among Sierra communities might help.

I return to the strong consensus that remains throughout the Sierra. The Barrios brothers' most significant achievement was to restore stability and peace to a region that found it hard to shake off the violent legacy of the revolutionary years. Sometimes wistfully, at other times solemnly, informant after informant related stories characterizing Gabriel Barrios as "a firm but fair man." Many believed that he was justified in using violence to combat violence. Most agreed that the Sierra suffered from banditry and that Barrios countered this by executing even those suspected of petty crimes. Guillermo Mejía, the Barrios family's servant, says that between 1924 and 1929, the Barrios brothers had a purge on robbers. Municipal presidents were asked to identify local delinquents, who were then taken away in the dead of night to meet an unknown fate. Mejía claims that the harshest punishments were reserved for bandits and cites one occasion when a gang derailed and robbed a night train by putting soap on a section of the Mexico-to-Veracruz railway track. Within a day, they had been caught and executed by Barrios's men. Beatriz Galindo, daughter of Barrios's jefe de armas in Amixtlán, recalls that those caught stealing cattle would be given one warning and that if they committed a similar crime, they would be shot without hesitation. Gabriel Barrios's son, Arnulfo, remembers as a boy hearing two commercial travelers talking about three corpses they had seen swinging from a tree. Locals had told them that the men had been caught stealing chickens.[44] Indeed, many serranos believe execution was Barrios's preferred way of dealing with suspects. A man in Tonalapa, in the heart of Barrios country, pointed out the tree where such hangings took place; across the Sierra in a small village near Libres, another informant did the same.[45] In another town, a huge maguey plant was said to have been used to hang criminals, and in Zacatlán, several informants suggested that Barrios's enemies were taken at night to a nearby hill and forced to dig their own graves before being shot in the back.[46]

Many informants described less violent forms of punishment in which antisocial behavior was punished by public humiliation rather than force. Mejía recalls a punishment that provokes a wry smile of recognition among many serranos: the *ley de cajones*. Gabriel Barrios argued that jailing persistent offenders was a waste of time and money; instead, he forced them to fill a basket with stones and carry it to Zacatlán, where the stones were used to pave the streets. Other areas benefited from what Mejía called a prisoner exchange, whereby miscreants were forced to perform public works in other communities. Several citizens in Zacatlán, including one of the Barrios brothers' revolutionary enemies, related the most striking example of a mild but effective retribution. The story concerns the son of a wealthy Zacatlán businessman who, after several drinks, thought it would be a good idea to ride around the central plaza on horseback, baring his backside to passersby. Barrios's men promptly threw him in jail and when the youth was sober he was brought before Barrios, who congratulated him on his horsemanship before fining him fifty pesos. The youth pulled a hundred-peso bill from his wallet and asked Barrios for change. Barrios said that he had none but that for the other fifty pesos the youth was at liberty to repeat his stunt in broad daylight before his troops.[47]

What should we make of these anecdotes? Unsurprisingly, the most positive impressions of Gabriel Barrios come from Zacatlán and Tetela, where the Barrios family lived and still lives. Yet further afield, and even among former enemies, a remarkably consistent picture emerges of a man with a no-nonsense approach who often stretched legal boundaries to bring a wayward region back to law and order. This widespread belief—which crosses social, ethnic, and geographic boundaries—suggests one of two things: that such a regime did exist throughout the

Sierra during the 1920s, or that stories of Barrios's sense of justice were so commonplace that they were assumed to be true. The difference is important, as ultimately it was accusations of Barrios's use of excessive force that led to his downfall. Arnulfo Barrios believes that his father did hang petty criminals and appears quite at ease with the latter's image as a figure who used ruthless methods for laudable ends.[48] It is significant, however, that none of the informants ever witnessed such acts of tough justice themselves. Like Arnulfo, they reflect a general feeling among his father's contemporaries that such acts were committed. Another son, José María, claims that Barrios's reputation was manufactured in order to intimidate and that the idea that petty criminals were routinely hung is false. Given that José María is remarkably candid regarding his father's checkered history on other issues, his view of law and order should not be seen as purely defensive. José María argues that if his father's ultimate aim was to pacify and control the entire Sierra, this could not have been achieved by repression alone. He muses that his father's tough reputation served conflicting interests. Barrios could use the threat of violence as a deterrent, whereas his enemies could argue that such violence was an unacceptable price to pay for regional stability.[49] As things transpired, once the federal government felt secure in its position, it increasingly accepted the latter argument.

Barrios's capacity to enforce his will, whether through actions or threats, depended on serranos' believing he had the power to do so. He could maintain this image only if serranos received regular reminders of the omnipresence of his forces, reminders that might make wrongdoers think twice before committing a criminal act. At the district level, garrisons of the 46th Battalion were a visible deterrent; but within the community, it was the network of cuerpos voluntarios that needed to be taken into account. Who comprised the cuerpos and their leaders, how were they chosen, and what were their responsibilities? Answers to these questions offer a better understanding of the balance of power between the Barrios family, local armed groups, and community leaders.

Jefes de Armas: The Scope and Nature of the Security Network

Few armed groups could justifiably claim the moral high ground during the Revolution. Government and rebel forces alike resorted to theft or arbitrary confiscation of provisions in order to maintain their campaigns. Efforts to restore law and order depended upon the initiatives of the dominant forces within a region, and in significant sectors of the Sierra, the Brigada Serrana performed this role with varying degrees of success. As widespread violence abated, Barrios's federal troops slowly relinquished everyday law enforcement duties to the network of jefes de armas and cuerpos voluntarios. In the process, Barrios risked compromising the high standard of discipline that he maintained among his regular troops. Acutely aware of the dangers in allowing numerous armed groups to assume local jurisdiction, he sought to erect new checks and balances to restrain unauthorized actions. The key to this mechanism was the telephone.

Efforts to repair and extend the Sierra's telephone network had begun during the Revolution. The Guerra y Marina agreed with Barrios that the telephone was an effective means of countering rebel activity, and during the early 1920s, Barrios continued to argue that development of the network was essential for restoring regional stability. Access to the lines was strictly limited and reserved primarily for jefes de armas. With all lines leading to Cuacuila, the system acted as an efficient means of conveying information regarding local disturbances and enabled the Barrios family to act swiftly. Given that telephones were installed in every community that housed a cuerpo voluntario, the true extent of Barrios's law enforcement capacity becomes apparent. In a Guerra y Marina report sent to President Calles, the telephone network was described as comprising more than two thousand kilometers of cables, and with more than five hundred offices, there was a telephone in almost every community in the Sierra.[50] There were offices throughout the municipalities of Zacatlán, Alatriste, Tetela, Huauchinango, and Pahuatlán in the northwest; and Zacapoaxtla, San Juan de los Llanos, and Tlatlauquitepec in the southeast. Several offices were also located in the districts of Tulancingo in Hidalgo, Papantla in Veracruz, and Tlaxco and Huamantla in Tlaxcala. Even with a conservative estimate that only half of the telephone offices indicated the presence of cuerpos voluntarios, there were at least three thousand armed men deployed across five states, each group in immediate contact with the Barrios brothers.[51]

The most idealized image of the jefes de armas is painted by José María Barrios. He describes a typical jefe as a man whose personal qualities identified him as a natural leader within a community. He usually would be bilingual and literate, with no political or commercial interests to compromise his position of authority.[52] This description might most accurately be viewed as an aggregate of the characteristics of jefes as a whole, rather than qualities possessed by a single individual. For example, the telephone meant that reports could be conveyed in Nahuatl or Totonac. Monolingual leaders of indigenous communities were not, therefore, excluded from incorporation into the Barrios cacicazgo as jefes de armas. The nature of the communities in which they resided and the way they were recruited offer more useful indicators of the composition of this network of local law enforcement agents. An extreme example serves to illustrate the general point.

Of all jefes de armas, the Galindo Salazar brothers of Amixtlán enjoyed the Barrios family's closest confidence. Enrique Galindo was jefe de armas of Tepango, Zacatlán, in 1924, while Alfredo became jefe of Amixtlán in 1925.[53] After the 46th Battalion's departure from the Sierra, Alfredo was given power of attorney to administer the legal affairs of his compadre, Demetrio Barrios.[54] With another brother, Ramón Galindo, representing the Barrios family in the federal congress as diputado for Teziutlán, it is evident that there was a considerable bond of trust between the two families. Ramón Galindo's daughter, Beatriz, provides a fascinating vision of the social background of these most trusted jefes de armas. Originally from Tuxpan, Veracruz, Ramón Galindo Abarca, the brothers' father, settled in Amixtlán in the nineteenth century. He married into the family of the local jefe político and eventually acquired two thousand hectares of land in addition to many houses and commercial properties in the town. The family's agricultural interests included coffee and vanilla production and the raising of cattle. The Galindo children each had their own nanny, and Galindo Abarca hired teachers from Puebla city to give them "the best education available in Mexico." Beatriz Galindo believes that the family was very conscious of its social status:

> The men wore the finest French cashmere suits and rode thoroughbred horses. They always wore the finest clothes from the city, despite spending most of their time in the Sierra. When one of the brothers was working in Mexico City, he bought a winter coat for his sister in Amixtlán. When asked whether it was a bit too refined for the Sierra, he answered "for the Sierra, yes, but this coat is for my sister." The Galindo women made considerable efforts to go to the dances in Zacatlán to show off their finest black-and-white silks. Even though it was an eight-hour journey, the ladies always took care to ride sidesaddle through the villages along the road to Zacat-

lán, in order to maintain the image of their lofty social position. Everyone came out of their houses to see them, and to see their horses.[55]

How does this image of the Galindo family match the model of the jefe de armas described by José María Barrios? Certainly, if Barrios sought out individuals who commanded respect within the community, then the Galindo family fulfilled the requirement. Yet the Galindos were hardly disinterested representatives of law and order. In as much as they controlled the area's political, judicial, commercial, and social life, they were in fact local caciques whose domination was reinforced by close personal ties with the Barrios family. The Galindo family may be an extreme example, but others such as the Flores family of Cuetzalan, the Lechugas of Huauchinango, and the Macips of Zacapoaxtla, suggest that in certain important locations, Barrios was inclined to adopt a pragmatic approach in his selection of jefes de armas. All four examples represented, to greater or lesser degrees, dominant factions within non-Indian communities. Barrios could not afford to brush aside their relative strength in preference for other, more compliant jefes de armas. To ignore their local domination would have been to risk increasing the factional violence that the appointment of jefes de armas sought to impede.

It appears, therefore, that the Barrios brothers were prepared to recognize local balances of power by seeking to incorporate those families or factions that could best produce a compliant response from their communities. In a similar way, important local figures also showed flexibility. Given their social status and self-perception, it seems strange that the Galindo brothers should have agreed to follow a family regarded by their social peers in neighboring districts as barbarous Indians. Beatriz Galindo denies any tension between the two families, which can be partially explained by the fact that they now form part of the same wealthy, mestizo society in Zacatlán. It was, however, with a slight sense of incredulity that she described Gabriel Barrios's habit of turning up unannounced at her father's house, expecting to be given a meal and a bed for the night. Barrios's rustic, if not indigenous, ways appear to have been tolerated rather than welcomed. It is likely that the Galindo family adopted a pragmatic approach. As it became clear that Barrios enjoyed full federal backing, it made sense to trade subordination in return for a form of patronage that would allow the Galindos to maintain their status within Amixtlán.

While pivotal to the regional political balance, municipalities such as Amixtlán represented the minority of communities that housed cuerpos voluntarios. More numerous were the small mestizo and indigenous pueblos that Moisés Sáenz encountered in his journey across the Sierra, where the "façade" of democracy prevailed. I believe that the secret of Barrios's success in obtaining acceptance of his overall authority was his willingness to meet such communities halfway. For example, in February 1925, Captain Leandro Amaro, federal commander of the Huauchinango garrison, reported that bandits in Tlaxcalantongo were robbing and hanging innocent people, and that the municipal president had asked him either to send a detachment of troops or to allow the local authorities to conduct their own armed defense. Demetrio Barrios authorized the largely indigenous community to muster its own force, comprising residents of "reputable character," with the sole objective of protecting their community. He responded in a similar fashion when Amaro reported that several individuals elsewhere had handed over their weapons and sought permission to become leaders of their community's voluntary forces. Barrios instructed Amaro to ensure that the volunteers restricted their actions to the maintenance of law and order in their localities, and ordered that incidents requiring a broader response be referred to Cuacuila.[56] These cases suggest that Sierra communities enjoyed a considerable degree of freedom in selecting their own jefes and cuerpos voluntarios.

What did it mean to become one of Barrios's men, as either a jefe de armas or a member of a cuerpo voluntario? The answer depended upon local circumstances. The Galindos obviously benefited from their position, but their "volunteers" did not. Members of the cuerpo voluntario in Amixtlán were none other than workers on Galindo's land who occasionally laid down their implements and picked up rifles. There is no suggestion, then, that in the case of Amixtlán membership in a cuerpo voluntario offered any significant opportunities for social advancement; the nature of the job might change, but social status remained unaltered.

In communities where authority relied largely upon consensus, did the sudden elevation of certain individuals alter the existing status quo? In Xochiapulco during the nineteenth century, membership in the national guard enabled the village youths to question the authority of the elders, whose legitimacy rested upon internal hierarchical structures.

Was this the case in the 1920s, or was the situation more akin to that noted by Paul Garner in highland Oaxaca, where during the Revolution village elders retained the power to mobilize and direct locally based armed groups?[57] The lack of evidence that Sierra youths were able to capitalize on their membership in cuerpos voluntarios requires explanation. It should be remembered that these groups were, first and foremost, civilian peacekeeping forces that only occasionally engaged in prolonged armed campaigns as auxiliaries of the 46th Battalion. Voluntarios had little opportunity to sustain any form of meaningful dialogue with external agents who might deliver them local political prestige. As such, the jefe de armas and his men were often viewed by their own community as a police force that was subordinate to the local authorities. In addition, the Barrios brothers remained acutely sensitive to any indications that jefes de armas were abusing their positions. We need not take this attentiveness as any form of altruism; it is more a measure of self-preservation that the Barrios family wanted to ensure that no one could establish a power base to challenge their regional authority. It was difficult to balance the need to maintain order with the imperative to prevent armed groups from taking the law into their own hands, particularly on the periphery where communities had few personal dealings with the Barrios family. Heavy-handedness by Barrios risked jeopardizing the cooperation that was essential to his regional operations. If a sufficient number of communities violently rejected his presence, his image as the only person who could deliver stability to the Sierra would be destroyed; and if he could no longer perform this role, the federal authorities would question the wisdom of allowing him to stay in the Sierra.

The very survival of the cacicazgo, then, depended upon striking a balance between cooperation and coercion. The task of appointing and monitoring the system of jefes fell to Bardomiano Barrios and, after his death, Demetrio. Upon his appointment, each jefe received a verbal or written description of his duties. Those sent to Ricardo M. Ramírez of Tetzitzilica and Arnulfo Sánchez of Rancho de la Palma, Tlaxco, are typical:

On behalf of General Gabriel Barrios and in agreement with the head-quarters, you have been chosen to become jefe de los voluntarios of your locality on the understanding that you always conduct yourself in an honorable manner and that you afford full guarantees to all law-abiding men so that they may dedicate themselves to lawful business. You are also expected to maintain good public order.[58]

Other appointments in 1923 carried reminders that the new jefes should set a good example and, in one case, permission was given to disarm the population to preserve the order and morality of the community. Most evidence confirms that the Barrios family appointed jefes to fulfill a role that was entirely connected with public security, the control of arms, and the suppression of bandits. They were not given license to act in place of or in contempt of existing local civil political authority.[59]

Alleged violence and abuse of power by jefes de armas were the main issues that provoked criticism against the Barrios brothers. Complaints ranged from individuals claiming victimization or wrongful imprisonment to whole communities petitioning for action to be taken against jefes for corruption, extortion, and even murder. Some accusations were sent directly to the federal president, others to the Guerra y Marina, state governor, or district magistrates.[60] The most striking example came at a time when the Barrios family's influence was beginning to falter. In October 1928, Bautista Molina of Papantla wrote to the president detailing numerous abuses of power that had taken place in the district under Barrios. He argued that most had been committed by jefes de armas who went unpunished because local authorities were afraid to complain. Rather than punish them, Barrios would move his jefes from one community to another. Molina claimed that the jefes offered security to no one but the landlords and the wealthy and that if anyone did complain, Barrios would say that he had the backing of the federal government to continue deploying the jefes.[61]

Molina's portrayal of a region living in fear must be balanced against the fact that many communities with complaints would appeal directly to Barrios himself. Several communities asked the Barrios brothers to remove or punish jefes de armas, and on several occasions they received positive responses.[62] One of the more unusual incidents occurred in March 1923, when Bardomiano Barrios instructed Simón Torres, jefe in Tlapacoya, to stop persecuting a man suspected of witchcraft.[63] A more typical example is this letter to Manuel Alvarado:

It has been brought to my attention that some of the soldiers under your command are committing abuses against people and property and are regularly drunk. As you appear to tolerate such abuses, I have a duty to warn you of the serious consequences should such a state of affairs be allowed to continue. I am strongly against such behavior, and this letter should be considered the only warning you will receive. Such abuses must be stopped completely, as they bring discredit not only upon commanders but also the government.[64]

Because this correspondence was private and confidential, there was no hidden political agenda attached to the choice of words used or the sentiments expressed. Thus, we can be fairly confident that the Barrios brothers were sincere in their desire to make representatives accountable. Occasionally, jefes de armas would notify Barrios of abuses committed by jefes in other settlements, and Barrios sometimes authorized them to take corrective action.[65]

Another way in which the Barrios family tried to control cuerpos voluntarios was to restrict their jefes' military potential. Correspondence with Pedro Becerril, jefe de armas in Chilocoyo, suggests that each of his men was rationed to one rifle and just sixteen bullets each year. In December 1923, as the de la Huerta rebellion broke, Bardomiano Barrios warned the jefe of Rancho de Rinconada to use the consignment of ammunition sparingly. There may have been a genuine shortage, but when the need arose Barrios had little problem in obtaining further supplies from the Guerra y Marina. More likely, the rationing was a precautionary measure reflecting a degree of uncertainty in Barrios's mind concerning the jefes' loyalty to him or to the federal cause. The danger of any group mounting a challenge against him would have been severely restricted by a shortage of ammunition and arms.[66]

As long as banditry remained a problem, the cuerpos voluntarios represented a vital reserve force of the 46th Battalion. Their usual duties, however, were more mundane: overseeing local fiestas, resolving cases of domestic violence, and controlling rowdy behavior.[67] As such, their actions often reflected and sought to uphold local social values. Daniel Carlos, jefe for Coyutla, Veracruz, for example, sought Demetrio Barrios's advice concerning the "loose behavior" of Señora Guadalupe Llano. The jefe explained that her immoral behavior in a house bordering the Parque Reforma was causing true indignation within respectable society and tarnishing the good name of her deceased husband.[68] In this and many other cases, the cuerpos voluntarios are revealed for what they most often were: local police forces that cooperated with the local judiciary in upholding law and order. The major difference between this situation and that envisaged under the Puebla constitution is that Carlos thought it natural to seek advice from Cuacuila not Puebla city.

The Balance of Power in Sierra Communities

It is worth recalling why Gabriel Barrios was allowed so much freedom in the 1920s. First and foremost, his military presence guaranteed that a significant region of the state of Puebla remained loyal to the federation. Second, and increasingly important as widespread military conflict decreased, he was able to take the place of civilian authorities in eradicating banditry and returning a semblance of law and order to the Sierra. If the Barrios brothers were to retain favor with their federal superiors, they needed constantly to remind influential political and military figures that they were producing the goods. Having the support of representatives in federal and state congresses helped, but in the end it was results, not political rhetoric, that strengthened their position. Again, Francisco Heredía's conclusions in an otherwise critical report on Barrios's political interference are pertinent: "A compensatory factor is that, with the exception of the incidents highlighted by the governor of the state of Puebla, the whole of the Sierra enjoys a situation of total peace, with complete security for all those using the roads within the region."[69] There was no better defense than success.

Yet how could Barrios create a region of near total peace and security? Charisma had its uses but did not travel well into areas where he was unknown and where politicians were hostile to incursions upon their turf. Coercion also had its place, and in those unsettled times of sporadic rebellion, it was convenient to label criminal activity as seditious. But surely José María Barrios is correct when he argues that no coercive force, no matter how strong, could have produced stability within the Sierra: "Killing people causes vengeance not peace."[70] The means by which Barrios gained cooperation from Sierra communities was by persuading them that, on balance, he was a force for good rather than evil. He did this by establishing a tough regime that delivered what serranos wanted above all else: the freedom and security to conduct their everyday activities without fear of violence. In her analysis of law and order within Guatemalan rural communities during a similar period, Rachel Sieder finds that indigenous communities prioritized judicial clarity over equity. Under the dictatorship of General Jorge Ubico, a strong state reached out to the countryside, producing a type of justice in which criminals were routinely killed. Sieder argues that within the predominantly Mayan province of Alta Verapaz, the dictator's harsh judicial legislation at least let everyone know where he or she stood. Although these laws were never intended to create social equality, Mayan campesinos were aware of the limits of legalized exploitation and were quick to use the local courts to protest against excessive abuses of *patrones* or other local officials. The very strength and pervasiveness of the centralized state impeded the local elite from colluding with the judiciary to thwart such appeals.[71] No such option was available in the Sierra Norte de Puebla during the 1920s. The federal government was still weak, the provincial government in chaos, and the local judiciary lacked the human and material resources to establish the rule of law. Bandits attacked without fear of retribution, municipal jails had insufficient guards to make them secure, and even minor security tasks, such as overseeing local fiestas, were too much for some communities. This is not to say that the Sierra degenerated into anarchy. To some degree or another, each community recognized the norms of responsible citizenship, and peer pressure often deterred miscreants. In this way, the judicial framework often survived the lack of institutional direction that undermined its authority. Problems arose in situations where peer pressure proved powerless to stop those who resorted to violence. In such circumstances, a greater authority was sought. Constitutionally, this authority resided in Puebla city with the state government; in practice, it lay in Cuacuila with the Barrios family. Communities in the Sierra believed that, as with President Ubico's sense of justice among Guatemalans, Barrios's firm hand had the capacity to resolve the situation.

Barrios's ability to perform this role depended upon a fine balance between cooperation and coercion. It is clear that the imposition of municipal presidents, councilors, secretaries, and jefes de armas created a network of compliant local representatives. Yet this was only part of the story. Many of the complaints the Barrios brothers received involved an officeholder within a community complaining against another: a municipal president against a secretary, a jefe against a municipal president, the ayuntamiento against a jefe de armas, and so on. It was this network of independent informers within a community that acted as a counterbalance against the abuses of officials. Telephone links to Cuacuila enabled the Barrios brothers to mobilize federal troops to quell actions that were prejudicial to their interests or to a community's well-being. The tenor of the letters issued to jefes de armas who overstepped their authority is unequivocal. They were expected to uphold the law rather than be above it. In this respect, Barrios was responsive to locally determined standards of decent behavior.

This is the point at which we might consider the true balance of power between various local political agents. Clearly, the Barrios brothers either directly or indirectly dominated political and social life in some communities. Yet in many others, they had little more than a tenuous grip on internal affairs. Even the network of cuerpos voluntarios, which represented the very fabric of the cacicazgo, was beyond Barrios's complete control. No single jefe or cuerpo might have been able to challenge Barrios's authority, but nor could Barrios compel each and every cuerpo to act in a way that contradicted community interests. The enduring image of the Barrios cacicazgo as a regime that used brutality to counter violent crime can be explained by the brothers' recognition of the value in retaining a degree of ambiguity between fact and fiction. Comparatively few serranos witnessed the summary executions for which the Barrios brothers are infamous. Yet the proximity of federal forces, and the persistent rumors that in a community over a distant ridge chicken thieves were being hanged, may have acted as a restraint on those tempted to challenge local authorities. Acknowledging that the Barrios family possessed this potential was not tantamount to unconditional acceptance of their right to wield such power, but for these communities, grudging acquiescence often held more promise than conspicuous opposition. During a period in which civil disorder and rebel activity were too great for any one community to withstand, it made sense to cooperate with Barrios for the greater prize of personal and regional security. Whether or not this represented a façade of local democracy, as Sáenz suggested, varied from one community to another. When serranos witnessed Barrios taking action to rectify abuses by his men, or appearing to concede to community demands that locally chosen forces should remain close to home, were serranos living an illusion, or did they perceive a real degree of influence over their own destiny? I suggest that the façade of governance was a two-way arrangement.

5 Postrevolutionary Socioeconomic Reform

The federal government's struggle for the hearts and minds of campesinos during the 1920s and 1930s has received considerable attention in recent years. The provision of education, roads, *ejidos,* and irrigation introduced new agents, concepts, and vocabulary into the countryside. Scholars such as Adrian Bantjes, Marjorie Becker, and Mary Kay Vaughan have analyzed the process of negotiation that such measures stimulated between groups at different levels of authority.[1] It is clear from their studies that essential to the success of federal projects in the 1930s was the link between national and state politics and its consequences at the local level. In return for his political support, for example, Lázaro Cárdenas allowed governor Maximino Avila Camacho considerable latitude to erect a conservative *caudillaje* in Puebla. Under this regime, political elites in some Puebla communities sought to re-impose control over "wayward" indigenous communities by forcing or convincing campesinos to reject the socialist education of SEP teachers.[2] Elsewhere in Puebla, campesinos were more successful in determining their responses to externally derived initiatives, often managing to stamp their own cultural identity on local policy implementation.

In many ways, the task facing government reformers in the 1920s was much greater, as the presence of the state within the community was both weaker and less defined than it would be a decade later. The paucity of federal funds placed additional burdens upon their shoulders. It was not until 1925 that President Calles was able to establish a central bank to provide capital for agrarian reform and technological developments.[3] Even so, schemes to modernize agriculture and the nation's economic infrastructure continued to suffer from inadequate investment and largely depended upon the voluntary labor of campesinos to bring otherwise unfeasible projects to fruition. Local elites took advantage of campesino reluctance to take on onerous duties and sought to reestablish earlier patterns of community labor, which they had traditionally controlled. Success in overcoming such opposition depended greatly upon the courage, skill, and determination of those proposing state reform, be it the construction of trails, the presentation of lessons on hygiene, or the drawing of lines in the dusty soils of future ejidos. Fortunes varied. Some reformers produced real changes in rural life while others became martyrs to the cause.

When Lombardo Toledano argued in 1928 that caciquismo had preyed upon the inherent insularity of the Sierra de Puebla, he was reflecting a common perception among social reformers within the federal government that campesino exploitation was made easier by a local elite's control of politics, commerce, and links with the world beyond.[4] There is little doubt that Lombardo Toledano saw Barrios as both a cause and an effect of the Sierra's backwardness. Certainly, it was during the late 1920s that the lasting image of Barrios as a force of repression and exploitation was first disseminated. This image reached a crescendo in 1930, when newspapers claimed that only by removing the 46th Battalion from the Sierra could its inhabitants be "released from the slavery under which they have suffered for so many years, and finally become part of the 'revolutionary family.'"[5] This image has never been questioned. Whether through lack of detailed analysis or the desire to portray caciquismo in a certain light, official history and the 1970s progressive literature on rural caciques emphasize Barrios's use of violence to maintain control.[6] More recently, Mary Kay Vaughan described him as "the regional strongman who protected the Sierra from outside interference."[7] While Vaughan's description has some merit, by shadowing earlier assumptions about Barrios, she risks lending weight to a two-dimensional portrayal of Sierra caciquismo. The evidence shows that the cacicazgo was much more complex than its contemporary critics would have us believe.

The negative image of Barrios emanated primarily from his decidedly anti-agrarian stance. His actions show that he had little time for the agrarista cause, and his resistance to the encroachment of *ejiditarios* into Sierra districts appears to fit a Marxist portrayal of caciques as figures who sought to continue campesino exploitation through perpetuating rural isolation. Yet this image ignores the fact that during the 1920s Gabriel and Demetrio Barrios orchestrated one of the most ambitious infrastructure development programs in postrevolutionary Mexico. By 1930, a comprehensive network of roads wove through the Sierra's valleys and mountain slopes, and it was along these very roads that many external influences penetrated the previously isolated region, conveying people, produce, and ideas with unprecedented ease. Furthermore, the brothers were involved in a large number of local initiatives that reflected and often foreshadowed federal government policies, including agricultural improvements, education, public health, and anti-alcohol campaigns.

If Barrios's enthusiasm for federal reform undermines his lasting image as an isolationist, should he be seen as a "modern" cacique who used his links with government departments to establish a more informal form of patronage characterized by a manipulative imposition of centrally driven initiatives? While this interpretation may come close to revealing the way he operated, we should not lose sight of the heterogeneity of the Sierra de Puebla. The degree to which these projects encountered local opposition varied. Road construction, for example, cut physical and psychological swathes across the region. Topography and politics largely determined route selection and, with little room for compromise, serranos were left to react as best they could to the demands made upon them and the consequences of increased exposure to the world beyond. Other projects were more contained, often based within specific districts or communities. Local initiatives were common and involved negotiations between different groups within communities and with external agents over their scope and nature. By analyzing Gabriel Barrios's role in these changes, I hope to clarify the present confusion among historians who alternatively portray him as a blunt instrument of federal hegemonic designs or as the henchman of a regional conservative elite determined to continue exploiting its neighbors. Moreover, the case of Barrios argues for a more subtle reflection on caciquismo in Mexico as a whole; one that takes into account political opportunism, personal convictions, ambition, compassion, and above all, a recognition of local circumstances and the boundaries between imposition and negotiation.

The Land Question in the 1920s

Previous studies on caciquismo place considerable emphasis upon the relationship between land tenure and popular support for caciques. That this was not an issue in the Sierra de Puebla demands explanation, especially given Barrios's image as an enemy of the campesino. Luisa Pare's study of interethnic and class relations in the district of Zaca-poaxtla, for example, provides evidence that Barrios's local allies con-ducted a vigorous, and sometimes violent, campaign to prevent cam-pesinos from the village of Atzalán from reclaiming land on the Apulco hacienda.[8] Such actions led Pare, and later Vaughan, to view Barrios as the sponsor of a local elite that sought to continue its exploitation of the campesino.

Evidence of Barrios's actions in other Sierra communities seems to corroborate this view. Throughout the 1920s, for instance, he fought agraristas in Palos Caídos y La Peñuela, a rural settlement some twenty kilometers north of Zacatlán. As early as 1923 friction had existed be-tween the local hacendado and campesinos. By October 1924 the dis-pute became formalized when petitions for land were lodged with the local agrarian commission.[9] Two months later, following claims that agraristas in the area had led an armed attack against laborers on a nearby farm, Barrios moved to disarm and arrest the agrarian leaders. In his official report, Barrios noted that although the culprits were in possession of land, they refused to work it and instead manufactured pulque for a living. Their idleness, Barrios suggested, was the source of their troublemaking.[10] For the agraristas of Palos Caídos, the die had been cast. In future years they would accuse Barrios's troops of in-timidation and of evicting their members and replacing them with cam-pesinos loyal to Barrios. The last report of such an incident was made more than three years after Barrios's forces had been transferred to Mexico City.[11]

On the other side of the Sierra in the municipality of Tepeyahualco, Libres, the actions of Ramón Arellano, a local trader and leader of an armed group said to be "volunteers of the 46th Regiment," first received widespread attention in July 1927 when the local agrarian committee accused Arellano of killing members of a civilian peacekeeping force during a local fiesta. Calling him a *pistolero* of the local hacendado, the committee alleged that this attack was just the latest incident of violence that Arellano had directed against the community. In November 1927 the agrarian committee complained to President Calles that Arellano was using his position to intimidate local agraristas. Demetrio Bar-rios responded to inquiries from his military superiors by stating that the accusations were untrue and politically motivated.[12] In February 1928 agraristas in Tepeyahualco repeated their charges against Arellano before the Secretaría de Gobernación. This time they broadened their charges by accusing Gabriel Barrios of personal responsibility for a campaign of violence against agraristas in their region.[13] Only after Arellano's mysterious death in June 1929 did agrarista complaints subside. And only much later did a full judicial inquiry find the cases against Barrios unproven, placing the blame for all atrocities upon the dead, and legally unrepresented, Arellano.[14]

Further serious allegations against Barrios concerned events occurring near land he rented on the hacienda El Paredón in the western Sierra district of Alatriste.[15] In October 1925 local agrarian leaders claimed that campesinos were victims of abuses committed by the hacendado and Barrios's troops. In a clear demonstration of the support that Barrios then enjoyed from his regional military commanding officer, General Juan A. Almazán responded by ordering a detachment of Barrios's own forces to police the situation.[16] Further land grants to campesinos in the area were made in 1928, and an uneasy truce lasted until 1932, when a campesino from El Paredón was killed. The Puebla city daily *La Opinión* alleged that the murder was committed by Barrios's cousin, Dario Barrios, who was occupying the ranch together with a group of armed men.[17] Subsequent investigations appear to have been inconclusive, and during the following year agrarian representatives accused Barrios's troops of similar atrocities. The tension culminated in November 1933 when, according to *La Opinión*, a group of Barrios's men massacred innocent campesinos in the nearby settlement of Corral Blanco.[18]

What do these violent incidents tell us about Barrios's attitude toward agrarian reform in the Sierra? First, it is important to distinguish the situation in El Paredón from that in Tepeyahualco. In the former, military officers under Barrios's direct control occupied a hacienda; as such, Hans Werner Tobler suggests that Barrios's tenancy reflected a broader phenomenon of hacendados attempting to limit agrarian reform by renting land to soldiers.[19] Arellano, conversely, was a jefe de armas who, as a pistolero of the local hacendado, already had a history of conflict with local campesinos. Caution needs to be taken, therefore, in making assumptions concerning the extent to which apparent officer-tenancy was a direct response to agrarian reform.

Given that Barrios had little sympathy for the agrarian cause, how do we explain the relatively small number of complaints by serranos concerning Barrios's actions to impede land reform? Had agrarian unrest existed, situations such as those at Atzalán would have been much more common. A possible explanation is provided by Miguel Lucas, who in 1919 commented:

> The agrarian problem that has served as a revolutionary banner for the people of other regions does not exist in this municipality [Tetela] and, perhaps, throughout the Sierra Norte de Puebla. Here, there are no large estates, there are no enemies of the small holder, and this is because in the past, whenever possible, the land has been divided and granted to serranos in small plots. Here in the Sierra, virtually all heads of families own their own plot of land that, if they tend it carefully, will provide them with sufficient for the needs of themselves and their families. If they are poor it is because they produce no more than is strictly necessary to survive.[20]

Miguel Lucas was reflecting the consequences of a generation of liberalism that had swept much of the western Sierra under the auspices of his father and mestizo Governor Juan N. Méndez. Through desamortización, inheritance, and defaults on debts, the Lucas family had acquired many small plots of land that they then rented to campesino families. The sale of these lands before and during 1919, and previous sales of land owned by the Méndez estate, had created a second generation of private landowners, among which were the Barrios brothers.[21]

Mallon suggests that nineteenth-century liberalism in the western district of Zacatlán assumed an individualist, entrepreneurial character, which she contrasts with a more popular, collective brand of liberalism that developed in central Sierra communities such as Tetela de Ocampo and Xochiapulco.[22] While Juan Francisco Lucas's commercial transactions reveal little evidence of this collectivism, Mallon's argument is still valid if one accepts that Lucas was not essential to the popular liberalism project. Although the phenomenon was by no means universal, western Sierra districts did include communities where campesinos were willing to abandon communal landownership in favor of individual enterprise. It is clear that Miguel, the son of the "Patriarch of the Sierra," strongly believed in a campesino's personal responsibility for the welfare of himself and his family. Some, such as the Barrios family, had good fortune and prospered, while others failed and reverted to becoming tenants. Barrios's attitudes toward land tenure and economic development were based upon his own experiences as a small landholder brought up in a liberal tradition. This philosophy led him to view agraristas in Palos Caídos and elsewhere as lazy and unwilling to invest in their own future. Barrios, therefore, saw no inconsistency in treating agraristas with disdain while at the same time enabling serranos to provide, to use Miguel Lucas's words, "sufficient for the needs of themselves and their families."

Miguel Lucas was inaccurate, however, in presuming that all communities in the Sierra viewed land tenure in the same way. The Sierra was a vast area of fairly isolated communities; in many localities, community land was not threatened by desamortización, as the climate, soils, and infrastructure made commercial agriculture unattractive. Where conditions were more favorable, land encroachment by mestizo immigrants in the nineteenth century had indeed led to violent interethnic clashes.[23] Yet it should not be assumed that the Revolution aroused the aspirations of an exploited Sierra campesino class, making it willing to fight for agrarian reform. Even in areas of previous conflict, revolutionary unrest was based more on political factionalism between mestizos than on landownership.[24] Although friction between dominant and weak sectors of serrano society was ever present, the fight for land was not the central issue that it was in areas of agrarian unrest.

Given the state of land tenure within the Sierra, Barrios never profitably used the fear of losing land, nor the promise of receiving land, to attract popular support. The majority of his Indian troops either owned land or lived in settlements where there was no immediate threat to communal ownership. This does not discount the possibility that, as Mallon suggests had happened in the past, some communities saw military service in Barrios's army as a means of legitimating their continued tenure of communal land through an informal agreement that rewarded military service to the federation with national recognition of traditional land rights. Daniel Nugent found a similar development among Namiquipans in Chihuahua. Yet in the cases of Namiquipa and, say, Xochiapulco, the issue of legitimate land tenure had long been linked to military service; in the former as a reward for fighting against Apaches, and in the latter for loyal service to the liberal cause as national guardsmen.[25] In the majority of Sierra communities, however, there was no direct connection between land tenure and military service, and it would have made no sense for serranos to introduce this factor into the equation at such a late stage. It seems equally unlikely that Barrios sought to secure his position in the Sierra by protecting the region's landowning elite from radical agrarian reform. While he certainly did this in some instances, the general lack of tension concerning land tenure in the Sierra made such a tactic unworkable. More promising perhaps is to view Barrios's anti-agrarianism as a measure taken by a regional cacique seeking to prolong his period of control. José María Barrios suggests that his father saw local leaders of agrarian committees as a threat: agents of external authority with access to federal patronage in the form of land grants.[26] As we will see, Barrios jealously guarded this prerogative. His authority depended upon serranos recognizing him as the main channel through whom federal patronage flowed. If this image were to be challenged, one of his principal methods of gaining campesino acquiescence would disappear. While Barrios's views on agrarian reform may have coincided with those shared by members of the landowning elite, the fact that they opposed many of his own initiatives suggests that the elites had little in common with Barrios. A class-based analysis of Barrios's actions does not reveal the full picture.

Rural Education Initiatives

Much of the responsibility for convincing campesinos that they had a vested interest in Mexico's future social and economic stability fell upon the SEP. Accomplishing this initiative depended upon eroding the innate suspicion and insularity that campesinos were deemed to harbor. Furthermore, innovation in the countryside was considered to be of little use if campesinos remained illiterate and unable to realize the full potential of such changes. Yet it appears that the campesinos were being educated not to foster social mobility, but merely to increase their efficiency within their present status. Ramón Ruiz places Secretary of Education José Vasconcelos and his successor, Puig Casauranc, at the forefront of an elite-led project that assumed the problems of the Mexican countryside were due to the character and behavior of campesinos rather than fundamental flaws in the structure of rural society. As such, they prescribed liberal doses of urban-based civility to wrest the campesinos from their slothful, degenerate ways.[27] Poorly paid, often badly trained teachers lived by their wits, trying to adapt SEP directives to suit local conditions. In attempting to gain local allies in the struggle to deliver meaningful changes, teachers often became more radical than SEP policymakers had intended, a process that might be seen as evidence of grassroots pressure to refashion SEP projects.[28]

Resolving the "Indian problem" was central to the broader agenda of rehabilitating the Mexican countryside. When Lombardo Toledano referred to the Sierra in 1928, he spoke of Nahuas or Totonacs who needed to be rescued from barbarism.[29] His choice of the word "barbarism" evoked conflicting emotions within mestizo society: a sense of superiority and perhaps pity toward the Indian, but also fear and suspicion unleashed by the mass mobilization of Indians and poor mestizo campesinos during the Revolution. As Vaughan explains, the federal rural school of the 1920s was asked "to discipline and channel the energies of the rebellious peasants."[30] Harnessing and defusing the Indian's unbridled passions informed the indigenismo tendency within SEP policies during the 1920s, a component that Guillermo de la Peña sees as fundamental to the ministry's ambitions of incorporating indigenous communities within broader society.[31] The corollary of these policies was that for campesinos to be accepted within a new national identity, urban society needed to be convinced that the Indian could be redeemed. The 1926 opening of the Casa del Estudiante Indígena in Mexico City was indicative of underlying trends.[32] It offered lodging and instruction to talented indigenous youths, in the hope that they would return to their communities and spread messages consistent with SEP policies. Although short-lived (the school closed because, among other reasons, it could not find enough "genuine" Indians to fill the classes), the emphasis on cultural and practical integration remained at the heart of the SEP's work during the 1920s. In another initiative, questionnaires were dispatched to rural municipalities to collect data and "authentic indigenous industrial products" for exhibition in museums. The aim was to stimulate "the social advancement of those indigenous who live within our national boundaries, bringing about their overall development, the conservation and perfection of their working skills, and even introducing new industrial activities that derive from those existing or from the natural products of the region. Such goals will also bring cultural and economic improvements."[33] By revealing evidence of a noble pre-Columbian past, SEP officials hoped that mainstream mestizo society would become convinced that education had the potential to rescue the Indian from degeneracy.

Throughout its early years, the SEP underwent a process of gradual transformation. Under Vasconcelos, rural education policies sought to make children literate, numerate, and familiar with basic methods of cultivation, "to inspire a love of the land among campesinos."[34] The emphasis on reading, writing, arithmetic, and in particular the notion of introducing the classics to children met with considerable resistance.

Parents, many of whom spoke little or no Spanish, saw such classes as irrelevant and tended to demonstrate their children's "love of the land" by keeping them away from the school and busy in the fields. Even before Puig Casauranc took over in 1924, the SEP had modified its approach to rural education. In this new approach reflecting the action pedagogy of the North American educationalist John Dewey, rural children would learn by example, and in the process would more fully appreciate the value of their labors within the broader community. Lessons in sobriety and personal hygiene were intended to transform Mexico's ethnically diverse youths into campesinos fully prepared to assume a productive role within a capitalist rural economy. Gender roles were reinforced. Boys were taught agricultural chores, while girls learned domestic sciences to help them provide a stable and healthy home environment. Although poorly coordinated, other government departments reinforced these messages. Civil engineers, agronomists, agriculturists, and physicians joined teachers in what they saw as the ambitious task of delivering Mexican campesinos, both young and old, from previous oblivion to assume their responsibilities within a new postrevolutionary future.[35]

Puebla's postrevolutionary educational authorities certainly faced a formidable task. Many schools had closed during the Revolution, and those that remained open were poorly attended. Provision of rural schooling in the Sierra was sporadic and incomplete. Federal, state, and privately sponsored schools coexisted, and the longevity of any one school depended greatly upon the community's enthusiasm to keep it going and its success in obtaining materials. Vaughan speculates that rural education failed to make significant improvements to Sierra life in the 1920s because although Gabriel Barrios supported rural schools, he also held "tight control over local government."[36] The inference is that Barrios's sponsorship of education was moved more by a desire to gain local political allies than to change rural society. Certainly, political patronage in support of education and public works was central to Barrios's participation in such projects; equally, he shared the federal government's desire to improve but not revolutionize rural society. Yet this conclusion is a long way from affirming the media's image of Barrios as the man responsible for keeping Sierra campesinos in slavery. This portrayal exaggerates his political control over the region and underestimates his desire to encourage efficient practices within the countryside. As we have seen, Barrios's political authority was neither as tight nor as uniform as has previously been supposed and, like others seeking to bring changes within the Sierra, he had to make compromises with rural communities. The nature of these negotiations provides a clearer picture of what motivated Barrios to become so heavily involved in these projects, how federal and state government representatives sought to achieve their objectives, and how local circumstances governed community reception and implementation.

During Carranza's presidency, Governor Alfonso Cabrera attempted to harness Barrios's intimate knowledge of the Tetela district to encourage communities to become more receptive to local educational initiatives.[37] In February 1920, gubernatorial candidate Pastor Rouaix asked Abraham Lucas to persuade Barrios to cooperate with educational development in the Sierra. A month later, Barrios responded positively to a similar request from the state government.[38] Across the Sierra in Cuetzalan, a lack of funds forced the municipal president to approach wealthy coffee merchants and local military commander Demetrio Barrios for loans of one hundred pesos to pay the wages of school directors.[39] By the time the state inspector of schools, Professor Carlos Barrios (unrelated), made a tour of inspection through the Sierra in September 1920, practical evidence of Barrios's help was beginning to emerge. From Cuetzalan, the hard-pressed Zacapoaxtla authorities were informed that a new school for boys had been opened on the Ranchería de Reyes-Ogpan as a result of Barrios's efforts.[40] Closer to home, Gabriel Barrios made great strides toward providing a basic education for his soldiers and equipping Cuacuila's schools to the highest standards. He arranged for one of Zacatlán's best teachers, Baudelio Candanedo, to take overall responsibility for education in Cuacuila.

Candanedo had begun his teaching career in 1905 and prior to the Revolution had been director of the school in Jicolapa, Zacatlán. After the Revolution, he became director of the Curso Normal Preparatorio and was made an SEP inspector in 1924.[41] It is likely that Candanedo, who was also an accomplished musician, had an important influence upon Barrios's overall attitude to rural education and the musical ambitions of the 46th Battalion band.[42] Education in nearby towns also began to receive Barrios's patronage. In Aquixtla, where the Galindo family had already taken a strong interest in local education, Barrios was personally involved in taking stock of the schools' teaching materials. In 1921, he arranged for the state government to supply Huehuetla's schools with books and equipment.[43] Meanwhile, the state government lacked funding to support rural education. In 1922, the government informed Zacatlán authorities that it had overturned an earlier decision to grant local authorities a monthly amount of two hundred pesos toward the costs of education.[44]

In June 1923, the celebrated Chilean poet Gabriela Mistral addressed a select audience in the public library in Zacapoaxtla. The SEP inspector for the district, Rafael Molina Betancourt, had recently returned to the area, and Mistral's visit was in support of his efforts to convince locals of the need to educate their children. As she extolled the virtues of books and their potential to enrich community life, Mistral had probably never heard of the person who would most immediately respond to her message—the "indito" Gabriel Barrios.[45] Within a month of Mistral's speech, the tiny mountain village of Cuacuila took delivery of materials to establish its own library, together with a further consignment of school supplies sufficient to satisfy the needs of the thousand Nahua children who lived in the immediate vicinity.[46] As state educators struggled with unrealistic objectives, Barrios capitalized upon a recent visit by José Vasconcelos to Tetela to convert fine words into action.[47]

I do not mean to suggest by these examples that Barrios had a coordinated program for promoting and supporting rural education beyond the immediate environs of Cuacuila. Elsewhere he reacted to requests in ways that strengthened his broader objectives of maintaining public order, making friends, and improving the potential of his fellow serranos. It was only in 1927, following Moisés Sáenz's tour of inspection, that Barrios began to show enthusiasm for the development of education on a broad, systematic scale. Sáenz, an advocate of action pedagogy, suggested that despite teachers' best efforts, educational policies bore little relevance to the everyday needs of serrano communities. He called upon federal departments to devise educational policies that would provide campesinos with practical skills. Only in this way, he argued, would Indian communities more fully embrace education and benefit from the civilizing influence it could deliver. Sáenz's philosophy must have struck a chord with Barrios, as it matched the practical approach Barrios sought to adopt in other initiatives. The Barrios brothers increased their support of rural education and began to gather statistics on the attendance and performance of children, as well as the quality, training, recruitment, and payment of teachers and school directors. In particular, correspondence between the brothers and their jefes de armas focused upon organized collection of community contributions to make up for budget shortfalls. The brothers became personally involved in fostering enthusiasm not only for the schools themselves, but for the range of community initiatives that teachers sought to introduce. Demetrio Barrios asked Salustio Cabrera, a pro-Barrios representative in the federal congress, to obtain maps of Puebla for distribution in isolated Sierra schools.[48] In another initiative, the Barrios brothers encouraged the establishment of local education committees to supervise the cultivation of crops, the sale of which would help to fund local education. In Zitlala, Zacatlán, this scheme enabled education funds to be used to extend small loans to vecinos wishing to improve their land.[49]

Following Moisés Sáenz's tour, something approaching a structured rural education program began to emerge. An unsigned report written in 1928 entitled "Guidelines for the Organization, Provision, and Inspection of Rudimentary Schools in the Sierra Norte de Puebla" bears the address of Barrios's ranch in Zacatempan. It defined educational objectives in line with federal and state constitutions: the reorganization of finances, channels, and levels of authority; regulations regarding the training, conduct, and duties of teachers and inspectors; the establishment of a regional education committee in Zacatlán to monitor the quality of personnel and the adherence to guidelines; and a series of practical proposals for putting such plans into action, among them the suggestion that regular teacher training courses should be held in Zacatlán to rectify any weaknesses identified by the school inspectorate. The report was sent to both federal and state governments.[50]

Although there is no evidence of government responses, several of these teacher-training courses did take place.[51] They appear to have encouraged local intellectuals and teachers to expound upon the peculiar problems related to education in an Indian area such as the Sierra. One paper addressed the difficulties of teaching in Totonac-speaking communities and encouraged all teachers to take heart in the knowledge that by spreading the national language they were serving the patriotic cause. From his experiences of teaching Nahua children in several Zacatlán communities, Candanedo spoke of how the prevalence of witchcraft in indigenous societies could be used by teachers who, through positive suggestion, might assume the role of "educative witches" in the minds of children. Other instructors focused upon teaching methods, the responsibility of the school for spreading propaganda about hygiene, and ways to encourage mothers to act as teachers within the home.[52] The scope of the topics makes it clear that those attending these meetings saw education as a civilizing influence to combat superstition and moral weakness.

Although law and order always remained Gabriel Barrios's priority, he quickly recognized that the SEP's emphasis on efficiency, honest toil, and sobriety were vital components in the struggle to obtain and preserve civil order within the Sierra. This interconnection can clearly be seen by analyzing events in the village of Jicolapa during the de la Huerta rebellion. Ariadna Acevedo-Rodrigo offers a fascinating snapshot of the everyday difficulties facing those who sought to educate the community's children. When federal school inspector Malaquías Piña visited Jicolapa in April and May 1924, he noted that although the two-story federal school was well lit and ventilated, the teacher, Luis Herrera, lacked dedication and was more concerned with running his business interests in Zacatlán than education. As a result, his assistant, Señorita Consuela Ortiz, found it hard to keep discipline and parents were reluctant to send their children to a school in which they spent more time fighting than learning anything useful. Attendance appeared to improve following the appointment of an additional female teacher in June 1924. The school plot of land was tended, and the completion of an irrigation channel to the orchard was the occasion of a small fiesta. Boasting a chicken coop, maize plot, and carpentry shop, the school was one of the more successful in the Zacatlán district. Even so, its effectiveness was hampered by a lack of continuity in teaching staff and insufficient funding. When Ortiz left in 1925, attendance again suffered as local parents claimed not to have the money to pay for a new female teacher and objected to their daughters being taught by Herrera's male replacement.[53]

What Malaquías Piña appears not to have noticed during his tour of inspection was that Jicolapa was a community with problems beyond education; in particular, it suffered periodic bouts of lawlessness. In January 1921, for example, Barrios had been sufficiently concerned about possible disturbances at the local fiesta that he billeted some of his men in the school for girls to ensure law and order.[54] On 5 April 1924, days before Piña's first visit, lawlessness reached new heights. The Puebla newspaper *Nuestro Diario*, reported that three armed men had raided a shop in Jicolapa, seriously injuring the owner and killing his wife. Demetrio Barrios and twenty of his troops detained the men and searched for accomplices. Whether this was a straightforward criminal act or one linked to the ongoing de la Huerta rebellion is not clear, but the paper did note that in preceding months, Jicolapa had suffered many such crimes. It concluded that only the death penalty could stop this "wave of bloodshed."[55]

Placed within the broader social context, Piña's observations may have reflected the underlying concerns and anxieties of a community in turmoil. Reticence to send children to school might well have been due to a lack of diligence on the part of the teacher; yet it also could have been a result of a heightened sense of insecurity within the community Similarly, lack of discipline in the classroom may have been a general problem, but it could equally have been a sign of Jicolapa's children playing out the violence that preoccupied their parents and had resulted in the recent injury and murder of their neighbors. The broader implication is that although there seems to have been enthusiasm among Jicolapa's population to provide their children with quality education, events within society had detrimental effects upon their resolve. Just as school attendance at many Sierra schools plummeted during the violent years of the Revolution, so too, during periods of social unrest in Jicolapa in 1924, parents kept their children by their side. Such sentiments are understandable and, perhaps, vindicate Barrios's priorities as regional military commander and patriarch. He would use his influence to help education when he could, but regional security was paramount. Without law and order, serranos would never be able to realize their communal and individual potential. Just as Vaughan draws connections between broader political events and the fortunes of rural teachers in the 1930s, it may be the case that a decade earlier Malaquías Piña had stumbled across similar, albeit more localized, connections.[56]

Although he sponsored their efforts, it seems unlikely that Barrios shared all the views of local educationalists. After all, despite regular trips to Mexico City and personal contact with several presidents of the republic, Barrios continued to display a preference for the rural life of his Nahua origins and apparently never fully mastered the Spanish language. Nonetheless, contributing to local educational initiatives enabled Barrios to monitor the direction and extent of the educational policies implemented at the local level in various parts of the Sierra.

Barrios accepted broader federal initiatives connected with education and morality, provided they encouraged personal development. Preempting a federal government campaign against alcoholism, for example, Barrios issued restrictions on the number of liquor outlets and quantities of alcohol sold in Sierra towns. *Aguardiente*, Barrios argued, fundamentally weakened the resolve of the independent serrano. As early as July 1928, several municipalities in the Sierra had adopted Barrios's lead on the restriction of pulque sales in order to promote "the improvement of our people and the implementation of healthy practices that will serve as an example for generations to come."[57] In subsequent months, Barrios instructed his network of jefes de armas to cooperate with municipalities in Libres and Chignahuapan to discourage alcohol sales. Barrios outlined his views on the anti-alcohol issue in a letter to a hostile state government concerned about a likely reduction in its taxes from alcohol sales. He explained that the municipalities had decided to restrict sales on Sundays and holidays "to avoid scandals and consequential lawlessness, and to encourage the humble classes and workers to abandon the habit of heavy drinking so that the next generation will develop into a healthy, strong, moral society, with the capacity to apply itself efficiently to its duties and various activities."[58] It is somewhat ironic that a cacique who would soon be accused by the state government of corruption and exploitation needed to convince the same officials that a sacrifice in tax revenues was a price worth paying for a moral rural society.

Helping Serranos to Help Themselves: Voluntary or Forced Labor?

Before the Barrios era, various visionaries had spoken fine words about the need to open up the Sierra de Puebla, but topography, politics, and lack of resources invariably thwarted their ambitions.[59] Demetrio Santa Fe was one such person, but he differed from his predecessors in that he enjoyed the confidence of individuals who could overcome such barriers. We have already seen in chapter 4 how his plans for community-based law enforcement units influenced the network that Barrios erected. In regional development, too, the Barrios brothers are said to have respected Santa Fe's "many ideas about the need for roads and schools."[60] Certainly, together with Abraham Lucas and Ricardo Márquez Galindo, Santa Fe composed part of the intellectual think tank behind Gabriel Barrios's approach to development. So effective were they that federal representatives soon began to see Barrios as a dynamo for change and pledged their considerable influence to support his initiatives.

Public works within the Sierra de Puebla had traditionally depended upon the colonial system referred to locally as *topiles,* in which serranos offered voluntary labor to complete works of mutual benefit.[61] By the time of the Revolution, this system had been corrupted, as local elites diverted the labors of the poor for their own benefit. Revolutionary disruption had enabled communities to take the law into their own hands, and it became increasingly difficult to persuade residents to perform topiles. While this refusal may have contained a large measure of social justice, it also damaged the communities' social and economic positions. As mountain tracks fell into disrepair, the already arduous journeys to local and regional markets worsened. Recognizing the urgent need to restore a legitimate system of community labor, in 1913 Demetrio Santa Fe urged that "without further delay we must sweep aside the unjust system of topiles that is common within indigenous villages, and ensure that local authorities require any future service to be provided without distinction of race or social group."[62] Part of the problem was that the organization of voluntary labor had always been in the hands of local ayuntamientos. As long as these authorities were controlled by local elites, the potential for abuse remained. Under Santa Fe's proposal, topiles would be replaced by a system that would continue to be under civilian control but would include all able-bodied members of a community.

The voluntary labor system of *faenas* that the state government subsequently sought to introduce closely resembled the model prescribed by Santa Fe. (Using the word *faena* may have been a deliberate attempt to distance the new system from the discredited topiles.) Lists of all eligible individuals were taken from electoral registers, and local judges were responsible for ensuring their participation in the work project, with a fine of fifty centavos imposed on those who refused to attend.[63] Given the disruption of voluntary labor during the Revolution, it is not surprising that correspondence between government officials reveals a reluctance among citizens to resume this onerous custom.[64] In an early example of "naming and shaming," a state government circular dated 23 February 1920 made serranos aware that Tlatlauquitepec's authorities had refused to cooperate in the construction of roads and tracks.[65] Similarly, the state government reminded Tetela de Ocampo's municipal president of the importance of local trail construction projects. In the absence of state funding, vecinos were reminded of their obligation to give voluntary labor to projects from which they would directly benefit.[66] In 1923, the local authorities in Cuetzalan went as far as to ask President Obregón if faenas were constitutional. Ever the politician, Obregón took refuge in rhetorical ambiguity: "According to our constitution, no one is obliged to give their personal services without fair payment; but, in my role as president, it is my duty to foster a spirit in which people might wish to give their spontaneous cooperation, expressed through modest quotas of work, towards projects of public interest and collective benefit."[67] What we see here, then, is a federal attempt to appropriate the local custom of voluntary labor. Works of communal benefit were also patriotic works to strengthen the nation. Sanitation, communications, and agricultural projects corresponded to the federal government's broader objectives to integrate and improve the infrastructure of the countryside. The fact that faena participation in the Sierra was intended to include all members of a community irrespective of ethnicity or class merely served to strengthen an image of common reward for common toil.

The overseeing of faenas offered Barrios an officially sanctioned means of using his military position to influence other aspects of Sierra life. As had been the case with law enforcement, the state government soon recognized that local judges lacked the authority and means to ensure faena attendance. Authorities began to ask Barrios to use federal troops or cuerpos voluntarios to add strength to the local judge's calls for faena attendance,[68] and it became common for Barrios's men to be present during days of faena labor (see figure 8). Particularly on major road construction projects, Barrios argued that his troops were needed to "protect" faeneros from the risk of attack by bandits and "enemies of progress." While some may have been reassured by the soldiers' presence, Victor Vega Bernal, then municipal president of Cuetzalan, argued that vecinos were willing to comply with faena duties but deeply resented the presence of armed men that made them feel like criminals.[69]

While Vega Bernal's argument has some merit, there is evidence to suggest that the faenas sought to lend a measure of dignity and social justice that Santa Fe had found lacking under previous systems. Faenas never questioned the Sierra's social order, but Barrios tried to ensure that all vecinos fulfilled their obligations. Prominent members of a community were assigned supervisory tasks or, in other cases, servants would take the place of their employers. Similarly, traders and other individuals whose businesses would have been harmed by faena attendance paid for a laborer to do their quota of work. As had happened

Figure 8. Barrios soldier guarding a group of faeneros (Courtesy of Jose María Barrios)

in the past, wealthier members of a community were often persuaded to make additional contributions of money and materials beyond the value of their labor quota to sustain the local effort.

Faenas represented a double attack on the privileges of the elite. That members of the *gente de razón* should take part in labors that in the past had been conducted solely by indigenous vecinos was anathema to many (see figure 9). To add insult to injury, Barrios's men increasingly directed faenas toward road building projects, thus challenging the elites' prerogative to control local labor resources. Prior to his conversion to the Barrios cause, Moisés Macip claimed that faenas in Zacapoaxtla could be obtained only by using "moderation, good sense, and exquisite tact."[70] He implied that Barrios had none of these qualities and that community cooperation could best be obtained by those with experience in handling such delicate matters. The state governor was not convinced and urged local authorities to cooperate with Barrios as long as he sought to use faenas for projects that were in the region's interests. Would it be too grandiose to portray Barrios as one means by which external authorities sought to erode the customary privileges of the Sierra rural elite? If so, this was not Barrios's intention. Had he been fully committed to social justice, he would have been less aggressive

Figure 9. Mestizo faeneros on a road construction project (Courtesy of Jose María Barrios)

toward agraristas. More likely, he was following his own agenda in which he sought to control and direct the nature of Sierra socioeconomic development. The elites' control of campesino labor, the factor that made such projects possible, represented as big a hurdle to Barrios as agrarismo. Both needed to be dismantled.

The response of indigenous communities to the resurrection of voluntary labor is more difficult to gauge. Thomson offers an extreme vision in which Agustín Cruz, a jefe de armas from Cuetzalan, "orchestrated a campaign of intimidation throughout the region," using whips, imprisonment, and death threats to ensure compliance with demands for funds and labor to construct the Zacapoaxtla road and local schools.[71] The evidence suggests, however, that the use of excessive force to ensure indigenous compliance was rare. More likely Cruz was a rogue representative who overstepped the boundaries of acceptable behavior in order to gain compliance.[72] The small number of Indian objections to faenas suggests that Barrios adopted a fairly flexible approach in convincing various communities to cooperate. The strength of Barrios's cacicazgo depended upon his ability to identify and incorporate more compliant sections of a population within his network of patronage. Backing such groups enabled him to influence community attitudes without having to interfere directly in the community's internal politics.

Long-term regional stability lay in selling the benefits of change, rather than the imposition of forced labor.

Taming the Serrano Landscape

Barrios's knowledge of the Sierra meant that he appreciated the campesinos' needs and concerns. Despite his flourishing military career, he remained a ranchero with a lifetime's experience of the specific challenges presented by the Sierra's climate and soils. In modifying federal policies designed to promote a self-reliant rural sector, Barrios was guided by two principles of local significance: his conviction that such an approach was the only true means of improving the life of the Sierra campesino, and his self-image as a benevolent patriarch who by ensuring local stability and facilitating improvements enabled serranos to maximize the potential of their land, whether private, rented, or communal.

Not surprisingly perhaps, the most ambitious agricultural project took place in the valleys below Barrios's home village, Cuacuila, when in 1917, a blueprint for irrigation and the provision of drinking water was adopted. As local military commander, Barrios organized the construction of an aqueduct to convey water from the Barranca Fría near Amixtlán to Tetela de Ocampo and outlying communities. In a feat of civil engineering that is still acclaimed today, Barrios's federal troops were lowered over the edge of the precipitous canyon where, suspended by ropes, they began the arduous task of cutting a water channel into the rock face. Faeneros later took over the excavations, and several lost their lives before the project was completed. The aqueduct transformed the agricultural potential of the Tetela region; light soil, susceptible to wind and rain erosion, was turned into land upon which planned cultivation based on irrigation could be sustained.[73] In another development, following a personal plea to President Obregón, Barrios acquired one hundred ploughs from the federal government. Obregón sent the ploughs "as a small gift from the nation," but no recipient was in any doubt that Barrios had obtained the ploughs and held the final decision regarding who should benefit.[74]

Other initiatives followed. In August 1925, Ubalde Barrios, a cousin of Gabriel's and an officer in the 46th Battalion, joined forces with the jefe de armas of Villa Juárez in organizing a community project to convert a derelict ranch into a self-sufficient rural community. A *junta agrícola* was formed and faenas were used to bring the project to a successful conclu-sion.[75] With the cooperation of the Dirección General de Agricultura y Ganadería, Barrios promoted measures to improve farming techniques within the Sierra and used his network of jefes de armas to establish forestry brigades throughout the region. In Libres, the local Unión de Obreros y Campesinos backed Barrios's suggestion that faenas should be used to renovate and repair local farm properties.[76] Similarly, the town reacted swiftly to Barrios's initiative to implement a federal policy encouraging agricultural diversification. Barrios stressed the potential of fruit, arguing that excess produce could be sold or bartered at local markets, thereby supplementing a family's income. In Libres, directives were issued that all households should without fail plant a minimum of five fruit trees within a period of ten days.[77] For his part, Barrios rarely lost the opportunity of emphasizing the Sierra's agricultural potential. His representatives in Mexico City delivered numerous boxes of locally produced apples, oranges, and fruit juice to a succession of presidents, senior officers, and politicians—tangible evidence that his, and the fed-eral government's, policies were working.

A simultaneous and arguably more far-reaching demonstration of Barrios's enthusiasm for federal attempts to develop rural Mexico was his role in road construction. Until the 1920s the topography of the Sierra had resisted the advance of modern transportation infrastruc-ture. While there were no technical difficulties in running rail and road routes across the meseta, once they reached the foothills of the Sierra, the number of possible routes was restricted. On the edges of the Sierra, at Honey, Beristaín, Zaragoza, and Chignahuapan, railway lines ended. Similarly, federal roads connecting Mexico City and Puebla city to Chig-nahuapan petered out once they reached the Sierra. Mules replaced trucks and railway wagons as the means of transport and, throughout the Revolution, the narrow mountain tracks exposed travelers to ban-ditry. In the space of a decade following the Revolution, however, the region's infrastructure dramatically changed. An undated report de-tailed the projects completed through a collaboration between Barrios's 46th Battalion and the Secretaría de Comunicaciones y Obras Públicas (SCOP):

1. Completion of the national highway from Mexico City to Tuxpan (via Tulancingo–Beristaín–Huauchinango–Necaxa–Villa Juárez–Agua Fría).
2. Partial completion of the national highway from Mexico City to Tecolutla

(via Apan–Hidalgo–Atotonilco–Chignahuapan–Tenango–Huehuetla–Coxquihui–El Espinal–Papantla).

3. Partial completion of the national highway from Mexico City to Tecolutla (via Chignahuapan–Aquixtla–Tetela de Ocampo–Huahuaxtla to Apulco, where it joined the Oriental to Tecolutla road).
4. Partial completion of the national highway from Oriental to Tecolutla (via Libres–Zaragoza–Zacapoaxtla–Apulco–Papantla).
5. Partial completion of the national highway from Oriental to Nautla (via Oyamales–Teziutlán–Martínez de la Torre–Jicaltepec).
6. Construction of the trans-Sierra state highway from Tulancingo to Jalapa, Veracruz (via Zacatlán–Chignahuapan–Tetela de Ocampo–Huahuaxtla–Zaragoza–Tlatlauquitepec–Teziutlán–Perote).
7. Construction of the state highway from Aquixtla to Cuyuaco.

Total distance accessible by car—more than 1,000 km.
Cost of road projects—$46,000.[78]

Under Barrios's stewardship, the dreams of previous generations who had wanted to break the Sierra's isolation became a reality.

Barrios had long stressed the strategic importance of improved communications in the Sierra, and this argument greatly strengthened his bargaining position when competing for scarce federal funding. Yet he was also keen to stress the sound economic reasons for investing in the Sierra's infrastructure: "The Sierra Norte de Puebla . . . is rich in all kinds of produce as a result of its humid climate. Given its proximity to the most important oilfields in the country, the Sierra is destined to reap considerable commercial rewards. The roads, which are being supported with great local enthusiasm, will be of enormous benefit, linking the central plains to the Gulf coast via the Sierra."[79] Each of the federal road projects in the Sierra during the 1920s connected Mexico City to the oil-producing coastline of Veracruz, and Barrios believed that Sierra communities would be well placed to capitalize on the heavy traffic plying these routes (see maps 4 and 5). The Huauchinango road had the added benefit of making the hydroelectric plant at Necaxa more accessible. As the major source of electricity for Mexico City, this installation was vital and fears of sabotage were high during the Revolution. Regional and local hopes that such projects would provide better security and communications for inter-serrano trade coincided with federal objectives for a better integrated and more secure economic infrastructure.

The sheer number of road-building projects conducted in the Sierra during the 1920s is evidence in itself of the high level of cooperation

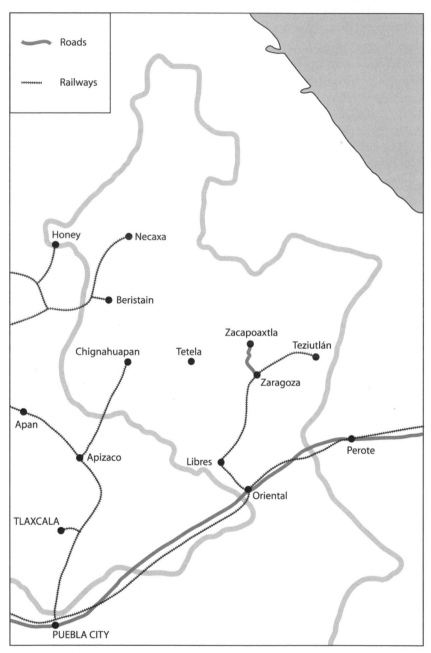

Map 4. Sierra transportation infrastructure in 1910

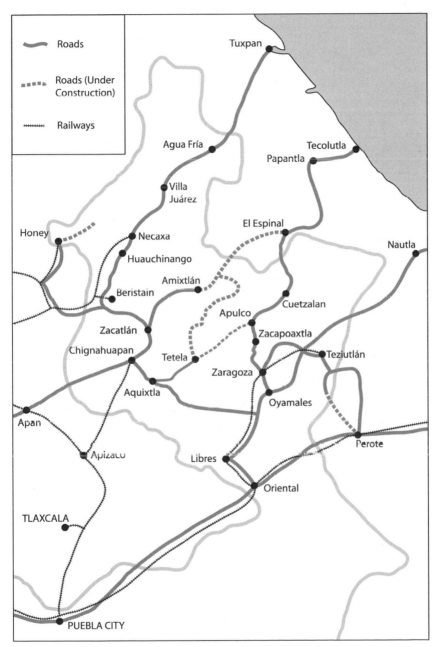

Map 5. Sierra transportation infrastructure in 1930

between the federal government and Barrios, but it does little to explain how they were completed. In the early days of Barrios's military command of the Sierra, he placed considerable emphasis upon the security issue and constantly urged local communities to do more to maintain thoroughfares in good order to facilitate the campaign against rebel forces. This argument struck a chord with his military superiors within the Guerra y Marina, and the ministry lent its weight behind Barrios's attempts to persuade the national executive to provide financial assistance for the proposed projects.[80] Perhaps in order to preempt accusations of corruption, Barrios quickly relinquished personal management of federal funding to his civilian representatives, most notably Demetrio Santa Fe and José María Flores, who became director of the Zaragoza-to-Tecolutla road construction project. Throughout the 1920s they maintained regular personal contact with presidents Obregón and Calles and facilitated the transfer of funds, machinery, and material from the SCOP to the projects within the Sierra.[81] Increasingly, requests for federal assistance stressed the importance of the roads to the national economy while pointing out that popular enthusiasm for the projects within the Sierra meant that unpaid labor could be recruited to reduce overall costs.[82] Barrios and his military forces were seen as vital for deploying materials and offering security for those working on the projects.

The arrival of the road was laden with symbolism: a triumph of technology over nature, of progress over backwardness. Reminiscent of José María Arguedas's fictional image of the Andean town of Puquio, the road brought rural indigenous society within the grasp of urban mestizo civility.[83] But like the situation in Puquio, the eclipse of one civilization by another was not clear-cut. Grid-planned streets may have been possible in some towns like Zacatlán, Chignahuapan, and Libres, but further in the Sierra, it was the road, the symbol of modernity, that had to yield to the forces of nature. Tortuous bends, steep gradients, and precarious bridges were required to negotiate a way through the landscape (see figure 10). Two officials were killed and Barrios narrowly missed the same fate when a bridge gave way, plunging their car into the torrents below. The road bisecting the center of Zacapoaxtla follows a precipitous ridge that the town saddles, while in Cuetzalan the same road hairpins its way down the slope toward the coast.

The inauguration ceremonies that took place as the roads penetrated rural communities were full of pomp and ceremony. Dignitaries flocked

Figure 10. The opening of a road bridge in the Sierra de Puebla (Courtesy of Arnulfo Barrios Aco)

to the Sierra to grab a little of the limelight and waxed lyrical about the significance of the roads for progress and modernity. Campesinos might have been forgiven if their attention strayed from speeches in a language that few understood to the noisy four-wheeled contraptions that sent man and beast scuttling. More often than not, the military band of the 46th Battalion would be on hand to add to the sense of occasion. Behind the stirring renditions of classical and popular music were subliminal messages of acculturation. Barrios's mestizo music teachers shared the SEP philosophy of "civilizing" the serranos, and through music, that most accessible and ubiquitous of genres, the sounds of the city were, by stealth, filling the valleys of the Sierra.

Those campesinos who had sacrificed valuable days to help construct the roads must have viewed these ceremonies with a mixture of pride and relief that the job was done. Yet when the band had stopped playing and the politicians had gone home, serranos were left with the task of adjusting to their new status. Roads literally cut through the heart of many Sierra communities, creating both opportunities and threats. For example, Zacapoaxtla, previously an important center of commerce within an isolated region, now became just another town along the road. Muleteers felt the bittersweet consequences of improved infrastructure. Competition with motor vehicles was futile, yet the increased security and volumes of commerce offered a new lease of life for those plying the dirt tracks to those communities that remained isolated deep in the Sierra.[84]

The road represented a beachhead for future projects. Barrios's approach was simple. Road construction activities created enthusiasm that acted as a catalyst for continued public works, such as irrigation, the piping of drinking water, the laying of sewer pipes, and the paving of streets. Local neighborhood committees were established to coordinate plans, petition for government support, and ensure successful completion of the enterprise. Residents of Libres showed particular enthusiasm for improving their environs. In July 1928, the town's saint's day coincided with the completion of paving work on three streets. Celebrations included the usual popular attractions: bullfights, dances, fireworks displays, and allegorical floats. Cockfights and basketball matches against neighboring villages and towns were also held. Teams from as far away as Perote, Veracruz came to compete, while special buses brought travelers from Puebla city to celebrate Libres's big day. Women from the town's high society perused stalls at a bazaar during a "noche mexicana," and a "literario-musical" evening was held in honor of the public works committee, which included a local teacher and had Barrios as its honorary president. Within a year, the completion of a project to provide Libres homes with drinking water gave similar cause for celebrations, and another evening of music and poetry was held at one of the local schools.[85]

The nature of the celebrations revealed steady social and cultural adjustments to recent developments. In 1926 as the Cristero rebellion began, several members of the community were arrested for distributing propaganda bearing sentiments such as, "If you are a true Catholic, do not attend the patriotic fiestas."[86] Two years later, although celebrations of the community's saint's day continued, the Catholic Church no longer had an ostentatious presence. Timing the annual fiesta, a traditional expression of civic pride, with the inauguration of paved roads served to fuse tradition with secular modernity in the same way as more established pastimes such as cockfighting were played alongside the new sport, basketball. Significantly, in both 1926 and 1928, the local teacher was at the forefront of initiatives, and the school was a center of community social life.[87]

Other towns farther into the Sierra celebrated similar events. Although Barrios was rarely personally involved in these schemes, most committees sought both his moral and material support. Negotiations concerning the extent of local participation in improvement projects were essential to the dialogue that developed between Barrios, Sierra communities, and federal agencies, and the range of compromises reached reflected the heterogeneous nature of community-state relationships. Interestingly, although some Indian communities in the Sierra sought to limit the intrusion of external influences, they offered little resistance to giving their faena labor for construction of nearby roads. Perhaps they saw these tasks as a price worth paying in return for minimal interference. Certainly, beyond offering faenas for major road projects, Barrios sought to encourage and facilitate other public works rather than to impose them upon communities. Above all, Barrios wanted communities' political support, which would hardly be facilitated by trying to force through unwanted changes. Provided they acquiesced to his general plans, Barrios deemed it wise to allow communities to determine the nature of their participation.

There is little evidence to show how rural, especially indigenous, communities decided upon their collective response to Barrios's requests. Subsequent anthropological studies of Sierra communities offer some insight, however. In 1961, Julio César Espínola studied the Nahua village of Xalacapan, located close to the new Zaragoza-Tecolutla national highway in the district of Zacapoaxtla. The timing of his study is significant. After 1930 the federal road through Zacapoaxtla deteriorated rapidly and only in the 1960s did the federal government begin to renovate it.[88] Espínola sought to observe the ways in which an indigenous community reacted to the modernizing influences of a non-Indian world. He found that internal negotiations regarding important decisions affecting the community were strongly influenced by those resisting integration within a national identity. By 1968, when Henry Torres Trueba conducted a study of Xalacapan, the battle between these opposing camps had become more defined.[89] One faction was in favor of cultural isolation, the other pushing for greater integration into the external capitalist system. At that time it seemed that the latter group held the upper hand. Certain individuals within Xalacapan had become bilingual and had developed economic and personal ties with mestizos in Zacapoaxtla. These people were prepared to counter cultural restraints in exchange for the economic and social rewards of increasing ties with the mestizo world. It is precisely this kind of division within Indian communities that Barrios had sought to exploit forty years earlier. By incorporating the groups favoring integration into his cacicazgo, Barrios was able use their influence to persuade communities to acquiesce to his proposals.

Just as Xalacapan underwent a period of transition in its relations with the non-Indian world, so would Barrios have confronted communities that were wary of outside interference. The lack of protests in the documentary records indicates that Barrios was generally able to find compromises that were acceptable to the communities and nonetheless secured labor for road construction. Other anthropological evidence from the 1960s offers interesting parallels with issues that Barrios confronted. Lourdes Arizpe's study of Zacatipan reveals a community with strong suspicions concerning the government's motives for linking the settlement to the federal highway at Cuetzalan. One vecino asked, "Who will benefit from a road that carries trucks?"[90] The question is identical to that posed by Sierra communities during the 1920s. Yet even in communities such as Zacatipan, underlying political and economic subordination to Cuetzalan forced compromises. Individuals in Zacatipan who wished to sell their goods in Cuetzalan's market had first to establish ties with the cabecera's merchants. With economic and political power often inextricably linked, if a Zacatipan trader wanted a license to sell aguardiente, for example, he would have to pledge political support to one group or another in Cuetzalan. Thus, economic ties gave *cuetzaltecos* political influence within Zacatipan without the need for more obvious intervention. In return, individuals in Zacatipan may have conceded a little but did not jeopardize the community's underlying sense of cultural autonomy.

In many ways, events in Zacatipan vindicate the position of those anthropologists calling for a revision of Eric Wolf's notion of closed corporate societies. These scholars warn against assuming that the presence of civil-religious hierarchical systems defines a community as inherently inward-looking and culturally inflexible. Rus and Wasserstrom show, for example, that after having survived many decades without them, indigenous communities in highland Chiapas chose to resurrect such systems in the early twentieth century so that they could take a greater measure of control over their own lives. Furthermore, Greenberg's study reveals how Mixe communities in Oaxaca have moved beyond viewing *cargo* sponsorship as a means of limiting disparities in wealth distribution. They have modified the *cargo* system by making distinctions between "good" and "bad" money, in order to accommodate the sudden influx of money among certain families without jeopardizing fundamental cultural values upon which the system rests.[91] Arizpe's study suggests that something similar was happening in Zacatipan, in that vecinos were able to react positively to the challenges represented by the road project through cultural evolution rather than isolation.

It is likely that the compromises made in Zacatipan in the 1960s were similar to those of many serrano communities in the 1920s that viewed loyalty to Barrios as a necessary evil in order to avoid greater assaults upon their limited autonomy. As already stated, Barrios did not attempt to dominate all aspects of serrano life. Even if he had wanted to, he lacked the resources and control network to accomplish such a feat. What he did demand, however, was a minimum level of cooperation from serrano communities, whether in suppressing banditry or giving faenas for a national highway project. Provided serrano villages met his demands, they were allowed to retain a large degree of autonomy. In this way, Barrios gained influence in both communities that were in favor of greater integration and those that opposed it.

Traditional Patriarch or Purveyor of Progress?

Gabriel Barrios's involvement in development programs during the 1920s might suggest that he was merely a shrewd judge of national trends, given that it occurred at a time when military expenditures were being diverted toward economic reconstruction. If Barrios had learned one lesson from the past, it was not to put all his eggs into the basket of military potential. Juan Francisco Lucas's diminishing regional influence in the late Porfiriato reflected his redundancy as a recruiting officer in times of peace. To retain influence, Barrios needed to extend his usefulness beyond the point when his services as a soldier became obsolete. Under the guise of promoting regional development, he found an effective method of prolonging his cacicazgo by appearing indispensable to the projects of other federal departments, such as the SCOP.[92] Yet as I have shown in this chapter, when it came to agrarian reform, other influences affected his attitude. These had much more to do with the political and familial background of his formative years in the western Sierra than with contemporary political expediency.

Inevitably, Barrios's efforts to develop a Sierra transportation and communications network eventually led to his own downfall. Roads brought new ideas, new political agents, and in 1930, new federal soldiers to replace Barrios's 46th Battalion, which was transferred with the Barrios brothers to Mexico City. Yet he had little choice other than to follow the path to his own loss of influence. Regional autonomy through continued isolation simply was not an option, even if Barrios had possessed the financial resources to sustain such a cacicazgo, which he did not. What Barrios did have was the military discipline, organizational skills, and network of allies that made him the natural choice to direct regional military and development projects. Combined with his strong conviction that serranos were best served by innovations that enabled them to become self-sufficient, Barrios's actions coincided with messages emanating from the SEP and other government departments during the 1920s. Agraristas were a different matter. While they may have argued that the Revolution was all about a struggle for land-based independence, this was not Barrios's experience. Barrios was raised in an environment that stressed the sacrosanct nature of private property and self-sufficiency. Faenas represented the means by which improvements in infrastructure and agricultural techniques could benefit the earnest campesino.

Where Barrios proved to be less progressive was in advancing the federal government's broader plan of incorporating campesinos within a direct, institutionalized system of state patronage. It was one thing to facilitate his own demise, completely another to hasten it. For as long as he could, Barrios ensured that the custom of regional patronage that had begun with his predecessor, Lucas, remained intact. Under this system, federal funds and materials for the construction of roads, telephones, irrigation canals, and other projects were channeled through him. His ability to secure materials, particularly for public works within specific communities, earned him a degree of goodwill that fed into his broader political and military ambitions. In this respect, one can question his willingness to be an accomplice in the federal government's efforts to establish its hegemony over the Sierra. More likely, he sought to retain for as long as possible the intermediary role that had made him so vital as a military leader during the Revolution. As federal agents came into the Sierra peddling wares that he sought to distribute, Barrios tried to negotiate a deal whereby they saw it as in their interests to seek his cooperation. In general, they appeared content to play along with his game of regional patronage in order to achieve their overall objectives. It is a matter of opinion whether this resulted in a net gain or a loss for those promoting change.

What is certain is that after Barrios was transferred out of the Sierra de Puebla in 1930, local elites had considerable success in imposing their own agenda with regional and national power brokers. As Vaughan notes, influential opponents of SEP policies in Zacapoaxtla turned the district against its teachers, and with the state government now controlled by the conservative Avila Camacho family, teachers became increasingly isolated and vulnerable. By 1935, there was not one SEP school operating within the district.[93] Similarly, fears that the Zaragoza-to-Tecolutla road would eclipse the commercial importance of Zacapoaxtla receded when the Avila Camacho brothers ensured that future funding for roads between the meseta and the Veracruz coast passed through their hometown of Teziutlán. A new patronage network was now being constructed, which left much of the Sierra to its own devices. Telephone lines and federal highways fell into disrepair, and it would be many decades before serranos again enjoyed the level of infrastructure developed in the 1920s.

6 The Downfall of the Barrios Cacicazgo

Obregón's assassination in July 1928 represented a major crisis for postrevolutionary order. For Calles, the imperative was clear: "I insist that it is absolutely indispensable, if we want peace and an institutional order in Mexico, . . . that we achieve revolutionary unification."[1] The formation of the PNR in 1929 heralded the beginning of a process that, discounting a few glitches, gave Mexico a degree of political stability for the rest of the century that most of its Latin American neighbors would envy. This stability resulted in part from the demilitarization of politics and the creation of a reliable, subordinate armed force. Obregón's reforms at the beginning of the 1920s began this initiative, and periodic military uprisings acted as timely reminders of the need to push it through. Simultaneously, the Puebla government was equally determined to take on those who threatened civilian political jurisdiction. Selected at the laborista convention that had so directly attacked Barrios, Governor Leonides Andreu Almazán wasted little time in pursuing these attacks to their logical conclusions. Almazán's alliance with the CROM provided a period of unprecedented, if short-lived, stability in Puebla politics, and this gave him a firm power base from which to launch an assault on Barrios's cacicazgo. While Almazán would soon lose the confidence of PNR national leaders, for a short time their objectives converged, allowing him to take on Barrios safe in the knowledge that the Guerra y Marina would not impede his efforts. The days when leaders such as Gabriel Barrios could use their military status to override civilian political authority were numbered.

Trade unions in Teziutlán, doubtless with Lombardo Toledano's encouragement, acted with uncharacteristic confidence in accusing Barrios of colluding with company owners in intimidating workers who sought to organize or join unions.[2] (By this time, Lombardo Toledano had turned against Barrios, as described at the end of chapter 3.) Across the Sierra in Zacatlán, Demetrio Barrios felt it necessary to deny publicly that troops had interfered on behalf of the municipal president, Angel Berrera, during the November 1928 elections.[3] In the past, the brothers had been able to shrug off similar accusations, but in the changed environment, every charge further jeopardized their position in the Sierra. In his first month in office, Almazán undermined the cornerstone of the cacicazgo by replacing jefes de armas and cuerpos voluntarios with his own security forces. The vital difference between these new groups and their predecessors was that they were placed under the control of municipal presidents loyal to the state government, rather than the Barrios brothers.[4] In an equally crucial move, Almazán declared void the elections in Zacatlán and Teziutlán and appointed juntas to take over the ayuntamientos.[5] Reflecting the mood of the times, La Opinión demanded an end to decades of oppression in the Sierra: "The moment has come to realize the Revolution's project of confronting cacicazgos, which are anathema to the modern age in which we live."[6] This stance directly contradicted the paper's previous praise of Barrios's initiatives in the Sierra, and considerable editorial space was given to explaining that the price Barrios demanded for such services—namely regional domination—was too high for postrevolutionary Mexico to pay.[7]

Reports from the Sierra suggested that Barrios would not relinquish his cacicazgo without a fight. According to the provisional municipal president of Pahuatlán, Barrios's men had terrorized state-sponsored public security forces, and ayuntamientos appointed by the state government were being replaced with others loyal to Barrios. Provisional federal president Portes Gil responded by asking the Guerra y Marina to restore stability and, if all else failed, to remove Barrios's forces from these districts.[8] The pressure on Barrios increased with the deployment of federal troops from the non-serrano 45th Battalion to Zacatlán, Teziutlán, and Libres. For the second year running, in 1929, the governor had intervened to impose his own ayuntamiento in Zacatlán, home of the 46th Battalion. The 45th Battalion was assigned to monitor the peaceful installation of provisional councils following the nullification of the 1929 elections. For a time Zacatlán had two ayuntamientos. Barrios loyalists occupied the municipal palace, while the governor's provisional ayuntamiento took up residence in a nearby hotel. Barrios supporters in Zacatlán sent appeals far and wide seeking assistance. They asked Governor Almazán to stop nonelected representatives from attempting to take over the council; warnings were dispatched to the president and Gobernación that the revolutionary pedigree of the people of Zacatlán would not allow them to stand by and see their rights violated, and similar letters were sent to the federal congress accusing Governor Almazán of trying to impose reactionaries upon the ayuntamiento. A complaint was sent to General Almada accusing the 45th Battalion of preventing a large public demonstration in support of the ayuntamiento from marching through the streets of Zacatlán. Demetrio Barrios sent letters and photographs of the demonstration to Ricardo Márquez Galindo in Mexico City, asking him to use the national press and his political influence to draw attention to events in the Sierra.[9]

The Barrios brothers had already lost the propaganda war, however, and Márquez Galindo's efforts were ineffective. Barrios had been harshly attacked in the national press, and the adverse coverage in Puebla provided cold comfort. Apparently acting as the state government's official mouthpiece, *La Opinión* published a lengthy article defending the governor's initiative against caciques. The paper heralded the deployment of the 45th Battalion to the Sierra as a victory of democracy over caciquismo, while a further article commented upon the strength of federal support for the governor's initiative.[10] By March 1930, the cacicazgo had run out of options. In a letter to Márquez Galindo, Demetrio Barrios described the situation in Zacatlán:

> The visitador de administración [Constantino Belmar], who is now acting secretary here in Zacatlán, is trying to agitate the communities, saying that they should reject their local authorities, kill their secretaries (who are also serving as teachers) and should not pay the teachers because the state government will provide for them, and that if the officials do not leave their positions, he will organize the deployment of troops to help remove them. . . . We are at a loss to know where we should complain: to the Standing Committee, Gobernación, the secretary of education, or the president. Complaints to the governor would be futile. Can you tell us if we still have sympathizers in the Standing Committee or, if not, where the various communities can send their complaints in order to resist these destructive labors?[11]

The content and tone of this letter depict a cacicazgo falling apart at the seams. Its foundations were being eroded by a combined political onslaught of federal and state governments using all the machinery at their disposal to secure their advantage. The very secretaries, local officials, and teachers who had pledged loyalty to Barrios in exchange for their posts were being threatened by a force more formidable than that of their patron. Demetrio Barrios was clearly unsure how much residual political support he and his brother enjoyed beyond the Sierra.

One of the brothers' remaining representatives in Mexico City, Diputado Salustio Cabrera, endeavored to enlist the help of an old ally, General Bravo Izquierdo, to dilute the Guerra y Marina's hostility toward the Barrioses. Bravo Izquierdo, then commander-in-chief of the infantry, expressed his continued support for Barrios and pledged never to act against his interests. He also promised to seek the backing of General Amaro, chief of the Guerra y Marina.[12] But times had changed, and even the help of influential friends in the ministry could not turn the tide of military subordination to civilian authority. The politicians held firm, and the non-serrano 45th Battalion remained in the Sierra long after Barrios's troops had left.

The order for Gabriel Barrios to transfer his battalion to Mexico City in May 1930 was the culmination of careful planning by the government. The federal government proceeded tentatively in dislodging Barrios's forces, showing that even though they acted from a position of strength, federal authorities were still unsure about the degree of support that Barrios had in the Sierra. The first step was the deployment of the 45th Battalion, partly to deter popular resistance. However, the battalion also sought to win public approval by improving public utilities, giving musical concerts, and establishing a forum for indigenous communities to voice their grievances, particularly those relating to alleged abuses by Barrios's troops.[13] This forum can be seen as part of a broader federal initiative to "bring salvation" to the Sierra's indigenous people.

Although *La Opinión* had previously praised Barrios's troops for their discipline and public-spirited endeavors, by the time they left the Sierra, the newspaper was describing them as "half savages." Indeed, the image of the savage Indian became a theme in the paper's coverage of events concerning not only Barrios's men, but also the region's indigenous population. In November 1929, the paper reported that police arrived in the Totonac village of Xochotla just in time to prevent villagers from sacrificing a nine-year-old girl. Allegedly, they intended to throw her heart into a nearby river in order to placate the rain god, who had caused much flooding in recent months. In February 1930, *La Opinión* stated that the governor was sending a cultural brigade to the Sierra to promote programs of education, hygiene, and anti-alcoholism in order to improve the lives of "our poor little Indian brothers." By April, these Indian brothers had become the "proletariat," many of whom walked around "semi-naked and lived in caves."[14]

State and federal officials were seeking to orchestrate a dramatic change in the public's perception of the Sierra's indigenous population, and this change reflected a decrease in the region's strategic importance. The Indian soldiers of the Sierra were no longer perceived as a force of stability and progress but as a barrier preventing the "proletariat" from enjoying the fruits of the Revolution. Barrios's Indian army had ceased to complement national interests. Amid a national political climate of centralization and anti-caciquismo, the 46th Battalion's presence in the Sierra de Puebla had become as much an obstacle to national ambitions as had Yaqui defiance against mestizo colonization in the Yaqui Valley. With indigenous resistance elsewhere often being depicted as a caste war, had Barrios refused to obey orders, it would have taken very little for *La Opinión* to portray events in the Sierra in the same light. Certainly, local mestizo political opponents would have provided the necessary "evidence" and—unlike when the gente de razón of Huauchinango lodged similar charges in 1920—they would have had a receptive hearing from federal and state governments that no longer needed Barrios's services.

When the order to redeploy the 46th Battalion to Mexico City arrived, the political shrewdness that Barrios inherited from Lucas saved him. He realized resistance ultimately would have been futile and costly in lives. When the orders were received, several weeks of frenetic activity in Zacatlán followed. The battalion had never been the professionally trained unit that Barrios pretended it to be, and the majority of the soldiers were still little more than peasants. Displaying their traditional reluctance to operate far from their communities, many arrived at Barrios's door asking to be excused from further military service. Occasional mobilization in the Sierra was one thing, transfer to Mexico City and beyond was a different proposition. Their places were taken by a new generation of serrano recruits, who viewed the move to the city as an opportunity to seek their fortune.

The transfer of the 46th Battalion to Mexico City on 27 May 1930 decisively ended the military hold that Barrios had enjoyed throughout the Sierra for more than a decade. As we have seen in the case of agraristas at El Paredón and Corral Blanco, Barrios's family and troops continued to be accused of harassing campesinos and deterring ejidal grants, even after the battalion's departure. Yet these were isolated incidents, and Barrios's influence rapidly declined throughout the majority of the Sierra. To survive in the absence of its leader, the cacicazgo network would have required much stronger ties of loyalty. Particularly outside his home constituency, Barrios had relied upon a varying and delicate balance of forces. The removal of his troops shifted the balance toward the source of power within each community, whether that be legitimate civilian authorities or local thugs seeking to fill the political vacuum. When in 1931, for example, campesinos from Xochiapulco forwarded pleas for state government action to curb the abuses of "Barrios's henchmen" in various communities, they were probably referring to the jefes and cuerpos voluntarios who had served Barrios during the 1920s.[15] Although Barrios's hand was still suspected, it is more likely that these actions reflected the personal ambitions of men who had previously been restrained by the need to appear loyal to the cacique.

Many of Barrios's former political allies within the Sierra managed to survive without him. Families such as the Galindos of Amixtlán and the Floreses of Cuetzalan had enjoyed influence before Barrios rose to power and were able to retain it after his removal. Julio Lobato, municipal president of Zacapoaxtla in 1930, found himself politically isolated when his patron, Barrios, withdrew from the area. Yet as Mary Kay Vaughan shows, throughout the 1930s he made the necessary transitions to become a powerful figure within local politics. A wide range of other retainers throughout the Sierra were forced to adapt to the new political situation. Immediate political patronage lay in allegiance to Governor Leonides Almazán, but by 1932 as the division between the PNR and the governor became apparent, the state elections offered alternatives for those with ambitions. Once again, the local political elites in the Sierra had to judge where best to place their support, but for the first time in more than a decade, Barrios's military presence was not a factor. This did not mean that internal, factional tussles disappeared, they merely were subsumed beneath the broader political contests taking place throughout the state of Puebla.

Life must have changed dramatically for those soldiers of the 46th Battalion who followed their leader to Mexico City. Instead of tending their crops or roaming the Sierra hunting for rebels, they suddenly found themselves in barracks at San Joaquín Tacuba performing ceremonial duties during visits by foreign dignitaries. Little wonder, then, that they participated so enthusiastically in the field exercises and other training programs of the Colegio Militar. On several occasions General Amaro, commanding officer of the colegio, congratulated Barrios on the dedication and enthusiasm with which the battalion conducted its duties. In December 1933, Barrios's battalion was deployed to the federal garrison at Arriaga, Chiapas. From there, units were sent to various communities where they performed duties related to maintaining regional security and providing support for communications projects. Troops assisted in the construction of a section of the Pan-American Highway near Cintalapa, and a recreation park there was named after Gabriel Barrios in recognition of the help that he and his men had given to the community.[16] President Lázaro Cárdenas commended the battalion for its construction work on the Southeast Railway in Pichucalco: "On behalf of the nation, I congratulate you and the men of the 46th Battalion for the patriotic labors that are contributing toward the advancement of the country." Yet the men who transferred with Barrios paid a high price. Exposed to the vagaries of the tropical climate, many of the Indian soldiers from the Sierra succumbed to malaria. In February 1936, for example, Barrios reported that 92 of the battalion's 415 troops were in the local military hospital.[17]

Throughout their years in Chiapas Barrios's troops assumed the role of troubleshooters, being swiftly deployed in small numbers to quell violent unrest and monitor local conditions. Almost inevitably, there was frequent tension with local agraristas. In August 1934, the Confederación Campesina y Obrera in Tuxtla Gutiérrez accused Barrios's forces of impeding land reform in the communities of Cintalapa and Jiquipilas.[18] In May 1935, Catarino Chacón, president of the Agrarian Executive Committee in Mexico City, took up the cause of the chiapaneco agraristas. He accused Barrios's forces of destroying Colonia "Moisés Enríquez" in Jiquipilas; arresting campesinos; and seizing land, equipment, and livestock. He reported, "The prisoners were then formed into a line and were sent, like criminals, to the prison in Tuxtla Gutiérrez. As they passed Barrios's garrison they were taunted and savagely humiliated by his troops." The local judge later released those arrested without charges. Despite this and further complaints made by Chacón, no action was ever taken against Barrios.[19] If anything, his battalion was seen as a necessary deterrent to violence within the Chiapas countryside. Several times troops were deployed to San Cristóbal de las Casas, San Juan de Chamula, and Salto de Agua to put down violent protests; most noticeably in July 1937 following demonstrations demanding the reopening of local churches.[20]

In June 1938, Barrios and his troops were transferred to Ixtepec, Oaxaca. Their duties included combating "banditry" and providing escorts on passenger trains. Short periods of deployment in Veracruz and Tlaxcala followed, after which the 46th Battalion returned to the state of Puebla and was based at the garrison in the southern town of Tehuacán.[21] During the battalion's time in Tlaxcala, Gabriel Barrios was recalled to Mexico City in preparation for his retirement from military service in February 1941. He returned to the Sierra de Puebla and, although lacking his previous influence, he resumed an active role in local affairs. He became president of a committee to organize the renovation of the irrigation channel that his troops had built twenty years earlier, he was chairman of the Tetela district's cattle-breeders association, and he was given the task of coordinating the Sierra's adult education programs promoted by the Avila Camacho brothers at both state and federal levels. He continued to live in the hilltop village of Cuacuila for many years, until ill health forced him to move to his house at Tonalapa in the valley below. He remained in the Sierra until the final days of his life.

On 2 May 1964, shortly after having been admitted to the military hospital in Mexico City, Barrios died from a stroke. Two days later he was buried with full military honors at the Panteón Francés de San Joaquín, within sight of the former convent that had served as the battalion's headquarters during its years in Mexico City. Yet after the military band had played its last note and the riflemen had fired their final volley over his grave, there were no visible signs of grieving. Because of his military duties, he had rarely been present as his children were growing up, and his paternal role was limited to that of provider and disciplinarian. Family intimacy was smothered by a demand for rectitude and respect, and this was reflected at the time of his death.[22] No one tended his grave; no monument, not even a nameplate, marks the spot where the mortal remains of the old soldier lie.

Who was manipulating whom in the Sierra Norte de Puebla during the 1920s? Serrano folklore maintains that as Juan Francisco Lucas lay close to death, he handed control of his Brigada Serrana to Gabriel Barrios with one simple piece of advice: "In all your actions as commander, remain loyal to the federal government." Try as his political opponents might to prove the contrary, there is no evidence that Barrios ever strayed from this instruction. When, in the spring of 1930, Barrios finally received orders to muster his troops for redeployment to Mexico City, there was no serious likelihood of him disobeying. It was this underlying respect for his superiors that ultimately saved him from the fate suffered by leaders like Manuel Montes and, later, Saturnino Cedillo.

Yet such loyalty was only one side of a complex relationship of interdependency between Barrios and the federal government. For much of the 1920s, the federal government, rightly or wrongly, saw Barrios as the key that would unlock the valuable military potential of the Sierra's indigenous communities. Furthermore, given the instability of regional politics during this time, Barrios represented one of the few political and military elements in the state of Puebla with whom the federal government might do business. This being the case, far from acting as a local agent of federal authority, Barrios often had as much freedom as those with more tenuous loyalties toward the federation. Particularly during and immediately following the de la Huerta rebellion, Barrios could do no wrong. His military chiefs protected him from criticism, and federal officials were wary of prejudicing regional development in the Sierra by investigating allegations against Barrios too rigorously. Irrespective of any personal ambitions for the Sierra, the most significant factor governing the manner in which Barrios used his influence was his dependency upon federal government funding. Unlike regional leaders elsewhere, Barrios never enjoyed the patronage of a strong provincial figure. Volatility in Puebla politics and the agrarian agenda of leading figures within the state made such an arrangement impossible. As Barrios diversified from a purely military role, a variety of government departments contributed toward the upkeep of his network of patronage and were inclined to overlook the less savory details of his control in exchange for broadly acceptable results. This delayed the inevitable moment when the federal government came to view Barrios's presence in the Sierra as more of a liability than an asset.

In recent years, several scholars have urged a more flexible approach toward the study of regional and local power brokers. Luis Roniger argues that no single definition of Mexican caciquismo can encompass a style of leadership that employed coercion, reciprocity, and flexibility in an infinite variety of ways. Similarly, Claudio Lomnitz-Adler questions the value of using dichotomous labels such as "traditional" and "modern," suggesting that styles of leadership depended upon the constituency being controlled.[23] Certainly, in his study of politics in post-revolutionary Tamaulipas, Arturo Alvarez Méndez finds it difficult to categorize Portes Gil within existing criteria.[24] The realities of politics within the Sierra de Puebla during the 1920s underline the limitations of previous approaches toward postrevolutionary caciquismo. Given that the most prominent feature of Barrios's relationship with the federal government was its ever-changing nature, trying to tie him down to one camp or another negates the very essence of his power base. Enrique Márquez describes the pragmatism of Gonzalo Santos in San Luis Potosí, a cacique who moved to claim the political void left by others. Within the broad spectrum of postrevolutionary rural leadership, there was room for opportunists, *hombres líquidos* who possessed sufficient foresight to adapt their style of leadership to reflect the changing environments and individual circumstances of their territories.[25] In the 1920s, Gabriel Barrios portrayed himself as such a figure: a necessary intermediary who could bridge the gap between the emerging state and the Sierra's indigenous communities. His ultimate fall in 1930 was an indication that central and regional political authorities finally believed that they could establish a lasting presence within the region.

As I have stressed throughout this book, the relationship between Barrios and external authorities was only one element within a much more complicated equation of rural politics. One of the main reasons why Barrios's relationship with the state varied so much was because of the diverse local pressures he faced. Post revisionist historians are right, therefore, to criticize the previous top-down approach to such relationships. Pointing out the weaknesses of such an approach, however, does not make it obsolete. In the case of Barrios, many of his staunchest followers were attracted by his charisma, cultural affinity, and patronage. Just as Lucas had sustained his image as the "Patriarch of the Sierra" by responding to his supporters' needs, so Barrios was required to accept the responsibilities that accompanied his inherited legitimacy. Whether a serrano had problems with a neighbor, an official was faced with vecinos refusing to do faenas, or an entire community was plagued by banditry, all came to Cuacuila in search of a solution. By organizing the building of schools and irrigation channels, improving water supplies, and encouraging agricultural innovations, Barrios maintained the same form of benevolent patronage that Lucas had employed to protect serranos from enforced conscription and desamortización. In certain communities, then, Barrios could be seen as a leader who encompassed features found at both extremes of the dichotomy: a patriarch, but one who used the formal bureaucratic structures of the state to distribute favors. Yet charismatic styles of leadership work best on a small scale among a homogenous constituency sharing the cultural and social values of their leader. In Zacatlán and Tetela, there is little doubt that Barrios struck a chord with the local Nahua customs and social norms that he knew so well. It is also true that he rarely missed an opportunity to convert such sensibility into political capital. Many indigenous communities, however, did not recognize him as one of their own, and the duality of his ethnic origins was more likely to cause resentment than admiration among elite sectors of Sierra society. Among these groups, Barrios's function as a link to the machinery of government may have become more important than any personal qualities he possessed.

If this were the only element in the local political equation, it would be possible to question the wisdom of viewing regional leaders as purely charismatic or bureaucratic while still sustaining the premise that they retained the ability to manipulate local campesinos. By scrutinizing the diversity of Barrios's popular support, however, we begin to address some of the issues raised by those advocating political agency among campesinos. The heterogeneity of Sierra communities demanded that Barrios remain flexible in his overtures toward them. It is worth remembering as well that he needed their support every bit as much as they needed the benefits that his privileged position bestowed. If opposition from within the Sierra ever reached a level that caused the federal government to doubt Barrios's ability to maintain regional stability, then moves to dismantle his cacicazgo would surely have swiftly followed. The singular characteristics of each community governed the reception it gave Barrios, and the members of each community decided the extent to which they were willing to compromise their own autonomy for what Barrios could offer. What seems clear, however, is that many shared a bottom line. As much as they might spout patriotic rhetoric, they steadfastly refused to be used, by either Barrios or the federal government, as foot soldiers in distant battles. Agreeing to fight on familiar rather than foreign territory might seem cold comfort, but the vital difference was that in doing so they were not fighting the federal government's battles—or even Barrios's battles. By mobilizing only within the Sierra they were fighting their own battles against local threats to their families and communities. Seen from this perspective, ostensibly loyal military service to the government can more accurately be viewed as a form of local armed resistance.

Military service, of course, was the most prominent feature in Sierra communities' engagement with broader political trends between 1910 and 1926. But we should not assume that when the need for soldiers had passed, the spirit of resistance suddenly disappeared. If Mary Kay Vaughan fails to uncover the same degree of self-determination among communities in Zacapoaxtla during the 1930s that had characterized their grandfathers' generation, this was, she argues, because the contemporary political environment discouraged such forms of resistance. This is not to say that community resistance was impossible, only that it had to find other ways of expressing itself. During the 1960s, anthropologists observed real debates being conducted within Zacapoaxtla's indigenous communities regarding how they should respond to the challenges created by the renovation of the federal road. It is likely that these debates had never stopped, but just as Barrios had done, that individual Sierra communities needed to find other ways of determining their own destinies at any given moment. As such, should we not see Sierra communities as *comunidades líquidas* that adapted their postures to contemporary circumstances?

The picture I paint of the Sierra Norte de Puebla during the 1920s is full of ambiguity. I portray a cacique who was neither one thing nor another, a semi-autonomous military leader who periodically lost political control of the area he commanded. Similarly, I show that successive federal administrations were never quite sure how much they could control Barrios and were consistently hesitant in trying to establish a direct relationship with the region's indigenous communities. On occasion particular communities appeared to be strident in their demands, at other times, they seemed submissive and susceptible to manipulation. Rather than clarifying the state of rural politics and society, the struggles that took place within the Sierra appear to muddy the picture still further. Yet if most historians of this period can agree upon one thing, it is that politics is anything but an exact science. Trying to apply generic formulas to explain the postrevolutionary Sierra is doomed to failure, and by recognizing this, we might gain a better understanding of how campesinos experienced this turbulent and traumatic period in their lives.

Notes

Introduction

1. García Martínez, *Los pueblos de la sierra*, 28. Whereas James Taggart distinguishes the serrano indigenous from their neighbors in Tlaxcala by referring to them and their language as Nahuat, I prefer to follow the lead of historians with whom this book directly relates and distinguish the serrano Nahua (the people) from Nahuatl (their language). See Taggart, *Nahua Myth and Social Structure*. I thank an anonymous reader for pointing out this possible source of confusion.

2. Interviews with Bardomiano Barrios's daughter, Carlotta Barrios Cabrera, Zacatlán, Puebla, 16 Oct. 1993 and 23 Aug. 1999.

3. Interview with Gabriel Barrios's sons, José María Barrios Nava and Arnulfo Barrios Aco, Tetela de Ocampo, Puebla, 24 Aug. 1999.

4. Although various legal documents, including an affidavit that Barrios sent to his military superiors in 1938, give years of birth between 1876 and 1889, more convincing is the fact that Bardomiano's year of birth is given as 1890 on his death certificate. Widely recognized within the family as two years older than Bardomiano, Gabriel was most likely born in March 1888. Archivo Histórico de la Defensa Nacional—cancelados (hereafter ADN, C), exp. 2-1145, fols. 432, 1274, 1310, 1409; Archivo General de Notarías del Estado de Puebla (hereafter AGNP), Tetela, caja 18, vol. 7, no. 60. Inaccessibility of parish records prevented further investigation, and Barrios's birth does not appear in any records held by the Church of Jesus Christ of Latter-Day Saints.

5. ADN, C, exp. 2-1145, fol. 1274.

6. See Schryer, *Rancheros of Pisaflores*.

7. AGNP, Tetela, caja 13, vol. 1, no. 18.

8. AGNP, Tetela, caja 12, vol. 1, no. 40. Abraham Lucas had inherited the land following the death of his father two years earlier.

9. Bardomiano Barrios's estate amounted to $12,660 at a time when the

average minimum wage for an agricultural worker was one peso per day. See AGNP, Zacatlán, caja 15, vol. 4, no. 121; AGNP, Chignahuapan, caja 7, vol. 4, no. 41.

10. While these may have been philanthropic gestures to women in financial difficulties, they also made good business sense. Having paid three hundred pesos for the rights to one estate in 1927, Barrios sold part of this property for one thousand pesos just six years later.

11. AGNP, Chignahuapan, vol. 18, nos. 916, 917. In 1960 he sold the ranch in two equal portions for twenty-one thousand pesos.

12. ADN, C, exp. 2-1145, fols. 1274, 1327.

13. Friedlander, *Being Indian in Hueyapan.* These determinants are still recognized by Indian intellectuals themselves. See Gutiérrez, *Nationalist Myths and Ethnic Identities*, 48.

14. Interview with Guillermo Mejía Cabrera, Tetela de Ocampo, Puebla, 22 Dec. 1993.

15. Ibid.

16. Space restrictions do not permit me to list the many relevant studies, but a good starting point is Brading, *Caudillo and Peasant in the Mexican Revolution.*

17. Thomas Benjamin provides a succinct summary of these studies in "Regionalizing the Revolution."

18. Schryer, *Rancheros of Pisaflores,* 7.

19. The following studies offer a good indication of the tenor of this debate: Ankerson, "Saturnino Cedillo," 140–41, and *Agrarian Warlord;* Falcón, *Revolución y caciquismo;* Márquez, "Gonzalo N. Santos."

20. Knight, "Peasant and Caudillo in Revolutionary Mexico," 58.

21. Ankerson, "Saturnino Cedillo," 140–41. The parameters and origins of this dichotomy can be traced to the seminal article by Hansen and Wolf, "Caudillo Politics."

22. Schryer, *Ethnicity and Class Conflict;* Friedrich, *Agrarian Revolt in a Mexican Village.* Other examples include Joseph, *Revolution from Without,* 222–24; and LaFrance and Thomson, "Juan Francisco Lucas."

23. Garner, "Federalism and Caudillismo."

24. Joseph, *Revolution from Without,* 222–24; Rus and Wasserstrom, "Civil-Religious Hierarchies in Central Chiapas," 468; Siverts, "Caciques of K'ankujk," 351.

25. Pare, "Caciquismo y estructura de poder."

26. Otero, *Farewell to the Peasantry.*

27. Miller, *Landlords and Haciendas.*

28. Wasserstrom, "Rural Labor and Income Distribution"; de la Peña, "Commodity Production."

29. Joseph and Nugent, *Everyday Forms of State Formation.*

30. Vaughan, "Cultural Approaches to Peasant Politics," 303.

31. Henderson, *Worm in the Wheat.*

32. Márquez Carrillo, "Los orígenes de Avilacamachismo."

33. Vaughan, *Cultural Politics in Revolution.*

34. Stern, *Resistance, Rebellion, and Consciousness,* 3–25.

35. For a thoughtful essay on the changing image of the "Indian," see de la Peña, "Articulación y desarticulación de las culturas."

36. Rugeley, *Yucatán's Maya Peasantry.*

37. Guardino, *Peasants, Politics, and the Formation of Mexico's National State.*

38. Thomson with LaFrance, *Patriotism, Politics, and Popular Liberalism;* Mallon, *Peasant and Nation.*

39. Scott, *Weapons of the Weak.*

40. Mallon, *Peasant and Nation,* 281, 317.

41. Quayson, *Postcolonialism.* In his recent resume of the historiographical applications of subaltern studies, Quayson highlights many pertinent issues facing the historian.

42. Stoll, *Rigoberta Menchú.*

43. Beverley, *Subalternity and Representation,* 71.

44. Mallon, *Peasant and Nation;* Beverley, *Subalternity and Representation,* 37.

45. Vaughan, "Cultural Approaches to Peasant Politics."

46. Nugent, introduction to *Revolt in Mexico,* 21.

47. A short description of my methodology can be found immediately preceding the bibliography.

48. Campbell, *Zapotec Renaissance;* Rubin, *Decentering the Regime.*

49. Vaughan, "Cultural Approaches to Peasant Politics." 298.

Chapter 1: The People and History of the Sierra Norte de Puebla

1. Beaucage, "Anthropologie économique des communautés indigènes."

2. Barrios Bonilla, *El café en Cuetzalan.*

3. For details of the long history of commercial and political interrelations between the tierra caliente and the tierra templada, see Ducey, "Village, Nation, and Constitution," 469.

4. Gerhart, *Guide to the Historical Geography of New Spain,* 390. The majority of the demographic details for the colonial period are taken from Gerhart. For more details on Otomí settlement, see Soustelle, *La famille otomi-pame.*

5. García Martínez, *Los pueblos de la sierra.*

6. Juárez Cao, *Catolicismo popular y fiesta.*

7. Gilly, "Chiapas and the Rebellion," 262.

8. Slade, "Kinship in the Social Organization"; Taggart, *Nahua Myth and Social Structure;* Buchler, "La organización ceremonial."

9. Thomson, "Montaña and Llanura"; LaFrance and Thomson, "Juan Francisco Lucas"; Thomson, "Agrarian Conflict in the Municipality of Cuetzalan";

Thomson, "Bulwarks of Patriotic Liberalism." Thomson's studies of Juan Francisco Lucas and "Pala" Agustín Dieguillo provide evidence that mestizo encroachment was not always met with passive submission. See also Arizpe, *Parentesco y economía en una sociedad Nahua.*

10. Quoted in DePalo, *Mexican National Army,* 140.

11. Archer, *Army in Bourbon Mexico,* 94.

12. Ibid., 95–101.

13. Guardino, *Peasants, Politics, and the Formation of Mexico's National State,* 134, 168.

14. Rugeley, *Yucatán's Maya Peasantry,* 177; Reed, *Caste War of Yucatán,* 34. While these interpretations differ in their emphasis on the Mayas' motives for rebelling, they agree that elements of local creole society feared for their race.

15. Rus, "Whose Caste War?"

16. Members of wealthy families in Zacapoaxtla still delight in showing visitors their private collections of furniture and clothing from this period.

17. Friedlander, *Being Indian in Hueyapan.*

18. Thomson, "Popular Aspects of Liberalism in Mexico," 282.

19. Thomson, "Montaña and Llanura."

20. Ducey, "Village, Nation, and Constitution."

21. Thomson with LaFrance, *Patriotism, Politics, and Popular Liberalism,* 268–78. This benign image masks the facts that Lucas gained great personal wealth and was not slow to repossess land should a campesino default on his rent.

22. Thomson, "Agrarian Conflict in the Municipality of Cuetzalan."

23. Mallon, *Peasant and Nation,* 87.

24. Williams, *Problems in Materialism and Culture,* 38; Mallon, *Peasant and Nation,* 61–62.

25. Gilly, "Chiapas and the Rebellion," 267.

26. Thomson, "Pueblos de Indios," 97.

27. Ducey, "Village, Nation, and Constitution," 485–87.

28. Thomson with LaFrance, *Patriotism, Politics, and Popular Liberalism,* 309.

29. Thomson, "Popular Aspects of Liberalism in Mexico," 283.

30. Sayer, "Everyday Forms of State Formation," 377.

31. Mallon, *Peasant and Nation,* 44–46.

Chapter 2: Indigenous Militarism within the Sierra

1. Interview with Demetrio Barrios's son, Vicente Barrios Vargas, Zacatlán, Puebla, 25 Nov. 1993.

2. Interview with José María Barrios Nava, Tonalapa, Tetela de Ocampo, Puebla, 6 Nov. 1993.

3. ADN, H, XI/333-21/43, historia de la unidad—46/o BTN. INF. This file provides an overview of the battalion's military history from 1917 to 1942. See

also ADN, C, XI/III/2-1301 and ADN, C, XI/III/2-1145. The army continued to be known as the Brigada Serrana until 1919, after which it adopted various titles before finally being incorporated into the federal army as the 46th Infantry Battalion in January 1922.

4. Lozoya, *El ejército mexicano*, 53–57; Gruening, *Mexico and Its Heritage*; Garciadiego Dantan, "La política militar del Presidente Carranza"; Hernández Chávez, "Origen y ocaso del ejército porfiriano."

5. *El Monitor*, 15 Feb. 1921, p. 2; Gómez, *El centinela.*

6. For recent analyses of the de la Huerta rebellion, see Plasencia, *Personajes y escenarios de la rebelión Delahuertista*; Castro, *Adolfo de la Huerta.*

7. García de León, *Resistencia y utopía*; Benjamin, "Una larga historia de resistencia," 196.

8. Campbell, *Zapotec Renaissance*, 72–79.

9. Hu-DeHart, *Yaqui Resistance and Survival.*

10. Knight, *Mexican Revolution*, 375.

11. Hu-DeHart, *Yaqui Resistance and Survival*, 9.

12. Aguilar Camín, "Relevant Tradition," 95.

13. Bantjes, *As If Jesus Walked on Earth.*

14. LaFrance, "Politics, War, and State Building."

15. Thomson with LaFrance, *Patriotism, Politics, and Popular Liberalism*, 289.

16. Archivo privado de Arnulfo Barrios (hereafter APAB), see the certified copy dated 8 Nov. 1933 compiled by Colonel Jesús Millan, p. 1.

17. Interview with Guillermo Mejía Cabrera, Tetela de Ocampo, Puebla, 22 Dec. 1993. Señor Mejía believes that the conflict arose from the political subordination of Cuacuila to Otlatlán during the early twentieth century. This fostered resentment among *cuacuileños* who deemed their treatment by Otlatlán authorities to be unfair.

18. APAB, see the certified copy dated 8 Nov. 1933 compiled by Colonel Jesús Millan, p. 3. This battle took place in Cuacuila on 20 May 1915. The Márquez forces numbered 1,200 and carried with them a field gun and two machine guns. Within three hours the Márquez attacking force had been repelled, leaving forty dead with a further sixty taken prisoner.

19. ADN, C, 2-425, fol. 399, and 2-1145, fol. 10.

20. APAB, see the certified copy dated 10 Nov. 1933 compiled by Colonel Jesús Millan, p. 14.

21. For a definitive version of Gabriel Barrios's military career, including campaigns, promotions, and postings, see ADN, C, 2-1145, tomo 6, fols. 1374–79.

22. Fideicomiso Archivos Plutarco Elías Calles y Fernando Torreblanca (hereafter FAPEC-FT), serie 130102213, exp. 7: CARRANZA, Venustiano, leg. 1/2, fol. 6, inv. 1074; quoted in Castro, "La Muerte de Carranza."

23. Among the most virulent published accusations of Barrios's denial of

Carranza is that of Castillo, *Puebla y Tlaxcala*. This version is also reflected in Guzmán, *Muertes históricas*, 81–102.

24. Carranza, *La verdad sobre la muerte de Carranza*. Luis Cabrera agrees with Julia Carranza's verdict on the role Barrios played in the death of her father (see Urrea, *La herencia de Carranza*, 114–19). Magistrate González's ruling that as a result of the manifesto declared by Carranza on 6 May 1920, he could no longer enjoy the presidential powers afforded under the constitution is reported in *El Universal* (Mexico City), 20 May 1920, p. 9.

25. Interview with Arnulfo Barrios Aco, Tetela de Ocampo, Puebla, 24 Sept. 1993. Arnulfo Barrios insists that his father received two telegrams from Obregón ordering him to capture and kill Carranza should he pass through the Sierra. As yet, documentary evidence to substantiate this claim remains elusive.

26. Archivo General de la Nación, fondo Obregón y Calles (hereafter AGN, O-C) 826-H-9. There is some disagreement about the spelling of General Maicotte's name. Although it usually appears as Maycotte, headed and signed personal correspondence in 1921 show him using the surname Maicotte (see letter dated 7 Sept. 1921).

De la Huerta did reflect later, however, that such an attack could not have taken place because the supply lines of rebel forces in Puebla city were severely stretched (see Brush, "De la Huerta Rebellion in Mexico," 183).

27. ADN, C, XI/III/2-754, fol. 14. For details of the campaign against Hernández in 1922, see AGN, O-C 816-P-45. For correspondence between Calles and Hernández, see FAPEC-FT, gav. 41, Hernández, Lindoro (Gral.), exp. 91, leg. 1/2, inv. 2727.

28. ADN, C, 2-754, tomo 1, Vega Bernal, Salvador, see archive note of report by Colonel Dinórin dated 16 Feb. 1918; interviews with Salvador Vega Rodríguez, Cuetzalan, Puebla, 14 Dec. 1993, and Baudelio Rivera, Cuetzalan, Puebla, 16 Dec. 1993; Knight, "Peasant and Caudillo in Revolutionary Mexico," 49.

29. Archivo Municipal de Tetela de Ocampo (hereafter AMT), caja 42, see telegram dated 1 Feb. 1922 from Joaquín Palomino to Barrios; Biblioteca Luis Cabrera, Archivo RHAM (hereafter BLC RHAM), caja 1922, telegrams received/sent in 1922, see telegram dated 25 April 1922 from General A. Elizondo, *jefatura* in Puebla, to Barrios; telegram dated 24 Aug. 1922 from Barrios to the jefatura, Puebla; and telegram dated 25 Aug. 1922 from Barrios to jefatura, Puebla; FAPEC-FT, exp. 93, inv. 543, see memo dated 30 May 1922 from Barrios to Calles; BLC RHAM, caja 1922, telegrams sent January 1922; ADN, C, XI/III/2-754, fol. 14; ADN, C, 2-1145, tomo 1, fol. 164.

30. AGN, O-C 241-W-L-25; ADN, C, 2-754, fols. 291–93, see declaration dated 9 March 1924 made by Vega Bernal to the Guerra y Marina; BLC RHAM, caja 1924, telegrams received March–April 1924. On 22 Mar. 1924, Major Demetrio Barrios, in Xochiapulco, confirmed that Salvador Vega Bernal had surrendered all the arms and ammunition under his control to the Barrios army.

31. For details of the death of Bardomiano Barrios Cabrera, see AGN, O-C 408-P-20; ADN, C, X / III 2 / 15-1879, fols. 92, 100.

32. BLC RHAM, caja 1927, telegrams for October 1927.

33. Thomson with LaFrance, *Patriotism, Politics, and Popular Liberalism,* 280; ADN, H, XI / 481.5 / 223, c. 120 (1917), fol. 33, see letter dated 30 Mar. 1917 from Castro to Carranza. Carranza ordered General Castro to reestablish the Catholic Church in Tetela de Ocampo.

34. Archivo privado de Vicente Barrios (hereafter APVB), summary of Demetrio Barrios's actions in the 1920s dated 1 Jan. 1931; BLC RHAM, caja 1927, telegrams from Demetrio Barrios to the jefatura dated 22 Oct. and 25 Oct. 1927 regarding "bandoleros fanáticos" attacking the town of Aquixtla.

35. ADN, C, 2-1145, tomo 2, fol. 318.

36. ADN, H, XI / 481.5 / 224, c. 121 (1918), fol. 88, see letter dated 26 Feb. 1918 from Cabrera to Carranza.

37. Henderson, *Worm in the Wheat,* 78–79.

38. ADN, C-64: D / III / 2-425, tomo 2, fol. 384. In 1914, Huertista generals concluded that Lucas's sons should not succeed their father. Abraham was deemed too young and unsuited to military command, while Miguel was said to be an alcoholic.

39. Archivo del Congreso de la Unión (hereafter ACU), *Diario de los debates,* periódico extraordinario, 26 July 1921, p. 4.

40. For examples of frustrated attempts to investigate charges, see Archivo Municipal de Zacatlán (hereafter AMZn), caja 3, 31, Gobernación; ADN, C, 2-1145, tomo 5, fols. 1017–93.

41. ADN, C, 2-1145, fol. 233. This report was made by Brigadier General Arturo Viqueras on 3 June 1920 and sent to Brigadier General Ricardo Reyes Márquez of the jefatura de operaciones militares in Puebla.

42. AGN, O-C 408-P-20, leg. 3, telegram dated 16 Aug. 1926 from Governor Tirado to President Calles; ADN, C, 2-1145, tomo 1, fols. 36–55, contains correspondence relating to Manjarrez's charge; ADN, C, 2-1145, tomo 4, fol. 913–22.

43. ADN, C, 2-1145, tomo 4, fol. 842.

44. AMZn, caja 2, 43, Justicia; see correspondence dated 21 Oct. 1920, which confirms that after a search of the *padrones de vecinos,* Berriozábal could not be found on any of the lists relating to the municipality of Zacatlán.

45. ADN, C, 2-1145, tomo 5, fols. 1017–93.

46. ACU, *Diario de los debates,* periódico extraordinario, 23 April 1923, pp. 15–17; ADN, H, caja 120, fols. 73–78. As early as June 1917 General Medina accused commanders of the Brigada Serrana of falsifying troop numbers, see ADN, C, 2-1145, tomo 4, fols. 807–12; See also letters dated 20 Nov. 1917 and 20 Jan. 1918 sent from the soldiers to the jefatura in Puebla located in ADN, C, 2-1145, tomo 1, fol. 133; letter dated 10 March 1920 from Soledad Pérez, concerning her son, Vulfrano Luna, who was killed on 18 April 1919, located in ADN, C, 2-1145,

tomo 4, fol. 828. Correspondence relating to money saved by Barrios is located in ADN, C, 2-1145, tomo 1, fols. 133, 139 and tomo 4, fols. 807–12; interview with José María Barrios Nava, Tonalapa, Tetela, Puebla, 23 Oct. 1993.

47. ADN, C, 2-1145, tomo 1, fols. 133–35.

48. ADN, C, 2-1145, tomo 1, fols. 14–26.

49. AGN, O-C 241-W-L-25.

50. ADN, C, XI / III / 2-1145, tomo 1, fols. 150–58; tomo 2, fol. 260; tomo 4, fol. 874.

51. ADN, C, XI / III / 4-5129, tomo 1, fol. 211.

52. O'Malley, *Myth of the Revolution;* Benjamin, *La Revolución;* Brunk, "Remembering Emiliano Zapata"; Knight, "Popular Culture and the Revolutionary State"; Martin, "Contesting Authenticity."

53. See Masferrer Kan, "Religión y política en la Sierra Norte de Puebla"; González de la Rama, "Los papeles de Díaz Manfort."

54. Marentes Bravo, *Relatos revolucionarios,* 8.

55. Interview with Guillermo Mejía Cabrera, Tetela de Ocampo, Puebla, 22 Dec. 1993.

56. Interview with Señora Posada, Tetela de Ocampo, Puebla, 5 Oct. 1993.

57. Upon the suggestion that Barrios had a woman in every port (*una mujer en cada puerto*), one informant, who wishes to remain anonymous, reflected for a moment and replied, *"Mejor decir, una mujer en cada puerta."* (Better said, a woman in every doorway.)

58. Archivo Municipal de Cuetzalan (hereafter AMC), caja 140A, Presidencia, exp. 2, 33, see letter dated 17 July 1919.

59. *Excélsior,* 4 Jan. 1924, p. 1.

60. AGN, O-C 241-W-L-25; ADN, C, XI / III / 2-1145, fol. 233; BLC RHAM, caja 1924, telegrams received March–April 1924.

61. BLC RHAM, caja 1927, telegrams for October 1927.

62. Thomson with LaFrance, *Patriotism, Politics, and Popular Liberalism,* 282–85.

63. Ankerson, *Agrarian Warlord;* Falcón, *Revolución y caciquismo;* Márquez, "Gonzalo N. Santos," 369–70.

64. Fowler-Salamini, *Agrarian Radicalism in Veracruz* and "Revolutionary Caudillos in the 1920s"; Knight, *Mexican Revolution,* 56. Frans Schryer shows that this kind of political opportunism was also evident at a more local level, see Schryer, *Rancheros of Pisaflores,* 7, 76–77.

65. Thomson, "Agrarian Conflict in the Municipality of Cuetzalan," 205–58; Valderrama Rouy & Ramírez Suárez, "Resistencia étnica," 189–206.

66. Thomson with LaFrance, *Patriotism, Politics, and Popular Liberalism,* 303.

67. For examples of such violence, see AMT, caja 424 (a report by the military commander of Tetela de Ocampo on 19 June 1914); AMT, caja 429; 12 (On 20 Sept. 1915, Villistas raided Tenampulco demanding the "loan" of money and

provisions.); ADN, H, 481.5 / 223, c. 120, fol. 73 (On 9 June 1917, citizens of Tetela complained of abuses by General Medina's men.) ADN, C, 2-1145, tomo 4, fols. 821–22 (On 9 March 1920, Barrios's troops were accused of committing atrocities in Tetela de Ocampo.).

68. Thomson with LaFrance, *Patriotism, Politics, and Popular Liberalism,* 292, 298.

69. The collection of essays in Joseph and Nugent, *Everyday Forms of State Formation* illustrates the point. See also Scott, *Weapons of the Weak;* Taylor, *Drinking, Homicide, and Rebellion,* 169–70.

70. Guardino, *Peasants, Politics, and the Formation of Mexico's National State,* 42.

71. Mallon, *Peasant and Nation,* 79–80.

72. Nugent, *Spent Cartridges of the Revolution,* 55, 94.

Chapter 3: Politics from the Center and Implications for the Sierra

1. Gruening, *Mexico and Its Heritage,* 468–69. Tirado achieved his dream, as the gold lettering on marble statues in the plaza in Puebla city testifies.

2. Carr, *El movimiento obrero,* 147.

3. Fowler-Salamini, "Revolutionary Caudillos in the 1920s," 226.

4. Barbosa Cano, *La CROM,* 223.

5. Evans, *Rosalie Evans Letters.*

6. Henderson, *Worm in the Wheat;* Márquez Carrillo, "Los orígenes de Avilacamachismo."

7. From 30 April 1920, when Alfonso Cabrera ceased to be recognized as governor, Colonel C. García held the provisional governorship for a week, followed by General R. Rojas, who occupied both the governorship and military command of Puebla until 17 July 1920. The state Supreme Tribunal had, in fact, designated Lic. Roberto Labastida as Cabrera's replacement, only to have the federal government override its decision.

8. Carr, *El movimiento obrero,* 66; Hernández Enríquez, *Historia moderna de Puebla,* vol. 2, 46, 64–65.

9. Wenceslao Macip, federal diputado for the district of Zacapoaxtla, nominated Manjarrez for the post of provisional governor.

10. General Almazán arrested Manjarrez on 2 Dec. 1923, and the federal government imposed Vicente Lombardo Toledano as interim governor. His governorship was interrupted almost immediately when Delahuertistas gained military control of Puebla city and imposed their own governor, Francisco Espinosa Fluery. Reinforced by troops from Tlaxcala, Almazán retook the capital on 22 Dec. 1923.

11. AGN, O-C 428-P-22.

12. Quoted in Sánchez López, "La institucionalización," 9.

13. Ibid., 10. Sánchez López incorrectly includes Gabriel Barrios in this group.

14. Ibid., 16.

15. Carr, *El movimiento obrero*, 42.

16. *El Machete*, 18 May 1925, quoted in Barbosa Cano, *La CROM*, 32, 285–87.

17. Hernández Enríquez, *Historia moderna de Puebla*, vol. 2, 102–3. Montes had been an officer in José María Sánchez's agrarian army and had ambitions of assuming his former leader's place at the center of Puebla state politics. Montes took an active part in organizing a campesino army from Huejotzingo to combat the Delahuertistas.

18. Sánchez López, "La institucionalización," 34–36, 44–45.

19. *El Machete*, 10 Sept. 1927, quoted in Barbosa Cano, *La CROM*, 40.

20. *El Monitor*, 3 May 1920, "Extra."

21. *El Universal de Puebla*, 10 May 1920, p. 3.

22. ACU, *Periódico de la comisión permanente*, leg. 28, 23 June 1920, no. 112. p. 6.

23. ACU, *Diario de los debates de la cámara de diputados*, 25 Nov. 1920, p. 5.

24. BLC RHAM, caja 1923, correspondence for Jan. 1923. General Juan Andreu Almazán took over as jefe de operaciones militares for Puebla on 1 Jan. 1923.

25. AGN, O-C 101-B-10, letter dated 26 Nov. 1924 from Cruz to Obregón; ADN, C, 2-1145, fols. 119–203, correspondence between May and July 1925. In answer to complaints that Barrios was impeding agrarian reform, Cruz replied to Calles that Barrios was not involved and that the case was more accurately described as a boundary dispute between neighboring settlements.

26. BLC RHAM, caja 1926, letters for June 1926, see letter dated 11 June 1926 from Amaya to Barrios.

27. BLC RHAM, caja 1926, letters for June 1926, see letter dated 27 Oct. 1926 from Amaya to Barrios; BLC RHAM, caja 1927, correspondence for April 1927, see letter dated 8 April 1927 from Almada to Barrios.

28. BLC RHAM, caja 1926, letters for June 1926. On 8 June 1926 Bravo Izquierdo addressed a letter to his "estimado amigo y compañero" Gabriel Barrios, reporting that he had recently handed over military supplies to "nuestro buen amigo" Ricardo Márquez Galindo; also see letter dated 9 June 1926 from Bravo Izquierdo to Barrios.

29. Archivo privado de Abraham Lucas (hereafter APAL), letter dated 21 Feb. 1917 from Abraham Lucas to his niece, Elena, and correspondence dated 10 Oct. and 16 Oct. 1916 between the Partido Liberal del Estado de Puebla and Abraham Lucas; AMT, caja 9, Gobernación, exp. 44, 45, letter dated 10 July 1918 from the Centro Directivo de los Clubs Liberales del Estado de Puebla reveals that Márquez Galindo was its president.

30. AMT, caja 28, exp. 30, 1291, Gobernación, see Partido Liberal Independiente circular dated 10 Oct. 1920; AGNP, vol. 2, 1920-1, caja 12, 119. See also documents dated 8 Nov. 1920 written by the Partido Liberal Independiente "Benito Juárez," Xaltatempan, Tetela de Ocampo.

31. *El Monitor,* 16 March 1921, p. 1; *El Universal,* 17 March 1921, p. 11; *El Monitor,* 27 Jan. 1921, p. 1.

32. *El Monitor,* 27 May 1921, 11 June 1921, 25 June 1921, 9 July 1921.

33. FAPEC-FT exp. 93, inv. 543; *El Monitor,* 28 Aug. 1921, p. 6.

34. *El Monitor,* 9 Jan. 1922, pp. 1, 4, and 27 Jan. 1922, p. 1.

35. *La Opinión,* 28 April 1930, p. 5.

36. AMT, caja 28, exp. 30, Gobernación, 1291.

37. AMT, caja 50, Gobernación, 685, see letter dated 23 June 1926 from the municipal president of Tetela to the municipal president of Puebla city. The campaign was endorsed by the Partido Laborista del Estado and the federal and state Alianzas de Partidos Socialistas. BLC RHAM, caja 1926, miscellaneous correspondence for July 1926. Evidence that funds from the 46th Battalion were diverted into Lucas's political campaign appears on a draft of the battalion's accounts for July 1926.

38. ACU, *Diario de los debates de la cámara de diputados,* 20 Nov. 1920, pp. 1–8; 25 Nov. 1920, pp. 3–12; and 26 Nov. 1920, pp. 1–24.

39. AMT, caja 44, Gobernación, document dated 9 June 1922; ADN, C, 2-1145, fol. 36.

40. ADN, C, 2-1145, fols. 409, 429, 459. Quintero reenlisted at the outbreak of the De la Huerta rebellion. Following a battle against a rebel unit on 22 Feb. 1924, Quintero was taken prisoner and, after a summary trial, was executed along with other prisoners.

41. ACU, *Diario de los debates de la cámara de diputados,* 25 Nov. 1920, pp. 3–12.

42. Hernández Enríquez, *Historia moderna de Puebla,* vol. 3, 17; AMC, caja 126, Presidencia, 1914. Thirteen members of the Tirado family lived in Cuetzalan in 1914.

43. ADN, C, 2-1145, fols. 913–14, letter dated 21 July 1922 sent to the jefe de operaciones militares in Puebla City.

44. ADN, C, 2-1145, fol. 922, letter dated 14 Aug. 1922 from Barrios to the jefe de la brigada, Puebla. This picture contradicts previous claims by historians that Barrios and Tirado were political allies. See Hernández Enríquez, *Historia moderna de Puebla,* vol. 3, 19; Sánchez López, "La institucionalización," 12. Further evidence suggests that any allegiance was highly unlikely: AGN, O-C 408-D-12, letter dated 4 Feb 1926 from Tirado to Calles; also see *Nuestro Diario,* 30 April 1924, p. 1, on the struggle for power in Zacapoaxtla.

45. Hernández Enríquez, *Historia Moderna de Puebla,* vol. 3, 73.

46. AMC, caja 151a, Seguridad Pública, 2049, see letter dated 3 Nov. 1922, vecinos from the Ranchería de Xiutecuapan.

47. AGN, O-C 816-P-45, see page 7 of the military report dated 1 May 1923 by General Almazán, jefe de las operaciones militares, Puebla. Given that Almazán was a strong defender of Barrios's actions in the Sierra, his report may well have been biased against Barrios's enemies.

48. AGN, O-C 408-P-20, legs. 1, 2.

49. BLC RHAM, caja 1925, letters July / August 1925, see letters from Flores to Demetrio Barrios dated 24 Aug. 1925 and 28 Aug. 1925.

50. BLC RHAM, caja 1925, letters for October 1925, see letter from Márquez Galindo to Barrios dated 1 Oct. 1925 and the letter from Flores to Demetrio Barrios dated 2 Oct. 1925.

51. AGN, O-C 408-P-20, leg. 3, see telegram dated 16 Aug. 1926 from Tirado to Calles together with extracts of telegrams detailing alleged abuses by Barrios.

52. AGN, O-C 408-P-20, leg. 3, no. 8844. Report dated 1 Sept. 1926 from Francisco Heredía to Calles.

53. AGN, O-C 408-P-20, leg. 3, no. 9274, memorandum dated 2 Sept. 1926 from Amaya to Calles.

54. BLC RHAM, caja 1926, letters received / sent for September 1926, see letter dated 4 Sept. 1926 from Molina to Barrios.

55. In doing so, Guerrero made it clear that various military chiefs in Puebla were undermining his authority. He claimed, for instance, that Barrios had written to his commander, Juan Almazán, asking his advice regarding recognition of Guerrero's appointments to the ayuntamiento in Zacatlán. AGN, O-C 428-P-22, see letter dated 13 June 1924 from Guerrero to Obregón.

56. AGN, O-C 104-P-106, leg. 1, telegram dated 24 June 1924 from Lombardo Toledano to Obregón.

57. AGN, O-C 104-P-106, leg. 2, see telegram dated 7 July 1924 from Villavicencio to Obregón.

58. Excélsior, 12 July 1924, p. 4. For similar incidents elsewhere see Excélsior, 16 June 1924, Edición 2ª, p. 8,

59. BLC RHAM, caja 1925, letters for January 1925, see letter dated 27 Jan. 1925 from Lombardo Toledano to Demetrio Barrios; also see letters for July / August 1925, letter dated 13 Aug. 1925 to Demetrio Barrios.

60. BLC RHAM, caja 1925, letters for October 1925, see letter dated 2 Oct. 1925 from Márquez Galindo to Demetrio Barrios.

61. ACU, Diario de los debates, vol. 2, no. 24, 9 Oct. 1925, pp. 1, 2.

62. ACU, Diario de los debates, vol. 1, no. 25, 19 Oct. 1926, pp. 7–9.

63. ACU, Diario de los debates, vol. 1, no. 30, 8 Nov. 1926, pp. 9–10.

64. For details of this ongoing controversy, see AGN, O-C 408-P-20, leg. 2, letter dated 28 Nov. 1925 from Leonardo Pimental to Calles; AGN, O-C 408-D-12, leg. 12, letters dated 4 Feb. 1926 and 27 May 1926 from Tirado to the presidencia; AGN, O-C 818-T-219, letters dated 26 July from Luis Romero to Calles and 28 July 1926 from Lombardo Toledano to Calles; AGN, O-C 408-P-20, leg. 3, letter dated 3 Aug. 1926 from Amaya to Calles.

65. BLC RHAM, caja 1926, correspondence for November 1926, letter dated 24 Nov. 1926 from Barrios to Márquez Galindo, diputado in the federal congress.

66. BLC RHAM, caja 1928, correspondence for 1928, see letter dated 15 Feb.

1928 from Miguel Andreu Almazán to Barrios. For other expressions of support and encouragement, see letters dated 15 Feb. 1928 from Pedro Lecona Soto; 16 Feb. 1926 from Miguel Angel Córtes, president of the Comité pro-Obregón, Tecamachalco, Puebla; 20 Feb. 1926 from Roberto Tirado Gutiérrez; 21 Feb. 1926 from Arturo Viqueros; and 20 April 1928 from the vecinos of Tlacuilotepec, Puebla.

67. AMT, caja 53, *La Voz de la Sierra*, no. 8, p. 2. Eight editions of *La Voz* were issued between 6 May 1928 and 24 June 1928.

68. BLC RHAM, caja 1927, letters for July 1927, see letter dated 20 July 1927 from vecinos of Teziutlán to the jefatura in Puebla; AGN, O-C 427-B-1, letter dated 24 Feb. 1928 from representatives of the Partidos "Plutarco Elias Calles" and the "Campesinos de la Sierra Norte" of Pahuatlán to Calles; ADN, C, 2-1145, fol. 405, letter dated 15 June 1928 from a representative of the Confederación Revolucionaria Socialista del Estado de Puebla in Chignahuapan; ADN, C, 2-1145, fol. 408, letter dated 13 July 1928 from the Partido Liberal Socialista Independiente Revolucionario de Puebla to Gobernación; AMC, caja 164, Gobernación, 14, circular dated 24 June 1928 from the Confederación Revolucionaria Socialista (the president was José María Sánchez) to the municipal president in Cuetzalan; *La Opinión*, 5 July 1928, p. 1.

69. Lombardo Toledano, "Estructura económica de la Sierra de Puebla."

70. BLC RHAM, caja 1926, letters for October 1926. Lombardo Toledano's letter dated 27 Oct. 1926 was forwarded to Barrios by General Amaya.

71. BLC RHAM, caja 1928, documents sent/received in August 1928, see letter dated 14 Aug. 1928 from the Guerra y Marina to Barrios.

72. *La Opinión*, 6 Oct. 1928, pp. 1, 6.

Chapter 4: Coercion and Compromise in Local Sierra Politics

1. Palacios, *Puebla*, 253–56; Congreso del Estado de Puebla, *Periódico oficial*, vol. 99, no. 14, 2 Oct. 1917, pp. 205–28.

2. ACU, *Diario de los debates*, leg. 32, vol. 1, no. 32, 16 Nov. 1926, p. 16.

3. Sáenz, *Escuelas federales en la Sierra de Puebla*, 82.

4. Ibid., 81.

5. Redfield, *Tepoztlán, a Mexican Village*, 66–68.

6. Sáenz, *Escuelas federales en la Sierra de Puebla*, 82.

7. Rus and Wasserstrom, "Civil-Religious Hierarchies in Central Chiapas"; Chance and Taylor, "Cofradías and Cargos."

8. BLC RHAM, caja 1923, letters sent/received April–June 1923, see letter dated 10 April 1923. On 22 March 1928 Demetrio Barrios sent a letter of introduction with Alfonso Lobato, informing the auxiliary municipal president of Tepeixco that Lobato was to become the community's secretary, see BLC RHAM, caja 1928, letters sent March 1928.

9. ADN, C, 2-1145, tomo 2, fols. 467–68.

10. BLC RHAM, caja 1925, letters sent/received November 1925.

11. BLC RHAM, caja 1926, letters received December 1926, see letter sent on 2 Dec. 1926.

12. BLC RHAM, caja 1928, letters received March 1928, see letter dated 29 March 1928 from Arturo A. Sosa of Tlacuilotepec to Demetrio Barrios.

13. BLC RHAM, caja 1926, letters received August 1926, see letter sent 15 Aug. 1926 from J. Meza y Mora in Papantla to Demetrio Barrios in Zacatlán.

14. BLC RHAM, caja 1925, reports, January 1925.

15. BLC RHAM, caja 1928, letters sent/received January 1928. The following year, the people of Jopala were still appealing for a remedy despite an investigation by Barrios; see BLC RHAM, caja 1929, letters sent/received January 1929.

16. Ibid., caja 1929, official correspondence, April 1929.

17. Ibid., caja 1925, letters received June 1925, see letter dated 22 June 1925 from Marcos Colombus Jr. of Caxhuacán to Demetrio Barrios.

18. Ibid., caja 1926, correspondence for November 1926, see letter dated 20 Oct. 1926 from Miguel Manzano to Barrios.

19. Rivera Moreno, *Xochiapulco*, 179. Given her father's role in the events she describes, Rivera's account should not be seen as objective.

20. Mallon, *Peasant and Nation*, 281.

21. Vaughan, *Cultural Politics in Revolution*, 116–17.

22. ADN, C, 2-1145, fol. 166.

23. Vaughan, *Cultural Politics in Revolution*, 116. We cannot dismiss Gutiérrez as irrelevant in local politics. Indeed, Vaughan shows him to have been a committed revolutionary and leader of agrarian activism within his community.

24. The fact that Indian serranos did not necessarily understand or wish to become involved in the revolution is indicated by the comments of Don Pedro Xoltoc, a witness of a battle between the forces of Gabriel Barrios and Salvador Vega Bernal, see Arizpe, *Parentesco y economía en una sociedad Nahua*, 60.

25. AMT, caja 420, no. 15, see letter dated 25 May 1913; AMT, caja 424, see report dated 19 June 1914 from Ricardo Márquez Galindo to regional Carrancista commander Antonio Medina; Mejía Castelán, *Huauchinango histórico*, 289–93. The direct fiscal consequences of banditry in Huauchinango were meticulously recorded by local officials.

26. AMT, caja 411, see letter dated 24 Dec. 1913.

27. APAL, see Programa dated 4 Nov. 1913 written by Demetrio Santa Fe.

28. AMT, caja 2, exp. 130, Justicia. Perhaps this proposal reflected the fact that Tetela de Ocampo recorded no fewer than eighty-five cases of robbery in 1916.

29. APAL, see letter dated 20 July 1917 from Demetrio Santa Fe to Abraham Lucas and report dated 4 Sept. 1917 entitled "Confidencias. Guardias civiles y servicio de guarniciones."

30. ADN, H, XI/481.5/223, c. 120, fol. 143. This letter, dated 3 Oct. 1917,

followed a discussion between the two men in which provisional approval was given and preceded a formal request being sent to Congress; see ACU, debate, 30 Oct. 1917. Cabrera does not detail to whom the description "plague of rats" referred, but he may well have been reflecting a wave of criminality affecting Mexico City and provincial cities during this period; see Knight, *Mexican Revolution*, 392–406.

31. AMT, caja 4, Seguridad Pública, 27 Oct. 1917.

32. AMZn, caja 17, Seguridad Pública, 13 May 1922.

33. Archivo Municipal de Libres (hereafter AML), Seguridad Pública, exp. 30, 1926, see letter dated 18 Dec. 1926 from Gen. Almada to the municipal president of Libres.

34. BLC RHAM, caja 1929, documents received / sent in May 1929, see letter to Esteban Islas, of Honey, Puebla, dated 2 May 1929.

35. AMT, caja 11, exp. 29, Justicia, see letter dated 22 Feb. 1918.

36. AMT, caja 16, Seguridad Pública, see letter dated 20 Oct. 1918.

37. AMT, caja 20, exp. 29, Seguridad Pública, see letter dated 24 Sept. 1919.

38. AMZn, caja 2, exp. 6, 21, Seguridad Pública, see letter dated 29 July 1920 from the municipal president to Barrios.

39. AMZn, caja 16, exp. 6, 18, Seguridad Pública, see letter dated 26 Oct. 1921.

40. *El Monitor*, 19 Jan. 1921, p. 2.

41. BLC RHAM, caja 1922, reports issued August 1922.

42. BLC RHAM, caja 1925, reports for May 1925.

43. Gruening, *Mexico and Its Heritage*, 326. This incident was reported to President Calles by a federal judge on 7 March 1927. For evidence of similar incidents see BLC RHAM, caja 1924, correspondence for October 1924, report dated 5 Oct. 1924 from Demetrio Barrios to General Roberto Cruz, jefe de operaciones militares, Puebla; BLC RHAM, caja 1925, telegrams received May 1925, letter from Captain Amaro dated 1 May 1925, regarding the death in custody of gang leader Juan Jiménez; AMZn, caja 6, exp. 17, report relating to the shooting of murder suspect Enrique Ponce Ibarra on 30 June 1927; BLC RHAM, caja 1928, correspondence for February 1928, report on the shooting of Joaquín Balderrabano on 19 Feb. 1928.

44. Interviews with Arnulfo Barrios Aco, Tetela de Ocampo, Puebla, 24 Sept. 1993; Beatriz Galindo de Sánchez (daughter of Ramón Galindo), Zacatlán, Puebla, 31 Dec. 1993 and 21 Aug. 1999; Guillermo Mejía Cabrera, Tetela de Ocampo, Puebla, 22 Dec. 1993.

45. Interviews with Alejandro L. Huerta Mora, Tonalapa, Tetela, Puebla, 23 Oct. 1993 and Señor Limón, Tepeyahualco, Libres, Puebla, 29 Nov. 1993.

46. Interview with Ciro Hernández García, Zacatlán, Puebla, 14 Dec. 1993.

47. Ibid.

48. Interview with Arnulfo Barrios Aco, Tetela de Ocampo, Puebla, 24 Sept. 1993.

49. Interview with José María Barrios Nava, Tonalapa, Tetela, Puebla, 6 Nov. 1993.

50. FAPEC-FT, Guerra y Marina, gav. 63, exp. 79, leg. 14/14, fols. 680–83. Although no date is given, from the description of the road network already completed, the report must have been produced toward the end of Barrios's period of control in the Sierra. In 1928 Barrios produced a telephone directory which confirms that almost five hundred telephones had been installed in the Sierra, see BLC RHAM, caja 1928.

51. AMZn, Presidencia, caja 14, 41, 745, Gobernación. A reply to a state questionnaire by the municipal president of Zacatlán reveals that the majority of the municipalities in the district had from one to three armed groups. All were licensed to carry arms and were responsible to Gabriel Barrios.

52. Various interviews with José María Barrios Nava, Tonalapa, Tetela, Puebla, during November and December 1993.

53. AGN, O-C 816-P-45, anexo no. 3, p. 1; BLC RHAM, caja 1925, correspondence September 1925, see letter dated 22 Sept. 1925 from Barrios informing the municipal president of Amixtlán of Alfredo Galindo's appointment.

54. BLC RHAM, caja 1931 onwards; see letter dated 5 Jan. 1945 from Demetrio Barrios to González Moreno of Hueytlalpan.

55. Interview with Beatriz Galindo de Sánchez, Zacatlán, Puebla, 31 Dec. 1993 and 21 Aug. 1999.

56. BLC RHAM, caja 1925, reports for February 1925, see Amaro's letter dated 28 Feb. 1925 and Barrios's reply sent on 1 March 1925.

57. Garner, "Federalism and Caudillismo."

58. BLC RHAM, caja 1921, letters sent/received January 1921.

59. BLC RHAM, caja 1923, letters sent/received January–March 1923, see letters sent by Bardomiano Barrios to seven jefes during February and March 1923; BLC RHAM, caja 1925, correspondence sent in October 1925, see Demetrio Barrios's letter of Oct. 1925 to Francisco Lechuga, jefe de armas of Cuamaxalco.

60. AMZn, caja 2, 42, no. 779, letter dated 29 July 1921. For other examples see ADN, C, 2-1145, fols. 864–68, letter dated 30 June 1920 accusing Simón Torres of committing innumerable crimes; AMZn, caja 2, 43, correspondence dated Dec. 1921 from Eloxchitlán, Ahuacatlán, to the Guerra y Marina regarding armed men under orders from Bardomiano Barrios terrorizing the neighborhood; AMZn, caja 5, 1, no. 153, letter dated 30 Aug. 1924 from municipal president to a local magistrate concerning a complaint by three women from San Cristóbal against the local jefe; BLC RHAM, letters received/sent May 1925, letter dated 4 May 1925 from the Guerra y Marina referring to an accusation by inhabitants of Tuazapa, Tetela, against abuses by a local jefe.

61. ADN, C, 2-1145, fols. 339, 397, 420, see letter from Molina to president dated 22 Oct. 1928.

62. For examples see AMZn, caja 16, 35, no. 1095, letter dated 16 Dec. 1921

from the junta auxiliar of Tomatlán; BLC RHAM, caja 1925, letters sent June–July 1925, undated letter from vecinos of the Ranchería El Pozo to Barrios against the actions of the jefe de armas; BLC RHAM, caja 1927, letters received December 1927, letter dated 13 Dec. 1927 from José Ibarra of Honey, Puebla, to Demetrio Barrios; BLC RHAM, caja 1928, letters received Nov. 1928, letter dated 24 Dec. 1928 from Joaquín Palomino of Coxquihui, Veracruz, to Barrios.

63. BLC RHAM, caja 1923, letters sent / received March 1923, see letter dated 21 March 1923 from Barrios to Torres, Tlapacoya, Puebla.

64. BLC RHAM, caja 1923, letters sent / received April–June 1923, see letter dated 11 April 1923 from Bardomiano Barrios to Manuel Alvarado, Camotepec, Puebla.

65. BLC RHAM, caja 1927, letters sent / received Nov. 1927, see letter dated 9 Nov. 1927 from Demetrio Barrios to Moisés Galindo of Agua Fría; see also caja 1928, letters received Feb. 1928, undated letter from Joaquín Palomino of Coxquihui, Veracruz, to Barrios.

66. BLC RHAM, caja 1923, letters sent / received April–June 1923, see letter dated 13 Dec. 1923 from Bardomiano Barrios to A. Barron, jefe de armas of the Rancho de Rinconada.

67. For examples of such duties see AMZn, caja 15, exp. 19, Gobernación; BLC RHAM, caja 1923, correspondence for March 1923; AML, legajo de oficios—varios, no. 5. (1929), Seguridad Pública, no. 686.

68. BLC RHAM, caja 1926, reports for May 1926, see letter from Carlos to Barrios dated 4 May 1926.

69. AGN, O-C 408-P-20, leg. 3, no. 8844, report dated 1 Sept. 1926 from Francisco Heredía to Calles.

70. Various interviews with José María Barrios Nava, Tonalapa, Tetela, Puebla, during November and December 1993.

71. Sieder, " 'Paz, Progreso, Justicia y Honradez.' " This situation is reminiscent of how indigenous communities used the judicial process in New Spain; see Taylor, *Drinking, Homicide, and Rebellion*.

Chapter 5: Postrevolutionary Socioeconomic Reform

1. Becker, *Setting the Virgin on Fire*; Bantjes, *As If Jesus Walked on Earth*.

2. Vaughan, *Cultural Politics in Revolution*, 107–36.

3. The funds to establish the bank derived primarily from the recovery of the silver mining industry, taxation of oil revenues, and the introduction of income tax (see Oñate, "Struggle for the Central Bank").

4. Lombardo Toledano, "Estructura económica de la Sierra de Puebla."

5. *El Nacional Revolucionario*, 7 June 1930, secc. 2ª, p. 3; *La Opinión*, 28 May 1930, p. 1; AGN, Instituto Nacional de Estudios Históricos de la Revolución Mexicana (hereafter INEHRM), caja 13, exp. 20.

6. Hernández Enríquez, *Historia moderna de Puebla*, vol. 3; Cordero y Torres, *Historia general del estado de Puebla*, 92, and *Diccionario biográfico de Puebla*; INEHRM, *Diccionario histórico y biográfico*; Pare, "Inter-ethnic and Class Relations."

7. Vaughan, *Cultural Politics in Revolution*, 118.

8. Pare, "Inter-ethnic and Class Relations," 415–16.

9. AGN, O-C 816-P-45, p. 4, *Periódico oficial del Estado de Puebla*, 1924; item no. 19 refers to documentation dated 21 Oct. 1924 notifying the hacienda owner that a petition had been received by the local agrarian commission.

10. BLC RHAM, caja 1924, telegrams sent / received December 1924, see telegram sent on 25 Dec. 1924 by Barrios to General Cruz, jefe de operaciones militares, Puebla.

11. ADN, C, 2-1145, fol. 398, see letter dated 18 Oct. 1928 from the Comisión Nacional Agraria to Guerra y Marina; AMZn, Justicia, 10, 16, 1502. In a letter dated 30 June 1932 from Governor Leonides A. Almazán to the municipal president of Zacatlán, it appears that one source of friction in the area was land disputes between the ejido of Palos Caídos and neighboring agraristas in Peñuela; ADN, C, 2-1145, fol. 544, see letter dated 13 Sept. 1933 from the vecinos of Pueblo Nuevo y Peñuela to President Abelardo L. Rodríguez.

12. BLC RHAM, caja 1927, correspondence for November 1927, see letters dated 3 Nov. 1927 from the jefatura in Puebla to Barrios, and 23 Nov. 1927 from Demetrio Barrios to the jefatura.

13. BLC RHAM, caja 1928, documents for March 1928, see letter dated 22 March 1928 from Gobernación to the jefatura in Puebla; BLC RHAM, caja 1927, documents sent / received July 1927, see letter dated 14 July 1927 sent to the Guerra y Marina from the local agrarian committee of Tepeyahualco and letter dated 27 July 1927 sent to Barrios from Alvarez Contreras, commander of the garrison in Libres; AML, Justicia, exp. 18, April 1928.

14. ADN, C, 2-1145, fols. 433–43, 692–94. All cases were investigated during February and March 1932.

15. *Periódico oficial del estado de Puebla*, 1920, p. 28. Sections of the hacienda had already been auctioned in 1920 to pay off debts, and several grants were subsequently made to agraristas.

16. BLC RHAM, caja 1925, letters for October 1925, see letter dated 24 Oct. 1925 from Almazán to Barrios.

17. *La Opinión*, 11 July 1930, p. 4, and 15 July 1930, p. 6.

18. ADN, C, 2-1145, fols. 682–91, 941–42; *La Opinión*, 10 Nov. 1933, p. 1.

19. Tobler, "Peasants and the Shaping of the Revolutionary State."

20. AMT, caja 20, exp. 30, Fomento, see letter dated 24 Sept. 1919 from Miguel Lucas to Carlos B. Zetina.

21. AGNP, Tetela, caja 12, vol. 1, no. 46, 30 June 1919. Greater details of trans-

actions relating to the Lucas estate are given in Thomson with LaFrance, *Patriotism, Politics, and Popular Liberalism,* 261–78.

22. Mallon, *Peasant and Nation,* 32.

23. The main area of agrarian conflict was the municipality of Cuetzalan, where the relatively mild climate enabled the cultivation of coffee. In the late nineteenth century, non-Indian migrants came into the area and interethnic conflict ensued as Indian communities fought to retain their lands. Such developments, however, were uncommon in the harsher climates of the upper Sierra. See Barrios Bonilla, *El café en Cuetzalan;* Thomson, "Agrarian Conflict in the Municipality of Cuetzalan"; Valderrama Rouy and Ramírez Suárez, "Resistencia étnica."

24. Brewster, "Caciquismo in Post-revolutionary Mexico"; Thomson, "Agrarian Conflict in the Municipality of Cuetzalan."

25. Nugent, *Spent Cartridges of the Revolution,* 50.

26. Interview with José María Barrios Nava, Tonalapa, Tetela, Puebla, 6 Nov. 1993.

27. Ruiz, *Mexico,* 26–27. Such an approach was nothing new; Justo Sierra prescribed similar remedies during the Porfiriato, and evidence suggests that such initiatives brought significant changes to rural society in some areas; see French, *Peaceful and Working People.* Vaughan also discusses the element of continuity between the policies of Justo Sierra and Vasconcelos (Vaughan, *Cultural Politics in Revolution,* 23–29).

28. Vaughan, *State, Education, and Social Class in Mexico,* 179.

29. Lombardo Toledano, "Estructura económica de la Sierra de Puebla."

30. Vaughan, *Cultural Politics in Revolution,* 4.

31. De la Peña, "La ciudadanía étnica."

32. For an interesting analysis of how the Casa del Estudiante Indígena fitted into broader indigenista policies, see Timmons, "The Only Good Indian."

33. AML, Fomento, Jan. 1923, see copy of SEP circular no. 6, dated 29 Jan. 1923, sent to all municipal authorities.

34. Loyo, "Lectura para el pueblo."

35. Knight, "Popular Culture and the Revolutionary State," 403–5.

36. Vaughan, *State, Education, and Social Class in Mexico,* 185.

37. AMT, caja 26, exp. 54, Seguridad Pública.

38. APAL, 1920, see letter dated 10 Feb. 1920; AMT, caja 26, exp. 54.

39. AMC, caja 146, Hacienda, see letter from the municipal president dated 1 March 1920.

40. AMZx, Instrucción Pública, exp. 22, 49 (1920), see letter dated 14 Sept. 1920 from Miguel Molina to the municipal president of Zacapoaxtla.

41. The biographical details are taken from Secretaría de Cultura, *Profr. J. Baudelio Candanedo Castillo.*

42. BLC RHAM, caja 1927, expediente on schools for 1927–29, see letter dated 3 May 1928 from the director of federal schools in Puebla city to Cuacuila's teacher, Baudelio Candanedo.

43. BLC RHAM, caja 1921, correspondence for January 1921, see memo dated 14 Jan. 1921 from the municipal president of Aquixtla to Barrios; AMZn, Instrucción Pública, caja 16, 26, 169, letter dated 19 Oct. 1921 to the provisional municipal president of Zacatlán.

44. Archivo del Congreso del Estado de Puebla (hereafter ACP), sección de leyes, p. 246, dated 8 April 1922. Presumably, the grant became a casualty of the mounting political pressure that culminated in the removal of Delahuertista Governor Manjarrez.

45. AMZx, Instrucción Pública, exp. 18, 1923.

46. BLC RHAM, 1923, telegrams received/sent July 1923, see telegram dated 26 July 1923 from José Galvez to Barrios.

47. AMT, caja 46, Gobernación, no. 322, see documents dated 20 March 1923.

48. BLC RHAM, caja 1928, letters for September 1928, see letter dated 16 Sept. 1928 from Demetrio Barrios to Salustio Cabrera.

49. BLC RHAM, caja 1929, see letter dated June 1929 from M. Becerra to Demetrio Barrios; BLC RHAM, caja 1930, minutes of a meeting held at the presidencia, Concepción, Atlequizayan, on 5 May 1930. A similar scheme was organized in the barrio of Concepción, Zacatlán.

50. BLC RHAM, caja 1928, report dated 17 July 1928.

51. BLC RHAM, caja 1928, Instrucción. Demetrio Barrios invited all teachers who had assisted in "Education Orientation Courses and Examinations" to attend a lunch to be held in Zacatlán on 29 Dec. 1928.

52. BLC RHAM, caja 1929, see paper dated 30 July 1929 entitled "La Castellanización del indios," paper dated 13 Sept. 1929 entitled "La Brujería," and various leaflets in the Sección Pedagógica.

53. Acevedo-Rodrigo, "Time and Discipline in Mexican Schools."

54. AMZn, caja 15, exp. 19, Gobernación.

55. *Nuestro Diario,* 8 April 1924, p. 5.

56. BLC RHAM, caja 1928, letters for March 1928. Demetrio Barrios also provided more tangible support for the school in the form of essential teaching materials. See letter dated 11 March 1928 from Angel Samuel Zambrano to Demetrio Barrios.

57. AML, Gobernación, exp. 28, 1928.

58. BLC RHAM, caja 1928, correspondence January–December 1928, see letter dated 22 Oct. 1928 from Barrios to the secretary-general of the state government.

59. AMT, caja 39, state government circular dated 16 June 1921; M. M. Vargas, *Proyecto de una vía de comunicación;* Arriaga, *Expediente geográfico-estadístico,* gives details of a proposal to build a national highway linking Zacapoaxtla with Tecolutla in the tierra caliente; AMT, caja 21, exp. 49, see letter dated 19 Dec. 1919

stating that a lack of funds prevented the state government from helping to improve local roads.

60. Interview with Guillermo Mejía Cabrera, Tetela de Ocampo, Puebla, 22 Dec. 1993.

61. The use of *topiles* in the Sierra de Puebla differs from its more common usage to describe a local official. I thank an anonymous reader of my manuscript for highlighting this difference.

62. APAL 1913, see Programa dated 4 Nov. 1913.

63. For examples of correspondence reminding judges of their responsibility to organize faenas, see AMZn, caja 1, 3, 327, Justicia, letter dated 24 Aug. 1919, and caja 5, 38, 836, Gobernación, letter dated 20 June 1920.

64. For examples of vecino resistance to faena directives, see AMC, caja 137, exp. 2, Gobernación, 104, report from municipal president dated 31 Aug. 1918; AMZx, Fomento 58, 16, correspondence from Xochitlán dated 4 Oct. 1920.

65. AMT, caja 44, Fomento Circular no. 8.

66. AMT, caja 26, exp. 7, Gobernación.

67. AGN, O-C 816-Z-20. Obregón's reply, dated 13 Aug. 1923, was sent to the municipal president of Cuetzalan, who had sought an opinion on the constitutionality of faenas.

68. *El Monitor,* 29 Sept. 1921, p. 1, reported that thirty of Barrios's men had been deployed to protect faeneros working on the Zaragoza-to-Zacapoaxtla road; AGN, O-C 816-Z-20, see correspondence dated 22 Nov. 1922.

69. AMZx, Fomento 18 (1923), see letter dated 25 May 1922.

70. AMZx, Fomento 1921, no. 1380.

71. Thomson with LaFrance, *Patriotism, Politics, and Popular Liberalism,* 308.

72. Nowhere in Barrios's extensive correspondence with his jefes de armas is there evidence that Cruz enjoyed a position of importance in the cacicazgo, as Thomson claims.

73. AMT, caja 86, exp. 1, Secretaría de Comunicaciones y Obras Públicas (SCOP), see letter dated 28 Sept. 1943; interview with Alejandro L. Huerta Mora (*presidente de aguas* in charge of the Solidaridad committee maintaining the canal), Tonalapa, Tetela, Puebla, 8 Nov. 1993. This canal was renovated in 1943, with Barrios and his son José María as the project's central organizing figures.

74. AGN, O-C 605-T-6, see letter from Obregón dated 21 March 1922.

75. BLC RHAM, caja 1925, letters for August 1925, copy of a declaration of intent signed by the junta on 21 March 1922.

76. AML, Fomento (1928), exp. 19, 21, 23, 27; AML, Beneficencia, (1928), exp. 5; AML, Gobernación, (1928), exp. 33.

77. AML, Fomento, circular 4, dated 13 Feb. 1928.

78. FAPEC-FT, Guerra y Marina, gav. 63, exp. 79, leg. 14/14. fols. 680–83. Although the report carries no date, judging by the advanced state of the projects mentioned, it must have been produced in 1929 or 1930. The total cost of the

road projects stated in the report would appear to be a considerable under-estimation given that federal funding for the Zaragoza-Tecolutla project alone amounted to forty thousand pesos (see AGN, O-C 816-Z-20, letter from José María Flores to Obregón dated 26 May 1924).

79. AGN, O-C 816-P-45, military report dated 1 May 1923.

80. Perhaps the most comprehensive case made by the Guerra y Marina for Barrios's initiatives is contained in Colonel Antonio Guerrero's wide-ranging military report of the Sierra Norte de Puebla dated 1 May 1923, in AGN, O-C 816-P-45, pp. 3, 5–6, 9–11, and appendix 13. The report repeatedly stresses the military and economic benefits of the different road construction projects in the Sierra, the willingness of serranos to provide unpaid labor, and the need for SCOP to support such enthusiasm.

81. There are numerous cases in which the national executive responded positively to requests for "material as well as moral support." An exchange of correspondence between Obregón, Flores, and SCOP during November 1921 is typical (see AGN, O-C 816-Z-20, November 1921).

82. See for example, correspondence between the municipal president of Cuetzalan and President Obregón, 18 March 1922, AGN, O-C, 816-Z-20.

83. Arguedas, *Yawar Fiesta.*

84. ADN, C, 2-1145, tomo 1, fol. 169.

85. AML, Gobernación, exp. 28, 1928, no. 143,; AML, Fomento, exp. 9, 1929, no. 210.

86. AML, Gobernación, exp. 14, 1926, no. 227, see telegram dated 13 Sept. 1926 from the municipal president to the state governor.

87. See Becker, *Setting the Virgin on Fire,* and Vaughan, *Cultural Politics in Revolution,* for discussions on the use of the school as a public space. See Benjamin, *La Revolución,* for a discussion on the importance of sports in the construction of the postrevolutionary state.

88. Espínola, "Ensayo de antropología apliada." Various informants commented upon how roads were neglected after Barrios left the Sierra. José María Barrios argues that after his father's departure "almost everything went to ruin" as political ambitions took precedence over community projects. Francisco Landero Alamo from Zacapoaxtla claims that during the presidency of Manuel Avila Camacho, the Zacapoaxtla-to-Cuetzalan road deteriorated to the extent that it was passable only by mule. Jaime Mora from Cuetzalan agrees, stating that Barrios's departure made it easier for those opposed to road-building schemes to use their connections with the state government (interviews with José María Barrios Nava, Tonalapa, Puebla, 6 Nov. 1993; Francisco Landero Alamo, Zacapoaxtla, Puebla, 10 Dec. 1993; Jaime Mora, Cuetzalan, Puebla, 13 Dec. 1993).

89. Torres Trueba, "Faccionalismo en un municipio mexicano."

90. Arizpe, *Parentesco y economía in una sociedad Nahua,* 65.

91. See, e.g., Chance and Taylor, "Cofradías and Cargos"; Rus and Wasserstrom, "Civil-Religious Hierarchies in Central Chiapas"; Greenberg, "Capital, Ritual, and Boundaries," 67–81.

92. For examples of Barrios using his influence to obtain government resources, see FAPEC-FT, 93, 543, letter dated 23 July 1921; AGN, O-C 816-Z-20, letter dated 28 Feb. 1922.

93. Vaughan, *Cultural Politics in Revolution*, 116–24.

Chapter 6: The Downfall of the Barrios Cacicazgo

1. Benjamin, *La Revolución*, 141.

2. ADN, C, 2-1145, fols. 381–83, 388–89, 402–3, see letters from the CROM dated 7 Nov., 15 Nov., and 20 Dec. 1928.

3. BLC RHAM, caja 1928, letters for December 1928, see declaration dated 13 Dec. 1928. The complaint was lodged by the Pro-Andreu Almazán group in Puebla City. BLC RHAM, caja 1929, documents for February 1929, letter dated 25 Feb. 1929 from the municipal president of Zacatlán to Demetrio Barrios informing Barrios of the imposition.

4. BLC RHAM, caja 1929, letters sent/received May 1929; see, e.g., letters dated 2 May 1929 and 12 May 1929 from the state government to Esteban Islas, jefe de armas of Honey, Puebla.

5. AML, Gobernación, exp. 10, 1929, see letter dated 15 Feb. 1929 from the state government to the municipal president of Libres; BLC RHAM, caja 1929, documents for February 1929, see letter dated 25 Feb. 1929 from the provisional municipal president to Demetrio Barrios; BLC RHAM, caja 1929, letters for May 1929, see letter dated 8 May 1929 from Eliseo W. Dominguez to Demetrio Barrios; BLC RHAM, caja 1930, correspondence for January 1930, see letters dated 22 Jan. and 23 Jan. 1930 from the jefatura to Barrios giving notice of the governor's actions in various communities within the district of Huauchinango.

6. *La Opinión*, 13 Sept. 1928, editorial, p. 3.

7. *La Opinión*, 6 Oct. 1928, pp. 1, 6.

8. BLC RHAM, caja 1930, correspondence for January 1930, see letter dated 26 Jan. 1930 from the jefatura in Puebla to Barrios; ADN, C, 2-1145, fol. 344.

9. BLC RHAM, caja 1930, telegrams for February 1930, see telegrams dated 14 Feb., 15 Feb., and 21 Feb. 1930.

10. BLC RHAM, caja 1930, correspondence dated 18 Feb. 1930 between José María Flores and Barrios; *La Opinión*, particularly between 19 Feb. 1930 and 28 Feb. 1930.

11. BLC RHAM, caja 1930, see letter dated 31 March 1930 from Demetrio Barrios to Ricardo Márquez Galindo.

12. BLC RHAM, caja 1930, see letter dated 6 March 1930 from Bravo Izquierdo to Barrios.

13. ADN, C, XI/III/2-1145, tomo 3, fols. 610, 651; BLC RHAM, caja 1930, telegrams for February 1930, see telegram from Colonel Escobedo to Demetrio Barrios dated 24 Feb. 1930; *La Opinión*, 25 Feb. 1930, p. 1; 20 April 1930, p. 4; 15 June 1930, p. 4; and 28 June 1930, p. 4.

14. Ibid., 28 May 1930, p. 1; 20 Nov. 1929, p. 1; 19 Feb. 1930, p. 1; and 1 April 1930, p. 4.

15. AMZx, Gobernación 1 (1931), see letters from the Confederación Campesino "Emiliano Zapata" of Puebla to Manuel Molina dated 23 Feb. and 30 March 1931; AGN, Aberlardo L. Rodríguez, 541.5/92. Similar complaints were made three years later; see letter to president dated 21 Nov. 1934.

16. ADN, H, XI/333.21/43, fol. 31.

17. APVB, see entries for 1936; ADN, H, XI/333.21/43, fols. 36–38; interviews with Vicente Barrios Vargas, Zacatlán, Puebla, 25 Nov. 1993, and José María Barrios Nava, Tonalapa, Tetela de Ocampo, Puebla, 6 Nov. 1993.

18. AGN, Aberlardo L. Rodríguez, 552.5/50-1, see letter to the president dated 8 Aug. 1934.

19. ADN, C, 2-1145, tomo 3, fols. 705–10, 762; AGN, Lázaro Cárdenas, 503-11/77 and 542.1/2552.

20. ADN, H, XI/333.21/43, fols. 37–38.

21. ADN, H, XI/333.21/43, fols. 38–40; ADN, C, 2-1145, tomo 6, fols. 1271–1327.

22. ADN, C, 2-1145, fols. 1313, 1327. Delays in receiving compassionate leave, for example, had prevented him from being present at his wife's deathbed.

23. Roniger, "Caciquismo and Coronelismo"; Lomnitz-Adler, *Exits from the Labyrinth*, chap. 17.

24. Alvarado Méndez, *El portesgilismo en Tamaulipas*, 324–25.

25. Márquez, "Gonzalo N. Santos," 389–91; Brewster, "Caciquismo in Postrevolutionary Mexico," 128.

Glossary

agrarismo: agrarian reform movement

agrarista: agrarian reformist

Aguaprietista: supporter of the Plan de Agua Prieta, which called for the overthrow of President Carranza

aguardiente: liquor distilled from sugarcane

amparo: grant of legal protection

ayuntamiento: town council

cabecera: administrative center of a district

cacicazgo: a cacique's network of supporters

cacique: local political boss

caciquismo: system of politics based on caciques

campesino/a: peasant

cargo: civil / religious responsibility

caudillo: political leader with armed supporters

compadre/comadre: godfather / godmother

constitucionalista: supporter of President Venustiano Carranza

convencionista: supporter of Villa-Zapata alliance

creole: Mexican-born person of Spanish descent

cuerpo voluntario: armed local law enforcement unit

desamortización: privatization of communal land

diputado: political representative in congress

ejido: communal farmland granted to campesinos under agrarian reform

faena: voluntary community labor draft

gente de razón: literally, "people of reason"; a term describing the white elite, as opposed to mestizos or Indians

gobernador: governor

Guerra y Marina: Ministry of War

hacendado/a: owner of an hacienda, or rural estate

huaraches: sandals typically worn by campesinos

indito: derogative term for an indigenous person

jefatura: military headquarters

jefe de armas: local commander of security forces

jefe de operaciones militares: commanding officer of regional military forces

jefe político: political boss

junta agrícola: agricultural committee

junta auxiliar: emergency administration of a pueblo

laborista: supporter of Partido Laborista Mexicano

ladino: white or mestizo person

meseta: high plains

mestizaje: process of ethnic mixing through intermarriage

mestizo: person of mixed Spanish and Indian blood

municipio: municipality

norte: a cold wind from the north

obrero/a: worker

palacio municipal: town hall

pasado: village elder

pistolero: gunman

poblano: native of the state of Puebla

presidente municipal: municipal president (leader of local council)

pueblo: small town or village

serrano: inhabitant of a mountainous region, in this case the Sierra Norte de Puebla

sujeto: local authority subordinate to a municipio

suplente: deputy political representative in congress

tierra cálida: semitropical lowlands

tierra caliente: tropical lowlands

tierra fría: cool mountainous zone

tierra templada: temperate zone

topiles: term used in the Sierra de Puebla for a colonial system of voluntary labor drafts to complete projects of community benefit

traje de manta: white cotton shirt and pants worn by campesinos

vecino: inhabitant, resident

A Note on Sources

A range of national archives proved invaluable in constructing the narrative framework linking the Sierra to regional and national events. Within the Archivo General de la Nación (AGN), documents in the presidential collections (Gallery 3) proved to be a rich source of information relating directly to Barrios and more generally to the political, social, and economic concerns of Sierra communities. Similarly, the Fideicomiso Archivo Plutarco Elías Calles y Fernando Torreblanca contains a wealth of data on political, economic, and military matters during the 1920s. Although by no means complete, the archive's computerized catalogs provide a useful research tool. The Hemeroteca Nacional and the hemerotecas of the AGN and Biblioteca Lerdo de Tejeda together offer a comprehensive range of newspapers for the 1920s and provide insights into how events in the Sierra de Puebla were perceived in Mexico City.

For any scholar seeking information on military figures, the Archivo Histórico de la Defensa Nacional (ADN) is indispensable. When I began my research on Barrios in 1993, access to the archive was extremely restricted. In recent years a more relaxed approach has prevailed, and a letter of introduction clearly defining the motives and boundaries of research is usually sufficient to gain access to the extensive *cancelados* files (personal files of deceased members of the armed forces). Typically, each of these files contains information on the individual's family background; military actions; letters of complaint or praise from members of the public; and internal correspondence regarding career advancement, investigations, etc. It should be noted that few cancelado files exist pertaining to the military careers of soldiers who later rebelled against the government. Other collections are held at the ADN, but access is either denied or filtered by archivists who search on your behalf.

As historians of Puebla know, the absence of a state congressional archive severely hampers research into the political history of the state. Nonetheless, the Archivo General de Notarías provides valuable information and is well organized, while the state hemeroteca contains a rich, if incomplete, collection of regional newspapers of the 1920s. (Both archives are housed within the former state prison.) For those wishing to explore the relationship between the state government and local authorities, some evidence exists within the *Diario de los debates* held in the congressional library, but for more detailed information there is little alternative other than to spend lengthy periods in municipal archives. Given that the incumbent municipal president controls access and determines the budget for maintaining these archives, it is difficult to offer meaningful advice concerning the present state of municipal archives within the Sierra de Puebla. A letter of introduction from the state Gobernación office in the city of Puebla did open doors that otherwise would have remained closed to me. The bulk of my own research in the Sierra was conducted between 1993 and 1995. During this period the municipal archives in Tetela de Ocampo, Cuetzalan, and Libres were well organized and accessible; those of Zacatlán, Chignahuapan, and Zacapoaxtla less so. Other archives in the Sierra, particularly that of Teziutlán, were totally disorganized and hard to access.

Municipal libraries can be sources for both locally published books and historical documents relating to the district. Foremost to my mind is the Biblioteca Luis Cabrera in Zacatlán. In the late 1980s, the librarian was given documents by a member of the Barrios family who saved them from imminent destruction. This pile of insect-ridden papers that had lain in an attic for fifty years gathering dust reveals extensive detail on the nature of the Barrios brothers' relationship with political and military superiors, and more significantly, on those figures within Sierra communities with whom the brothers did business. The content of these documents is diverse, ranging from local government documents to a most intimate page on which Gabriel and Demetrio scribbled versions of the epitaph for Bardomiano's gravestone in the town cemetery. In much of this correspondence, political posturing is stripped away, laying bare a range of emotions: deference, insubordination, hope, fear, affection, and anger. Together, these documents open an invaluable and as yet neglected window to the social and political life of the Sierra in the 1920s. For those wishing to consult the archive, time is of the essence. My efforts to get state government funding to preserve the archive were thwarted by mutual suspicion between state and municipal authorities, and while the debate continues regarding where best to keep the archive, insects and the damp continue to ravage the documents. All translations from Spanish-language texts were made by the author.

Archival sources form only one part of a much richer seam of information that includes oral history, anecdote, and folklore. This diversity of evidence makes local history in the Sierra both fascinating and frustrating. By its very nature, oral history is subjective; it reaches into the darkest recesses of human memory and, for a variety of reasons, snapshots of the past emerge from the gloom. A range of often disconnected and contradictory influences impinge upon the processes by which these fragments are transformed into a version of the past. Cross-referencing and reevaluation of such accounts sometimes reveal hitherto hidden patterns of behavior but are equally likely to lead to a cul-de-sac. This does not mean that seductive, if unsubstantiated, evidence carries no historical significance. Even when no supporting evidence can be found, the fact that a sufficiently large and diverse number of people believe a certain event to have taken place carries historical significance in itself. In this respect, anecdotes and folklore reflect more than contemporary opinion; they reveal how serranos made sense of their own lives and the times through which they lived.

There is a tendency to place greater importance upon the accounts of informants who witnessed or lived through particular moments in history. Their versions of events carry authority and, it must be said, a degree of celebrity. Inevitably, the generation of the revolution is fast dying out to be succeeded by those who have strong impressions of the past based on what they were told. The recollections of certain individuals still carry greater weight than others, with greatest respect going to local intellectuals, typically schoolteachers and librarians, who have taken the trouble to gather evidence and present an image that extends beyond personal experiences to situate the community within a global history. "Those who know" are respected and sought out by those who would like to know; the process is self-perpetuating, because the more their views are recorded, the more authority they gain. I believe this value to be slightly misplaced because, although longevity or education may make people wiser, neither qualifies them as the primary authority on the past. Finding alternative points of view requires time and patience to seek out those who, when answering the knock on the door, meet the interviewer with a varying mixture of suspicion and surprise that anyone would ever be interested in hearing what they have to say. Throughout this book, I have recorded the opinions of many serranos who harbor deep sentiments regarding Gabriel Barrios and those who followed him. It goes without saying that when interviewing these informants, I did not challenge the validity of their version of history. The evaluation of all evidence, whether written or oral, took place elsewhere, on my terms and upon my own responsibility. I am aware of the pitfalls that academics have recently pointed out concerning scholarly analysis of indigenous people. I do not presume fully to understand the motives of those I study; what I have done is to look for signs and patterns of behavior that indicate connections between thoughts and actions.

Bibliography

Interviews

Graciela Ayala Gaytán, Puebla city, 10 Sept. 1993

Arnulfo Barrios Aco, Tetela de Ocampo, Puebla, various interviews between 24 Sept. 1993 and 24 Aug. 1999

Carlotta Barrios Cabrera, Zacatlán, Puebla, various interviews between 16 Oct. 1993 and 23 Aug. 1999

Ivonne Barrios Kuri, Tetela de Ocampo, Puebla, 24 Dec. 1993

José María Barrios Nava, Tonalapa, Tetela, Puebla, various interviews between 23 Oct. 1993 and 24 Aug. 1999

Vicente Barrios Vargas, Zacatlán, Puebla, various interviews between 25 Nov. 1993 and 23 Aug. 1999

Esperanza Cruz Perez, Otlatlán, Puebla, 2 Jan. 1994

María Dolores Lucas and Serafín Manzano Huerta, Puebla city, 5 Sept. 1993

Emma Flores, Cuetzalan, Puebla, 13 Aug. 1993

José Flores Huidobro, Cuetzalan, Puebla, 13 Dec. 1993

Beatriz Galindo de Sánchez, Zacatlán, Puebla, interviews on 31 Dec. 1993 and 21 Aug. 1999

Ciro Hernández García, Zacatlán, Puebla, 14 Dec. 1993

Alejandro L. Huerta Mora, Tonalapa, Tetela, Puebla, 23 Oct. and 8 Nov. 1993

Francisco Landero Alamo, Zacapoaxtla, Puebla, 10 Dec. 1993

Señor Limón, Tepeyahualco, Libres, Puebla, 29 Nov. 1993

Guillermo Mejía Cabrera, Tetela de Ocampo, Puebla, 22 Dec. 1993

Jaime Mora, Cuetzalan, Puebla, 13 Dec. 1993

María Peña, Zacatlán, Puebla, 30 Dec. 1993

Señora Posada, Tetela de Ocampo, Puebla, 5 Oct. 1993

Humberto Quintero Cortes, Cuautempan, Tetela, Puebla, 6 Oct. 1993

Baudelio Rivera, Cuetzalan, Puebla, 16 Dec. 1993

Alberto Toral, Zacapoaxtla, Puebla, 10 Dec. 1993
Salvador Vega Rodríguez, Cuetzalan, Puebla, 14 Dec. 1993

Archival Sources

Mexico City

Archivo del Congreso de la Unión (ACU)
Archivo General de la Nación (AGN)
Archivo Histórico de la Defensa Nacional (ADN)
Archivo Histórico de la Universidad Nacional Autónoma de México, J. Barragán
Archivo Histórico de la Universidad Nacional Autónoma de México, Jacinto B. Treviño
Archivo de Relaciones Exteriores
Archivo de Venustiano Carranza, Instituto de Estudios Históricos de México, Condumex S.A.
Biblioteca Vicente Lombardo Toledano
Fideicomiso Archivo Plutarco Elías Calles y Fernando Torreblanca (FAPEC-FT)
Hemeroteca Nacional, Universidad Nacional Autónoma de México
Records of the Department of State Relating to Internal Affairs of Mexico, Ref. No. MP 1370, Colegio de México

Puebla

Archivo del Congreso del Estado de Puebla (ACP)
Archivo General de Notarías del Estado de Puebla (AGNP)
Archivo Municipal de Cuetzalan (AMC)
Archivo Municipal de Libres (AML)
Archivo Municipal de Tetela de Ocampo (AMT)
Archivo Municipal de Zacatlán (AMZn)
Archivo Municipal de Zacapoaxtla (AMZx)
Biblioteca Luis Cabrera, Zacatlán, RHAM archive (BLC RHAM)
Hemeroteca del Estado de Puebla

Private

Archivo de la Palabra, Instituto Mora, PHO/1/35. Gen. Brig. Juan L. Cardona López
Archivo de la Palabra, Instituto Mora, PHO/1/85. Ignacio Suárez
Archivo de la Palabra, Instituto Mora, ref. 972.002.MIS.164. Santiago Arias Navarro
Archivo privado de Abraham Lucas, Puebla (APAL)
Archivo privado de Arnulfo Barrios, Tetela de Ocampo (APAB)
Archivo privado de Juan Francisco Lucas, Puebla
Archivo privado de Vicente Barrios, Zacatlán (APVB)

Works Cited

Acevedo-Rodrigo, Ariadna. "Time and Discipline in Mexican Schools, 1921–1934." M.A. thesis, University of Warwick, U.K., 2000.

Aguilar Camín, Héctor. "The Relevant Tradition: Sonoran Leaders in the Revolution." In *Caudillo and Peasant in the Mexican Revolution*, edited by David Brading, 92–123. Cambridge: Cambridge University Press, 1980.

Alvarado Méndez, Arturo. *El portesgilismo en Tamaulipas: estudio sobre la construcción de la autoridad pública en el México posrevolucionario*. Mexico City: Colegio de México, 1992.

Ankerson, Dudley. *Agrarian Warlord: Saturnino Cedillo and the Mexican Revolution in San Luis Potosí*. DeKalb, Ill.: Northern Illinois University Press, 1984.

——. "Saturnino Cedillo: A Traditional Caudillo in San Luis Potosí 1890–1938." In *Caudillo and Peasant in the Mexican Revolution*, edited by David Brading, 140–68. Cambridge: Cambridge University Press, 1980.

Archer, Christon I. *The Army in Bourbon Mexico, 1760–1810*. Albuquerque: University of New Mexico Press, 1977.

Arguedas, José María. *Yawar Fiesta*. Buenos Aires: Editorial Losada, 1941.

Arizpe, Lourdes. *Parentesco y economía en una sociedad Nahua (Nican Pehua Zacatipan)*. Mexico City: Instituto Nacional Indígena, 1973.

Arriaga, F. J. *Expediente geográfico-estadístico*. Palacio, Mexico: Imprenta del Gobierno, 1873.

Bantjes, Adrian A. *As If Jesus Walked on Earth: Cardenismo, Sonora, and the Mexican Revolution*. Wilmington, Del.: Scholarly Resources, 1998.

Barbosa Cano, Fabio. *La CROM: de Luis N. Morones a Antonio J. Hernández*. Puebla: Universidad Autónoma de Puebla, 1980.

Barrios Bonilla, G. Marcos. *El café en Cuetzalan*. Mexico City: Instituto Nacional Indigenista, 1991.

Beaucage, P. "Anthropologie économique des communautés indigénes de la Sierra Norte de Puebla (Mexique): les villages de basse montagne." *Canadian Review of Sociology and Anthropology* 10, no. 2 (1973): 114–33.

Becker, Marjorie. *Setting the Virgin on Fire: Lázaro Cárdenas, Michoacán Peasants, and the Redemption of the Mexican Revolution*. Berkeley: University of California Press, 1995.

Benjamin, Thomas. "Regionalizing the Revolution: The Many Mexicos in Revolutionary Historiography." In *Provinces of the Revolution*, edited by Thomas Benjamin and Mark Wasserman, 319–57. Albuquerque: University of New Mexico Press, 1990.

——. *La Revolución: Mexico's Great Revolution as Memory, Myth, and History*. Austin: University of Texas Press, 2000.

——. "Una larga historia de resistencia indígena campesina." In *Paisajes rebeldes: una larga noche de rebelión indígena*, edited by Jane-Dale Lloyd and Laura Pérez Rosales, 181–210. Mexico City: Universidad Iberoamericana, 1995.

Beverley, John. *Subalternity and Representation: Arguments in Cultural Theory.* Durham, N.C.: Duke University Press, 1999.

Brading, David, ed. *Caudillo and Peasant in the Mexican Revolution.* Cambridge: Cambridge University Press, 1980.

Brewster, Keith. "Caciquismo in Post-revolutionary Mexico: The Case of Gabriel Barrios Cabrera in the Sierra Norte de Puebla." *Journal of Latin American Studies* 27, no. 1 (1996): 105–28.

Brunk, Samuel. "Remembering Emiliano Zapata: Three Moments in the Post-humous Career of the Martyr of Chinameca." *Hispanic American Historical Review* 78, no. 3 (1998): 457–90.

Brush, David A. "The de la Huerta Rebellion in Mexico 1923–1924." Ph.D. diss., Syracuse University, 1975.

Buchler, Ira R. "La organización ceremonial de una aldea mexicana." *América Indígena* 27, no. 2 (1967): 237–63.

Campbell, Howard. *Zapotec Renaissance: Ethnic Politics and Cultural Revivalism in Southern Mexico.* Albuquerque: University of New Mexico Press, 1994.

Carr, Barry. *El movimiento obrero y la política en México 1910–1929.* Vol. 2. Mexico City: SEP, 1976.

Carranza, Julia. *La verdad sobre la muerte de Carranza.* San Antonio, Tex.: Quiroga, 1920.

Castillo, Porfirio del. *Puebla y Tlaxcala en los días de la revolución.* Mexico City: Zavala, 1953.

Castro, Pedro. *Adolfo de la Huerta: la integridad como arma de la revolución.* Mexico City: Siglo Veintiuno, 1998.

——. "La muerte de Carranza: dudas y certezas." *Boletín* 34, May–Aug. (2000): entire edition.

Chance, John K., and William B. Taylor. "Cofradías and Cargos: A Historical Perspective of the Mesoamerican Civil-Religious Hierarchy." *American Ethnologist* 12, no. 1 (1985): 1–26.

Cordero y Torres, Enrique. *Diccionario biográfico de Puebla.* Mexico City: n.p., 1972.

——. *Historia general del estado de Puebla (1531–1963).* Vol. 2. Puebla: Bohemia Poblana, 1966.

DePalo, William Jr. *The Mexican National Army, 1822–1852.* College Station: Texas A&M University Press, 1997.

Ducey, Michael T. "Village, Nation, and Constitution: Insurgent Politics in Papantla, Veracruz, 1810–1821." *Hispanic American Historical Review* 79, no. 3 (1999): 263–93.

Espínola, Julio César. "Ensayo de antropología apliada entre los Nahuas de la Sierra de Puebla. *América Indígena* 25, no. 1 (1965): 79–116.

Evans, Rosalie. *The Rosalie Evans Letters from Mexico.* Indianapolis: Bobbs-Merrill, 1926.

Falcón, Romana. *Revolución y caciquismo: San Luis Potosí, 1919–1934*. Mexico City: Colegio de México, 1984.

Fowler-Salamini, Heather. *Agrarian Radicalism in Veracruz, 1920–38*. Lincoln: University of Nebraska Press, 1978.

———. "Revolutionary Caudillos in the 1920s: Francisco Múgica and Adalberto Tejeda." In *Caudillo and Peasant in the Mexican Revolution*, edited by David Brading, 169–92. Cambridge: Cambridge University Press, 1980.

French, William F. *A Peaceful and Working People: Manners, Morals, and Class Formation in Northern Mexico*. Albuquerque: University of New Mexico Press, 1993.

Friedlander, Judith. *Being Indian in Hueyapan: A Study of Forced Identity in Contemporary Mexico*. New York: St. Martin's Press, 1975.

Friedrich, Paul. *Agrarian Revolt in a Mexican Village*. Englewood Cliffs, N.J.: Prentice-Hall, 1970.

García de León, Antonio. *Resistencia y utopía: memoria de agravios y crónicas de revueltas y profecías en la provincia de Chiapas durante los últimos quinientos años de su historia*. Vol. 2. Mexico City: Ediciones Era, 1985.

García Martínez, Bernal. *Los pueblos de la sierra*. Mexico City: Colegio de México, 1987.

Garciadiego Dantan, J. "La política militar del presidente Carranza." In *Memoria del congreso internacional sobre la revolución mexicana*, 211–36. San Luis Potosí: INEHRM, 1991.

Garner, Paul. "Federalism and Caudillismo in the Mexican Revolution: The Genesis of the Oaxaca Sovereignty Movement (1915–1920)." *Journal of Latin American Studies* 17, no. 1 (1985): 111–33.

Gerhart, Peter. *A Guide to the Historical Geography of New Spain*. Cambridge: Cambridge University Press, 1972.

Gilly, Adolfo. "Chiapas and the Rebellion of the Enchanted World." In *Rural Revolt in Mexico: U.S. Intervention and the Domain of Subaltern Politics*, edited by Daniel Nugent. Durham, N.C.: Duke University Press, 1998.

Gómez, Arnulfo R. *El centinela*. Mexico, n.p., 1924.

González de la Rama, Renée. "Los papeles de Díaz Manfort: una revuelta popular en Misantla (Veracruz), 1885–1886." *Historia Mexicana* 39, no. 2 (1989): 475–521.

Greenberg, James B. "Capital, Ritual, and Boundaries of the Closed Corporate Community." In *Articulating Hidden Histories: Exploring the Influence of Eric R. Wolf*, edited by Jane Schneider and Rayna Rapp, 67–81. Berkeley: University of California Press, 1995.

Gruening, Ernest. *Mexico and Its Heritage*. London: Stanley Paul, 1928.

Guardino, Peter. *Peasants, Politics, and the Formation of Mexico's National State: Guerrero 1800–1857*. Stanford: Stanford University Press, 1996.

Gutiérrez, Natividad. *Nationalist Myths and Ethnic Identities*. Lincoln: University of Nebraska Press, 1999.

Guzmán, Martín Luis. *Muertes históricas.* 3rd ed., vol. 1. Mexico City: Cia General de Ediciones, 1963.

Hansen, Edward C., and Wolf, Eric R. "Caudillo Politics: A Structural Analysis." *Comparative Studies in Society and History* 9 (1966–67): 168–79.

Henderson, Timothy J. *The Worm in the Wheat: Rosalie Evans and the Puebla-Tlaxcala Valley of Mexico, 1906–1927.* Durham, N.C.: Duke University Press, 1998.

Hernández Chávez, Alicia. "Origen y ocaso del ejército porfiriano." *Historia Mexicana* 39 (1989–90): 257–96.

Hernández Enríquez, Gustavo A. *Historia moderna de Puebla.* Vols. 1–3. Puebla: Comunicación y Análisis, 1986.

Hu-DeHart, Evelyn. *Yaqui Resistance and Survival.* Madison: University of Wisconsin Press, 1984.

INEHRM. *Diccionario histórico y biográfico de la revolución mexicana.* Vol. 5. Mexico City: INEHRM, 1992.

Joseph, Gilbert M. *Revolution from Without: Yucatán, Mexico, and the United States 1880–1924.* Cambridge: Cambridge University Press, 1982.

Joseph, Gilbert M., and Daniel Nugent, eds. *Everyday Forms of State Formation: Revolution and the Negotiation of Rule in Modern Mexico.* Durham, N.C.: Duke University Press, 1994.

Juárez Cao Romero, Alexis. *Catolicismo popular y fiesta: sistema festivo y vida religiosa de un pueblo indígena del estado de Puebla.* Puebla: Universidad Autónoma de Puebla, 1999.

Knight, Alan. *The Mexican Revolution.* Vol. 2. Cambridge: Cambridge University Press, 1986.

——. "Peasant and Caudillo in Revolutionary Mexico 1910–17." In *Caudillo and Peasant in the Mexican Revolution,* edited by David Brading. Cambridge: Cambridge University Press, 1980.

——. "Popular Culture and the Revolutionary State in Mexico, 1910–1940." *Hispanic American Historical Review* 74, no. 3 (1994): 393–444.

LaFrance, David. "Politics, War, and State Building in Mexico's Heartland: The Revolution in Puebla, 1913–1920." Wilmington, Del.: Scholarly Resources, in press.

LaFrance, David, and Guy P. C. Thomson. "Juan Francisco Lucas: Patriarch of the Sierra Norte de Puebla." In *The Human Tradition in Latin America,* edited by William Beezley and Judith Ewell, 1–13. Wilmington, Del.: Scholarly Resources, 1987.

Lombardo Toledano, Vicente. "Estructura económica de la Sierra de Puebla. Teziutlán." *La Revista Teziutlán,* 1928.

Lomnitz-Adler, Claudio. *Exits from the Labyrinth: Culture and Ideology in the Mexican National Space.* Berkeley: University of California Press, 1992.

Loyo, Engracia. "Lectura para el pueblo, 1921–1940." *Historia Mexicana* 33, no. 3 (1984): 298–345.

Lozoya, Jorge A. *El ejército mexicano.* Mexico City: Centro de Estudios Internacionales, Colegio de México, 1970.

Mallon, Florencia E. *Peasant and Nation: The Making of Postcolonial Mexico and Peru.* Berkeley: University of California Press, 1995.

Marentes Bravo, Carlos. *Relatos revolucionarios.* Puebla: SEP, 1985.

Márquez, Enrique. "Gonzalo N. Santos o la naturaleza del 'tanteómetro político.'" In *Estadísticas, caciques y caudillos,* edited by Carlos Martínez Assad, 385–93. Mexico: Instituto de Investigaciones Sociales, Universidad Nacional Autónoma de México, 1988.

Márquez Carrillo, Jesús. "Los orígenes de Avilacamachismo: Una arqueología de fuerzas en la construcción de un poder regional: El estado de Puebla, 1929–1941." Tesis de licenciatura, Universidad Autónoma de Puebla, 1981.

Martin, JoAnn. "Contesting Authenticity: Battles over the Representation of History in Morelos, Mexico." *Ethnohistory* 40, no. 3 (1993): 438–65.

Masferrer Kan, Elías. "Religión y política en la Sierra Norte de Puebla." *América Indígena* 46, no. 3 (1986): 531–44.

Mejía Castelán, Sandalio. *Huauchinango histórico.* Puebla: Editorial Cájica, 1965.

Miller, Simon. *Landlords and Haciendas in Modernizing Mexico: Essays in Radical Reappraisal.* Amsterdam: CEDLA, 1995.

Nugent, Daniel. *Spent Cartridges of the Revolution: An Anthropological History of Namiquipa, Chihuahua.* Chicago: University of Chicago Press, 1993.

——., ed. *Revolt in Mexico: U.S. Intervention and the Domain of Subaltern Studies.* 2nd ed. Durham, N.C.: Duke University Press, 1998.

O'Malley, Illene. *The Myth of the Revolution: Hero Cults and the Institutionalization of the Mexican State, 1920–40.* New York: Greenwood Press, 1986.

Oñate, Abdiel. "The Struggle for the Central Bank: Mexico's Negotiations with the International Bankers, 1923–1925" Paper delivered at the annual meeting of the Society of Latin American Studies, Cambridge, April 1999.

Otero, Gerardo. *Farewell to the Peasantry?: Political Class Formation in Rural Mexico.* Boulder, Colo.: Westview Press, 1999.

Palacios, E. J. *Puebla. Su territorio y sus habitantes.* Mexico: n.p., 1917.

Pare, Luisa. "Caciquismo y estructura de poder en la Sierra Norte de Puebla." In *Caciquismo y poder político en el México,* edited by Roger Bartra, 31–61. Mexico City: Siglo Veintiuno, 1982.

——. "Inter-ethnic and Class Relations (Sierra Norte Region, State of Puebla)." In *Race and Class in Post-colonial Society: A Study of Ethnic Group Relations in the English-Speaking Caribbean, Bolivia, Chile, and Mexico,* edited by John Rex, 375–420. Paris: UNESCO, 1977.

Peña, Guillermo de la. "Articulación y desarticulación de las culturas." In *Filosofía de la cultura,* edited by D. Sobrevilla, 101–29. Madrid: Editorial Trotta, 1998.

——. "La ciudadanía étnica en el México contemporáneo." *Revista Internacional de Filosofía Política* 6 (1995): 116–40.

———. "Commodity Production, Class Differentiation, and the Role of the State in the Morelos Highlands: An Historic Approach." In *State, Capital, and Rural Society: Anthropological Perspectives on Political Economy in Mexico and the Andes,* edited by Benjamin S. Orlove, Michael W. Foley, and Thomas F. Love, 71–100. Boulder, Colo.: Westview Press, 1989.

Plasencia, Enrique. *Personajes y escenarios de la rebelión Delahuertista (1923–1924).* Mexico City: Instituto de Investigaciones Históricas, Universidad Nacional Autónoma de México, 1999.

Quayson, Ato. *Postcolonialism: Theory, Practice, or Process?* London: Polity Press, 2000.

Redfield, Robert. *Tepoztlán, a Mexican Village: A Study of Folk Life.* Chicago: University of Chicago Press, 1930.

Reed, Nelson. *The Caste War of Yucatán.* Stanford: Stanford University Press, 1964.

Rivera Moreno, Donna. *Xochiapulco: una gloria olvidada.* Puebla: Gobierno del Estado de Puebla, 1991.

Roniger, Luis. "Caciquismo and Coronelismo: Contextual Dimensions of Patron-Client Brokerage in Mexico and Brazil." *Latin American Research Review* 22, no. 2 (1987): 71–100.

Rubin, Jeffrey W. *Decentering the Regime: Ethnicity, Radicalism, and Democracy in Juchitán, Mexico.* Durham, N.C.: Duke University Press, 1997.

Rugeley, Terry. *Yucatán's Maya Peasantry and the Origins of the Caste War.* Austin: University of Texas Press, 1996.

Ruiz, Ramón E. *Mexico: The Challenge of Poverty and Illiteracy.* San Marino, Calif.: Huntington Library, 1963.

Rus, Jan. "Whose Caste War? Indians, Ladinos, and the Chiapas 'Caste War' of 1869." In *Spaniards and Indians in Southeastern Mesoamerica,* edited by Murdo J. MacLeod and Robert Wasserstrom, 127–68. Lincoln: University of Nebraska Press, 1983.

Rus, Jan, and Robert Wasserstrom. "Civil-Religious Hierarchies in Central Chiapas: A Critical Perspective." *American Ethnologist* 7 (1980): 466–78.

Sáenz, Moisés. *Escuelas federales en la Sierra de Puebla: informe sobre la visita a las escuelas federales en la Sierra de Puebla.* Mexico City: SEP, Talleres Gráficos de la Nación, 1927.

Sánchez López, Rogelio. "La institucionalización. Una historia de los derrotados: Puebla 1929–1932." Tesis de licenciatura, Universidad Autónoma de Puebla, 1992.

Sayer, Derek. "Everyday Forms of State Formation: Some Dissident Remarks on 'Hegemony.'" In *Everyday Forms of State Formation: Revolution and the Negotiation of Rule in Modern Mexico,* edited by Gilbert M. Joseph and Daniel Nugent, 367–77. Durham, N.C.: Duke University Press, 1994.

Schryer, Frans J. *Ethnicity and Class Conflict in Rural Mexico.* Princeton, N.J.: Princeton University Press, 1990.

——. *The Rancheros of Pisaflores: The History of a Peasant Bourgeoisie in Twentieth-Century Mexico.* Toronto: University of Toronto Press, 1980.

Scott, James C. *Weapons of the Weak: Everyday Forms of Peasant Resistance.* New Haven: Yale University Press, 1985.

Secretaría de Cultura del Estado de Puebla. *Profr. J. Baudelio Candanedo Castillo: síntesis biográfica del ilustre maestro zacateco.* [Information sheet]. Puebla: Gobierno de Estado de Puebla, 1997.

Siedei, Rachel. "'Paz, Progreso, Justicia y Honradez': Law and Citizenship in Alta Cerapaz during the Regime of Jorge Ubico." *Bulletin of Latin American Studies* 19 (2000): 283–302.

Siverts, Henning. "The Caciques of K'ankujk." *Estudios de Cultura Maya* 5 (1965): 339–60.

Slade, Doris L. "Kinship in the Social Organization of a Nahuat-Speaking Community in the Central Highlands." In *Essays on Mexican Kinship,* edited by Hugo G. Nutini, Pedro Carrasco, and James M. Taggart, 155–85. Pittsburgh: Pittsburgh University Press, 1976.

Soustelle, Jacques. *La famille otomi-pame du Mexique central.* Paris: Institut d'ethnologie, 1937.

Stern, Steve, ed. *Resistance, Rebellion, and Consciousness in the Andean Peasant World, 18th to 20th Centuries.* Madison: University of Wisconsin Press, 1987.

Stoll, David. *Rigoberta Menchú and the Story of All Poor in Guatemala.* Boulder, Colo.: Westview Press, 1999.

Taggart, James M. *Nahua Myth and Social Structure.* Austin: University of Texas Press, 1983.

Taylor, William B. *Drinking, Homicide, and Rebellion in Colonial Mexican Villages.* Stanford: Stanford University Press, 1979.

Thomson, Guy P. C. "Agrarian Conflict in the Municipality of Cuetzalan (Sierra de Puebla): The Rise and Fall of "Pala" Agustín Dieguillo, 1861–1894." *Hispanic American Historical Review* 71, no. 2 (1991): 205–58.

——. "Bulwarks of Patriotic Liberalism: The National Guard, Philharmonic Corps, and Patriotic Juntas in Mexico, 1847–88." *Journal of Latin American Studies* 22 (1990): 31–68.

——. "Montaña and Llanura in the Politics of Central Mexico: The Case of Puebla 1820–1920." In *Region, State and Capitalism in Mexico,* edited by Wil Pansters and Arij Ouweneel, 59–78. Amsterdam: CEDLA, 1989.

——. "Popular Aspects of Liberalism in Mexico 1848–1888." *Bulletin of Latin American Research* 10, no. 3 (1991): 265–92.

——. "Pueblos de Indios and Pueblos de Ciudadanos: Constitutional Bilingualism in Nineteenth-Century Mexico." *Bulletin of Latin American Research* 18, no. 1 (1999): 89–100.

Thomson, Guy P. C., with David LaFrance. *Patriotism, Politics, and Popular Liberalism in Nineteenth-Century Mexico.* Wilmington, Del.: Scholarly Resources, 1999.

Timmons, Patrick. "The Only Good Indian Is an Educated Indian: Cultural Politics and Indigenismo in 1920s Mexico." M.Phil. thesis, University of Cambridge, 1998.

Tobler, Hans Werner. "Peasants and the Shaping of the Revolutionary State, 1910–1940s." In *Riot, Rebellion, and Revolution*, edited by Friedrich Katz, 487–581. Princeton, N.J.: Princeton University Press, 1988.

Torres Trueba, Henry E. "Faccionalismo en un municipio mexicano: estudio preliminar de las expresiones políticas, económicas y religiosas de faccionalismo en Zacapoaxtla, Puebla." *América Indígena* 30, no. 3 (1970): 727–49.

Urrea, Blas. *La herencia de Carranza*. Mexico City: Libros de México, 1982.

Valderrama Rouy, Pablo, and Carolina Ramírez Suárez. "Resistencia étnica y defensa del territorio en el Totonacapan serrano: Cuetzalan en el siglo XIX." In *Indio, nación y comunidad en el México del siglo XIX*, edited by A. Escobar, 189–206. Mexico City: Centro de Estudios Mexicanos y Centroamericanos, 1993.

Vargas, M. M. *Proyecto de una vía de comunicación de la Mesa Central a la Costa de Papantla pasando por el distrito de Tlatlauqui promovido ante de la H. Asamblea del Estado por el diputado de la misma C. Manuel M. Vargas, y llevado al Hon. Congreso de la Unión*. Puebla: Gobierno del Estado de Puebla, 1874.

Vaughan, Mary Kay. "Cultural Approaches to Peasant Politics." *Hispanic American Historical Review* 79, no. 2 (1999): 269–305.

——. *Cultural Politics in Revolution: Teachers, Peasants, and Schools in Mexico, 1930–1940*. Tucson: University of Arizona Press, 1997.

——. *The State, Education, and Social Class in Mexico, 1880–1928*. DeKalb, Ill.: Northern Illinois University Press, 1982.

Wasserstrom, Robert. "Rural Labor and Income Distribution in Central Chiapas." In *State, Capital, and Rural Society: Anthropological Perspectives on Political Economy in Mexico and the Andes*, edited by Benjamin S. Orlove, Michael W. Foley, and Thomas F. Love, 101–18. Boulder, Colo.: Westview Press, 1989.

Williams, Raymond. *Problems in Materialism and Culture: Selected Essays*. London: Verso, 1980.

Index

About the Author

Keith Brewster currently holds a research position at the Centre of Latin American Studies, University of Cambridge, U.K. He received his Ph.D. from the University of Warwick, U.K., in 1996, where he studied the political and social history of rural communities in postrevolutionary Mexico. He has published several articles in leading U.K., Mexican, and U.S. journals on a range of related topics, including caciquismo, indigenous resistance, and socio-economic developments in Mexico during the 1920s. His current research interests comprise two distinct topics: the role of spiritism within the Mexican military during the early twentieth century and the political manipulation of sport in postrevolutionary Mexico, with particular reference to Mexico's hosting of the 1968 Olympic Games and 1970 World Cup.

continued from front flap

Masterfully blending archival sources and oral history, Brewster captures life in the Sierra during the 1920s and examines the decision-making processes that determined how communities responded to new pressures, such as requests for soldiers or support for development projects. He shows that subaltern groups were able to shape and even resist state reforms, mustering evidence that the Sierra's indigenous communities drove hard bargains over issues affecting their everyday lives. Although many communities used Barrios as an intermediary, Brewster reveals that they did not universally accept his legitimacy but simply used his connections to pursue their own local agendas.

Brewster depicts the Sierra de Puebla of the 1920s as a scene of shifting balances of power where political, economic, social, and ethnic factors combined to produce the temporary ascendancy of different interest groups beyond and within the region. His study forces us to question assumptions about how power was exercised at the local and regional levels in postrevolutionary Mexico and will be of lasting interest to all concerned with the dynamics of caciquismo and the evolution of the Mexican political system.

Keith Brewster currently holds a research post at the Centre of Latin American Studies, University of Cambridge, UK.